HOW TO WRITE
BETTER RÉSUMÉS
AND COVER
LETTERS

SECOND EDITION

by Pat Criscito, CPRW

President and Founder
ProType, Ltd., Colorado Springs
and author of Barron's
e-Résumés,
Designing the Perfect Résumé,
Interview Answers in a Flash,
and *Guide to Distance Learning*

BARRON'S

The résumés in this book are real résumés used by real people to get real jobs. The names and contact information have been changed to protect their privacy.

All Web site addresses in this book were current on the date of publication. Because of the dynamic nature of the Internet, URLs can change. If you cannot find a site with the published address, use a good search engine to locate one that is up to date.

All inquiries should be addressed to:
Barron's Educational Series, Inc.
250 Wireless Boulevard
Hauppauge, New York 11788
www.barronseduc.com

Library of Congress Catalog Card No.: 2007030709

ISBN-13: 978-0-7641-3917-8
ISBN-10: 0-7641-3917-7

Library of Congress Cataloging-in-Publication Data

Criscito, Pat, 1953–
How to write better résumés and cover letters / by Pat Criscito – 2nd ed.
    p. cm.
ISBN-13: 978-0-7641-3917-8 (alk. paper)
ISBN-10: 0-7641-3917-7 (alk. paper)
1. Résumés (Employment) 2. Job hunting. I. Title.

HF5383.C742 2008
650.14'2--dc22   2007030709

PRINTED IN THE UNITED STATES OF AMERICA
9 8 7 6 5 4 3 2

Contents

About the Author

Pat Criscito is a Certified Professional Résumé Writer with more than 27 years of experience and résumé clients in 42 countries. As the president and founder of ProType, Ltd., in Colorado Springs, she has written more than 15,000 résumés in her career and speaks nationally on the subject, appearing regularly on television and radio shows, as well as at Harvard, Yale, Tulane, SMU, Thunderbird, and other major universities.

Pat is also the author of Barron's *Designing the Perfect Résumé* (a comprehensive idea book for designing your paper résumé), *e-Résumés* (your complete guide to a computerized job search), *Interview Answers in a Flash*, and *Guide to Distance Learning*. She is a contributing writer to *The Wall Street Journal's careerjournal.com*, *The Boston Globe*, *Colorado Springs Business Journal*, and other publications.

Because of her research, Pat is always on the cutting edge of job search science. She interviews human resource managers across the country and understands what they are looking for in a résumé and how to get a résumé read. In her books, Pat teaches you how to be successful in your job search and how to create and use electronic résumés. In this book, she passes on her expert knowledge of the résumé writing process from an insider's perspective.

Pat is an active member of the Career Management Alliance and National Résumé Writers' Association *(www.nrwa.com)*. For more information and to access the hyperlinks from this book in a handy online format, visit *www.patcriscito.com.* You will also find downloadable versions of all the forms in this book at the same site.

Chapter 1

Meet the Perfect Résumé

The job market itself defines the *perfect résumé,* which means résumés must evolve along with it. This new edition of *How to Write Better Résumés and Cover Letters* provides you with the latest résumé science, which means a lot of it will focus on the creation and use of résumés for the Internet, including Web résumés, blogging, and social networking. However, we can't ignore the paper version of your résumé for use in networking, interviewing, mailing to a well-researched list of companies, and the few times you will mail or fax a résumé in response to a job advertisement.

Whether you are a seasoned executive trying to condense a lifetime of experience onto two pages or a recent graduate struggling to find enough data to file a one-page résumé, this book will provide you with everything you will need to create the *perfect* personal branding instrument for your unique job search.

William Arruda, founding partner and president of the Reach Branding Club *(www.reachbrandingclub.com)* says, "Personal branding is a revolution in the way we manage our careers. It means identifying and communicating what makes you unique, relevant, and compelling so you can reach your goals. It's about differentiation, about using what makes you outstanding to stand out from the myriad others who offer seemingly similar services. Personal branding means using who you *are* to get what you want from life." To create a résumé that reflects this uniqueness, you need to highlight your unique promise of value, and this book will guide your through that process.

So just what is the perfect résumé? The *perfect* résumé is the one that fits your personality in both design and wording, tempered, of course, by the unique expectations of your industry and tailored to maximize the technologies of the Internet. It must contain the keywords of your industry, so your

> The perfect résumé is the one that fits your personality in both design and wording, tempered by the expectations of your industry and tailored to maximize the technologies of the Internet.

résumé appears at the top of a list of candidates in an electronic keyword search. It must be formatted to work on the Internet, and the wording must be dynamic and interesting to the human reader who will ultimately decide whether or not you deserve an interview.

Your paper résumé must be designed and written in such a way that it stands out in a stack of résumés on a busy executive's desk. It will help you get that all-important interview by making a strong first impression with a reader, and then by keeping that attention with dynamic sentences that convey your knowledge, skills, and abilities. It's that simple.

Having said that, you should know that writing your résumé is often one of the most difficult things you will ever do! Think about it . . . you must turn your life history into a one- or two-page advertisement that highlights a lifetime of experience, accomplishments, and education. Since we have been taught all of our lives to be modest and not to brag or be prideful, most people find this ultimate "pride" piece difficult to write.

Even if you have already made a first attempt at writing a résumé, it may not meet the expectations of today's technology or discerning hiring manager. The National Résumé Writers' Association *(www.nrwa.com)* publishes a test to help job seekers decide whether their résumés are ready for a job search. With their permission, let's evaluate your old résumé's effectiveness. Put a checkmark by every box that applies to you.

❏ My résumé uses the same marketing techniques used by companies to sell my unique "personal brand" to employers.

❏ My résumé is packed with industry-specific language and crucial key-words to ensure it will be searchable in an electronic database.

❏ My résumé emphasizes and quantifies my achievements to show not only what I have done, but also *how well* I have done it.

❏ My résumé reflects what I'm really good at doing, my unique value proposition.

❏ My résumé uses varied action verbs and powerful marketing phrases.

❏ My résumé contains superior grammar, spelling, sentence structure, and punctuation.

❏ My résumé emphasizes how I will benefit employers and meet their precise needs.

❏ My résumé engages the reader from the outset (on the first third of page one) and maintains interest throughout.

❏ My résumé clearly communicates my job target and the key strengths I bring to the table within the first few lines of text.

❏ My résumé utilizes accomplishment statements in a compelling way, using numbers when possible to quantify my achievements.

❏ My résumé communicates and targets my key transferable skills.

❏ My résumé minimizes my potential weaknesses and turns negative "red flags" into positive assets—things like gaps in employment, recent graduate with little real-world experience, lack of key skills for a new industry, self-employment, re-entering the job market after a long time raising children, older worker facing possible age discrimination, among others.

❏ My résumé uses an eye-catching, inviting, and original design (not a template).

❏ My résumé includes ASCII (plain-text) and electronic versions to enable use with e-mail, Internet, and e-forms.

❏ My résumé uses the most effective format, style, and strategy for my particular situation.

❏ My current résumé is getting enough (or the right type of) interviews.

How did you do? If you checked 14–16 boxes, your résumé writing abilities appear to be sound. You can still benefit from some of the strategies and tips in this book, or you might want to avail yourself of a critique from a professional résumé writer to be sure you didn't miss anything important.

If you checked 11–13 boxes, you have some distinct abilities that will help you write a résumé more solidly than most. Without the help of this book, however, you may leave out some critical components that can cost you interviews. Optimize your results by following all 12 steps in this book.

If you checked less than 11 boxes, you definitely need this book! You will miss opportunities that may be perfect for you unless you apply all the suggestions listed.

Writing the Perfect Résumé

Millions of paper and electronic résumés are distributed every day, and they all serve one purpose—to entice potential employers to open their doors for an interview. Every résumé is simply a marketing tool—your own personal advertisement to promote your personal brand. Just as the value of money is determined by what is printed on a piece of paper—there is a big difference between $1 and $100 bills—so is the value of your résumé determined by its content and format.

When writing the perfect résumé, you must ensure you include the things hiring managers and recruiters want to see on a résumé. According to a survey by CareerBuilder.com, that includes evidence of relevant work experience (77%), skills put into action (45%), problem-solving and decision-making capabilities (56%), leadership (44%), oral and written communication skills (40%), team building (33%), and performance and productivity improvement (31%).

You must also avoid the things they find irritating—spelling errors (59%), inaccurate information (29%), lack of customization to the position (30%), too much irrelevant information (21%), résumés longer than two pages (21%), as well as formatting errors, lack of organization, and irrelevant personal interests.

In my own résumé writing practice, I designed a 12-step résumé writing process over the years to help me clarify the experience, accomplishments, skills, education, and other background information of my clients and then to condense that person's life onto paper to create the perfect advertisement, always keeping in mind both the reader and the industry's expectations.

I shared that experience with my readers in a shortened form in the first edition of *Résumés in Cyberspace* (now titled *e-Résumés*). My 12-step writing process was then excerpted from the book in *The Wall Street Journal's National Employment Business Weekly* and was selected by their editors for the "Ten Best Articles of the Year" award. It is now permanently archived at their Web site, *www.careerjournal.com*.

With this book, I wanted to give you the whole story, to teach you how to create the perfect résumé from beginning to end. In this book you will find insider information from the world of résumé writers. You will learn:

- How to focus your résumé (Chapter 2, Step 1)

- How to define educational experiences to your advantage (Chapter 3, Step 2)

- How to research other sources to help you describe your past experience (Chapter 4, Step 3)

- How to fill your résumé with the buzzwords of your industry and make your résumé pop up in a keyword search in an electronic résumé database (Chapter 5, Step 4)

- How to organize your experience and describe your duties (Chapter 6, Step 5)

- How to emphasize your accomplishments (Chapter 7, Step 6)

- How to refine your information to the most relevant experience (Chapter 8, Step 7)

- How to develop dynamic, attention-getting sentences that will grab and keep your reader's attention (Chapter 9, Step 8)

- How to rearrange the information on your résumé so your reader is forced to see your most important items first (Chapter 10, Step 9)

- How to include related information to strengthen your qualifications (Chapter 11, Step 10)

- How to create a qualifications summary that will knock your reader's socks off (Chapter 12, Step 11)

- How to put it all together, including positioning, design, functional versus chronological résumés, executive résumés, and curriculum vitae (Chapter 13, Step 12)

Electronic Résumés

However, this book won't stop there. In order to manage your career today, you need both a paper résumé and electronic versions that can be used for attaching to e-mail messages, posting to Web sites, and filling out e-forms on the Internet. Chapter 14 will cover how to create and when to use ASCII text files, MS Word files, and PDF files.

You will learn what makes an electronic version of your résumé different and how to use it effectively to ensure that your résumé is selected from the thousands of résumés that companies receive every year. Just as one example, Jet Blue Airways receives 130,000 résumés a year, from which they must choose only 3,000 qualified people. You want to be one of the few chosen and not the many rejected.

Then I will add the latest information on how to use blogs, personal Web résumés, social networking sites (LinkedIn, Facebook, MySpace, Ecademy, Ryze, Friendster, and others), lense sites (Squidoo), and profile aggregating sites (Zoominfo, Ziggs) to build your online identity.

Since more than 75% of recruiters and hiring managers conduct a Google search on applicants before interviewing them, you must learn how to manage your online identity. That means controlling every word you write on the Internet and in e-mails, and choosing Web tools that will enhance the position of information *you choose* to appear when your name is Googled.

Cover Letters

What is a good résumé without an equally good cover letter? The answer is nothing. If your cover letter doesn't whet the hiring manager's appetite, your résumé may not get read at all.

Every résumé you send out, whether by mail, fax, or e-mail, needs a good cover letter. The last chapter will share some of the more common types and give you guidelines for including the right information to entice a hiring manager to continue reading.

Get Ready, Get Set, Write!

You have a wealth of résumé examples in this book from which to choose. Each chapter will provide you with sample wording to guide your creative process. If you find descriptions that work for you, please feel free to use them as a foundation for the words on your own résumé.

That doesn't mean that you should use every sentence verbatim. Accuracy is paramount in a résumé. Never use wording that you cannot explain or justify in an interview.

Unfortunately, cheating on résumés has become distressingly common. A study of 2.6 million job applications, conducted by the Society of Human Resource Management (SHRM), showed that 55% of all job applications contained false information, 44% lied about their work experience, 23% fabricated credentials or licenses, and 41% lied about their education. An FBI study found that approximately half a million people falsely claimed to have college degrees. Further studies show that nearly one-third of job applicants list dates of employment that are inaccurate by more than three months.

Don't get caught in that trap. A SHRM survey found that 96% of companies conduct some type of background screening, which can include reference checks, pre-employment drug/alcohol screening, fingerprinting, credit and driving history reports, INS verification, and background checks for criminal or terrorist activities.

An interesting development over the past few years has been the creation of companies that certify résumés for job seekers themselves *(www.careerexplorer. net/resume-background-check.asp,* or *www.restrust.net)*. A certified résumé is one that contains information that an individual has authorized to be verified as factual, which can include information relative to employment history, education and credentials (e.g., professional certifications, etc.), address history, criminal record, and civil records (bankruptcies, tax liens, civil judgments).

For a fee, trained staff research the information, and once all of the data is verified as accurate and correct, you are either provided with a report that will accompany your résumé, or the résumé is "stamped" with a unique identification code. An applicant can forward this certified résumé to a company with complete assurance that those who receive it will know the information they are receiving is accurate and correct.

This tool allows you to differentiate your résumé from others and shows recruiters that you are a serious candidate who actually has the credentials you claim. This is still a rather new concept, but as HR managers try to find means of narrowing down huge databases of résumés, I predict that "certified" résumés will catch on.

Throughout the book, you will find forms to help you collect information for your résumé. Please feel free to copy them as needed. If you would like to download PDF, MS Word, or WordPerfect versions of the forms, please go to *www.patcriscito.com* and follow the links to my books. When you see the title of this book, there will be hyperlinks to download the files. There are also lists of the Web sites provided in the book so you can quickly hyperlink to each site.

Now, let's get down to the business of writing a *perfect* résumé!

Chapter 2

Step 1
Focus

The first step in writing the perfect résumé is to know what kind of job you will be applying for. A résumé without a focus is never as effective as one that relates to a specific job description. If you don't know what you want to be "when you grow up," now is the time to see a career counselor. He or she can help you define where your skills and interests lie through tests and interest inventories.

You can either pay a professional career counselor for these services or approach your college's career services center for help. Some colleges and universities only work with currently enrolled students, while others provide their services to anyone who ever graduated from their institution. Some of these services are free and others are available for a fee.

For help in finding your alma mater's career services center, check the list of Web sites at the end of this chapter. To look into the credentials of a career counselor or coach, check the following Web sites:

- Career Management Alliance, *www.careermanagementalliance.com*
- Certified Career Coaches, *www.certifiedcareercoaches.com*
- Career Coach Institute, *www.careercoachinstitute.com*
- Career Counselors Consortium, *www.careercc.org*
- The Coach Connection, *www.findyourcoach.com*
- National Association of Colleges and Employers, *www.naceWeb.org*

If you are an active duty member of or are separating from a military service or are a reservist or a member of the National Guard, you are eligible for free career counseling through your service's transition assistance program. There are professional career counselors available on military bases, or you can use their online assistance program at *www.taonline.com*.

> *A résumé without a focus is never as effective as one that relates to a specific job description.*

Your Passion

Do you have a purpose for your life, something that drives you every day when you get out of bed? Or do you feel like something is missing, like you are just going through the motions every day? Marcia Bench of the Career Coaching Institute *(www.careercoachinstitute.com)* is convinced, "You will experience success in your life to the extent that you are clear about your life purpose."

Knowing your passion can help you determine the focus of your résumé. To help you find that focus, Marcia has developed a list of Clues to Your Life Purpose, which I will list here in shortened form with her permission. For more information on the clues, check Marcia's Web site, *www.careercoachinstitute.com/pdf/DiscoveringYourLifePurpose2.pdf.*

Clue 1: What do you love to do? That is, when you have spare time, how do you like to spend it?

Clue 2: What parts of your present job or life activities do you thoroughly enjoy?

Clue 3: What do you naturally do well? What has always come easily to you?

Clue 4: What are your ten greatest successes to date (in your eyes)?

Clue 5: Is there a cause about which you feel passionate?

Clue 6: What are the ten most important lessons you have learned in your life?

Clue 7: Are there some issues or perceived problems that have occurred over and over again? Out of one of these repeated issues may come your greatest lessons.

Clue 8: What do you daydream about doing? It is in your subconscious mind that your beliefs reside, as well as your deepest desires for success and fulfillment.

Clue 9: Imagine you are writing your epitaph. What things do you want to be remembered for at the end of your life? What things will your life be incomplete without? If you only had six months to live, what would you do differently than you are now doing?

Clue 10: What would you do if you knew you could not fail?

You should take the answers to the ten clues and evaluate them for any themes. Those themes can then be distilled down into an essence, the core of your purpose that is relatively unchanging. They represent your core values and core mission, which can be used to define your core competencies, the things you do very well. They will help you focus your résumé and give it a "theme."

Your Brand

Research by the Gallup organization suggests that the most effective people are those who understand and operate in their areas of natural talent, a.k.a. passion or unique value proposition or personal "brand."

Branding has been used in the corporate world since the first product was created and marketed, but the concept has only recently been applied to individuals. Just like for a business, your personal brand is what distinguishes you from other people. Think of Coke and Pepsi. They are not selling a bubbly brown water. They are selling their *brand*, what each one represents, their unique features (taste, bottle shape, logos) and benefits (refreshing, thirst quenching, satisfying).

By determining your passion, and consequently your *brand*, you can become a career activist, setting your own career direction by determining short- and long-term goals that have meaning for *you* and implementing them by acquiring the education, training, and experience you need to succeed. You are truly in charge of your career rather than being the victim of your employer's whims.

"By being your own career boss, you decide which positions you will take, how much effort you will invest in each job, and how you will handle the challenges you'll inevitably encounter. You control how you present yourself and your intellectual and emotional assets," say Kirsten Dixson and William Arruda in their book, *Career Distinction: Stand Out by Building Your Brand (www.career distinction.com).* "Just doing your job, and even doing it well, is no longer enough. . . . Every day, in everything you do, you tell the world about yourself, your values, your goals, and your skills. In fact, you already have a brand—even if you don't know what it is and even if it isn't working for you the way you'd like it to. Clarify and create your personal brand in order to achieve career distinction. Then, communicate that brand unerringly to those around you."

Peter Weddle, career researcher and consultant *(www.weddles.com),* feels, "Career activism is essentially a pair of commitments you make to yourself; bringing the best you can be at work each day and improving your personal best every day. Those promises provide the only real security there is in today's volatile and perilous workplace . . . because you are relying on yourself."

Your passion, or brand, becomes the focus for your résumé. Louise Kursmark, well-known career author and president of Best Impression Career Services *(www.yourbestimpression.com),* believes, "Truly powerful résumés need to convey a person's brand—what it is about him or her that is unique and differentiating. I strive to include branding statements in the summary of a résumé. Then, throughout the résumé, I show themes and trends during the person's career that reinforce the brand image, which creates a cohesive document that helps to distinguish the person from the competition."

Career Planning Internet Resources

The Internet is also a great source for do-it-yourself help in finding your passion. Although often not as effective as seeking help from professionally trained counselors, it can sometimes give you at least enough information to help you determine a focus for your résumé. Here are some of the career planning and assessment sites I recommend:

BGSU Career Planning Process *www.bgsu.edu/offices/sa/career/page17955.html*

Career and Technical Students Organizations . . . . *www.acteonline.org/resource_center/index.cfm*

Career Interests Game, University of Missouri . . *career.missouri.edu/students/explore/thecareerinterestsgame.php*

CareerBuilder Career Assessment . . . . *www.careerbuilder.com/jobseeker/resources/*
careerresourcesdetails.aspx?sc_cmp1=JS_CarRes_JobSee&crid=ca

College Board Online . . . . *www.collegeboard.com/csearch/majors_careers/profiles/index.html*

Excite Career Profiles . . . . *www1.excite.com/home/careers/industry_list/0,15624,,00.html*

IQ and Personality Tests . . . . *www.davideck.com*

Job Profiles.com . . . . *www.jobprofiles.org*

JobHuntersBible.com . . . . *www.jobhuntersbible.com/counseling/index.php*

Jobs for America's Graduates . . . . *www.jag.org/jag_career_corner.htm*

Keirsey Character and Temperament Sorter . . . . *www.keirsey.com*

LiveCareer Free Career Interest Test . . . . *www.livecareer.com/*

Mind Tools . . . . *www.mindtools.com/*

NextSteps.org, Youth Employment Center . . . . *www.nextsteps.org*

O*NET Online Occupation and Skill Search . . . . *online.onetcenter.org/*

Princeton Review Online . . . . *www.princetonreview.com/college/*

Princeton Review Career Quiz . . . . *www.princetonreview.com/cte/quiz/career_quiz1.asp*

QueenDom: The Land of Tests . . . . *www.queendom.com*

Quint Careers . . . . *www.quintcareers.com/test.html*

Self-Directed Search . . . . *www.self-directed-search.com/index.html*

Support for Learning *www.support4learning.org.uk/jobsearch/*

TypeFocus on Careers . . . . *www.typefocus.com*

U.S. News Self-Evaluation Questionnaire . . . . *www.usnews.com/usnews/work/articles/ccciss.htm*

The Objective Statement

Now that you know what you want to do for a living, take a blank piece of paper and write that focus/objective at the top. This can become your objective statement, should you decide to use one, or be used in the first line of the profile section of your résumé to give your reader a general idea of your area of expertise.

Objective statements are not required on a résumé, and often the cover letter is the best place to personalize your objective for each job opening. There is nothing wrong with using an objective statement on a résumé, however, provided it doesn't limit your job choices. As an alternative, you can alter individual résumés with personalized objectives that reflect the actual job title for which you are applying. Just make sure that the rest of your information is still relevant to the new objective.

Adding an objective statement to a résumé you will post on the Internet can severely limit your possibilities. It is better to be a bit more generic in stating your goals, although you still need to stay true to your passion/brand. In other words, if you want a sales or marketing position and you are willing to consider multiple industries, it is better not to state the industry or specialty of your expertise in your objective.

Having said that, never write an objective statement that is so imprecise that it says nothing at all about your focus. In your paper résumé, you should name the position you want so specifically that, if a janitor came by and knocked over all the stacks of sorted résumés on a hiring manager's desk, he could put yours back in its right stack without even thinking about it. That means saying:

A marketing management position with an aggressive international consumer goods manufacturer.

instead of:

A position which utilizes my education and experience to mutual benefit.

Here are some examples of specific objective statements for various industries:

- **AIRLINE PILOT:** Career as a United Airlines Flight Officer.

- **APPRAISER (entry-level):** Registered appraiser seeking an apprenticeship with a progressive appraisal service specializing in commercial real estate.

- **CHEF:** An executive chef position in a gourmet à la carte restaurant.

- **CUSTOMER SERVICE:** A customer service position in the airline industry, preferably in the Chicago area.

- **ELECTRICAL ENGINEERING:** A position in electrical engineering at the technician/integration level.

- **FACILITY MANAGEMENT:** A responsible physical security, facility/safety program management position.

- **FLIGHT ATTENDANT:** A career as a flight attendant with United Airlines.

- **GENERAL MANAGEMENT:** A management position where an MBA and 12 years of experience can be combined with positive interpersonal skills, initiative, and the capacity to motivate others.

- **HEALTHCARE MANAGEMENT:** To be an integral part of the management of a progressive, visionary healthcare organization.

- **INTERNATIONAL MANAGEMENT:** A senior management position in a marketing or related capacity for a multinational company with operations in Latin America.

- **MARKETING:** A challenging marketing and/or public relations position that utilizes international experience in a dynamic company whose vision is truly global.

- **MARKETING MANAGEMENT:** A marketing management position with the opportunity to develop and implement marketing strategies that will promote innovative products and/or services. Or: A management position in international sales/marketing in the entertainment industry.

- **MEDICAL ASSISTANT:** A position as a medical assistant that will also utilize back office skills and experience. Or: To work in a medical office where I can utilize my skills in both back and front office procedures.

- **PARKS AND RECREATION:** A permanent parks and recreation position that will utilize my knowledge, skills, and experience in outdoor education, natural resource interpretation, and/or park maintenance.

- **PHARMACEUTICAL SALES:** Eager to make the transition into pharmaceutical sales where a dynamic personality and strong work ethic could be used to grow market share and increase the profitability of a territory. Or: A challenging and rewarding career in pharmaceutical sales.

- **RESPIRATORY THERAPIST:** Registered Respiratory Therapist desiring a position with a progressive hospital that needs proven leadership, teaching, and clinical skills.

- **RETAIL SALES REP:** A retail kiosk coordinator position with Verizon Wireless.

- **SALES / ACCOUNT EXECUTIVE:** A sales and marketing position with the opportunity for advancement into management. Or: An account executive position focusing on new business development opportunities.

- **SEMICONDUCTOR MANUFACTURING:** A position with Intel as a Process Engineering Technician. Or: A position as a clean-room operator or an entry-level maintenance technician position.

- **SOFTWARE DEVELOPMENT:** A responsible position in software requirements analysis, testing, or training. Or: A challenging entry-level, object-oriented software development position.

- **SPORTS MANAGEMENT:** A challenging position in sports management and/or training in a hotel or resort.

- **SYSTEMS ENGINEERING:** A systems engineering position combining outstanding customer and communication skills with leading-edge information technology experience. Particularly interested in emerging system requirements engineering and architecture methodologies, strategic planning for information technology, and business process re-engineering for technology insertion.

- **TRAINING:** A challenging opportunity in corporate or industrial training.

You will notice that occasionally the job title is capitalized as if it were a proper noun. You have some creative license when you write and design a résumé, just like advertising copywriters do. You can choose to capitalize the job title to make it stand out, or you can use the grammatical conventions of capitalizing it only when you personify the title, as I did in the airline pilot and respiratory therapist objectives.

College Career Service Centers

As I mentioned, if you are presently a student at a college or university, your career services center is a great place to start a job search. In addition to skills and interest assessments, many of these schools maintain a résumé database of all their students that can be accessed by companies worldwide.

College career service centers are connected with many employers who list entry-level job openings and internships available to students of that particular school in job banks. Take advantage of those internships and other work experiences long before your graduation. Join student chapters of professional associations, like the American Marketing Association, American Geological Association, and so on. Doing so will produce marketable keywords that will help your electronic résumé pop to the top in a keyword search.

Sometimes colleges offer reciprocal services to students of other schools, but the only way to find out is to make a telephone call to the career center of the school nearest you. Alumni associations are another good place to start. There is an Internet site at *www.careerresource.net/carserv/* that is an excellent source for hyperlinks to hundreds of college alumni services. Check there first to see what type of support your alma mater provides. Colleges and universities often offer their alumni the same services as current students, while others limit free services to a year after graduation. Again, check your school just to make sure.

College career service centers may have a home page or a hyperlink from the university's main home page where you can find lists of the career resources available from your particular school. In addition, most major universities and colleges post their own job openings on the school's home page.

To locate online information about universities and colleges in general, including the addresses for their home pages, check the following resources:

Career Resource Home Page	*www.careerresource.net*
College and University Home Pages	*www.mit.edu:8001/people/cdemello/univ.html*
CollegeNET	*www.collegenet.com*
Index of American Universities	*www.clas.ufl.edu/au/*
Peterson's Education Center	*www.petersons.com*
U.S. Universities and Community Colleges	*www.utexas.edu/world/univ*

Résumé Sections

In the next chapter, we will begin the process of dividing your information into major headings. Before we start, let's review what those potential titles can be.

For instance, your *objective statement* (should you decide to use one) can be titled:

- Objective
- Goal
- Interests
- Career Objective
- Career Goal
- Job Target

Education is "Education," but it could also be:

- Credentials
- Professional Development
- Continuing Education
- Training
- Some other variation

The *profile,* or *qualifications,* section of the résumé can be called:

- Profile
- Qualifications
- Highlights of Qualifications
- Expertise
- Strengths
- Summary
- Synopsis
- Background
- Professional Background
- Executive Summary
- Highlights
- Overview
- Professional Overview
- Capsule
- Keyword Profile

The *experience* section could be headlined:

- Experience
- Relevant Experience
- Professional Experience
- Work History
- Employment History

- Employment Summary
- History
- Professional History
- Related Employment
- Business Experience
- Employment Record
- Career History

When you pull out your *achievements* into a separate section, you can use any of the following subtitles:

- Accomplishments
- Key Accomplishments
- Representative Accomplishments
- Related Accomplishments
- Highlights of Accomplishments
- Achievements in the same combinations

You might have noticed the addition of *related* or *relevant* before some titles. Use these adjectives when you want to drop some of your experience and focus on a certain industry or job function. Remember, your résumé is just an advertisement. It's not intended to give your reader every ingredient in the soup can. Its purpose is to provide enough information to prompt a hiring manager to pick up the telephone and call you for an interview. You can leave off entire jobs in a résumé. By using the words *related* or *relevant,* you automatically tell your reader that there is more to the story but you have intentionally chosen to leave something out because you thought it would be a waste of the reader's time.

Chapter 3

The second step in writing a résumé is to think about your education. That means all of your training and not just formal education (college, university, or trade school). The education section of your résumé will include degrees, continuing education, professional development, seminars, workshops, and sometimes even self-study.

Turn to the forms at the end of this chapter and list any education or training that you think might relate. If you participated in college activities or received any honors or completed notable projects that relate directly to your target job, then this is the place to list them. A business student might cite a marketing plan developed for a specific class, or a graphic designer might describe artwork created for a Web site and provide a link. Think also about relevant course work, volunteering, internships, clubs, honor societies, fraternities, and sororities.

Take advantage of internships, temporary jobs, and volunteering to gain valuable experience in your target industry. As little as five hours of volunteering or interning a week can add meat to your résumé. If you are working toward becoming a teacher, volunteer for after-school programs. If you want to be a nurse, then volunteer at hospitals, nursing homes, or hospices.

Showing high school education and activities on a résumé is only appropriate when you are under twenty and have no education or training beyond high school. Once you have completed either college courses or specialized technical training, drop your high school information altogether.

Which Came First . . .

If you are a recent college graduate and have little relevant experience, your education section will be placed at the top of your résumé. As you gain more experience, your education almost always gravitates to the bottom.

There is an exception to every rule in the résumé business!

There is an exception to every rule in the résumé business, however, so use your common sense. If you are trying to change careers and recently went back to school to obtain new credentials, your education section will appear at the top of the résumé even if you have years of experience. Think about your strongest qualifications and make certain they appear in the top half of page one of your résumé.

How you choose to list your school and degree can make a difference in how the reader perceives the importance of each item. For instance, in the following education section, the name of the university is prestigious, so I chose to list it first so the reader focused on the school. The job seeker had little real experience, so I provided valuable keywords by listing areas of study under each major. The GPA was relevant because he was competing for jobs through the school's career services center, which required GPAs on all résumés.

SOUTHERN METHODIST UNIVERSITY, Cox School of Business, Dallas, Texas
Bachelor of Business Administration, May 2007
- *Major in Management Information Systems* (166 credit hours, GPA 3.9): Database Design and Administration, Business Computer Programming, Advanced Programming Techniques, Systems Analysis Design, Information Systems in Organizations, and Telecommunication Design and Policy.
- *Minor in International Business:* Introduction to World Cultures, International Politics, International Economics, and the Global Perspective.
- *Awards:* SMU Scholarship, Who's Who Among Students in American Universities and Colleges.
- Selected for a special Electronic Commerce Honors Course that provided in-depth, hands-on experience in the use of the Internet to help companies achieve competitive advantage, transform relationships with customers, suppliers, and business partners, and empower global business.
- Completed a year-long mentoring program with a senior executive at Southwestern Bell as part of the SMU Business Associates Program.
- *Honors:* Beta Gamma Sigma National Honor Society for Collegiate Schools of Business, Alpha Iota Delta honorary member of Decision Sciences Institute, Golden Key Honor Society, Financial Management Association National Honor Society, Alpha Chi National Honor Society.

When the degree is more important than the university where it was earned, list your education with the degree first. Prioritize your degrees in order of importance, like this:

Ph.D. IN AEROSPACE ENGINEERING (2007)
University of Maryland, College Park, Maryland
- Dissertation: *The Optimization of Engine-Integrated Hypersonic Waveriders with Steady State Flight and Static Margin Constraints*
- Received a four-year postgraduate research assistantship in the Hypersonic Research Group

MASTER OF BUSINESS ADMINISTRATION, FINANCE (2006)
The Pennsylvania State University, University Park, State College, Pennsylvania
- Graduated *magna cum laude* with a GPA of 3.93
- Graduate Student Association Representative for the MBA program (2001 – 2005)
- Awarded a Graduate Assistantship in the Real Estate Department during the final semester

BACHELOR OF SCIENCE IN NURSING (2007)
Beth-El College of Nursing and Health Sciences, University of Colorado, Colorado Springs, Colorado
• Recipient of the Outstanding BSN Student Award for outstanding leadership, clinical, and academic achievement (May 2007)
• Hand picked by the university's nursing faculty to help teach Aging Simulations (February 2006)
• Beth-El College of Nursing nominee for the UCCS Student Achievement Award (May 2007)

The Devil's in the Details

Details, details, details . . . they really do matter. Something as simple as a date in your education can affect your job search. For instance, writing from–to dates (1999 – 2001) implies that you did not graduate. If you graduated with a degree, list only the year you graduated (2001). Computerized applicant tracking systems and Internet résumé databases are programmed to show that you have college study but not a degree if they see from–to dates.

If you are searching for a job that will utilize special language skills, cross-cultural experience, or international travel, the fact that you studied abroad or completed a foreign exchange program will be an important addition to your résumé. Study abroad falls under the "Education" category, while travel for recreation's sake could be included in a separate "International Experience" section on your résumé, if you are searching for a job that would make that experience valuable.

STUDIES ABROAD
Loyola University, Rome, Italy (Spring 2007)
• Classroom study integrated with European field experiences
ITESM, Monterrey, Mexico (Summer 2006)
• Intensive Spanish language and Mexican culture studies

When you did not complete a degree but have some college study, you can list the degree with the qualification that you have a certain number of credits left to finish, as in the first sample below, or classify the section as "Undergraduate Studies" like the second sample. Whichever method you choose, just make sure it is quite clear that you didn't graduate.

BACHELOR OF SCIENCE, MARKETING (2004 – 2007)
Hawaii Pacific University, Honolulu, Hawaii
• Two credits short of completing an undergraduate degree
• Selected for the Dean's List
• Relevant course work completed: Marketing Management, Public Relations, Marketing Research, Consumer Analysis, Principles of Advertising, International Marketing, Principles of Retail, Industrial Marketing, Production Management, Principles of Marketing.

OR . . .

UNDERGRADUATE STUDIES
Pikes Peak Community College, Colorado Springs, Colorado
- Banking and Finance Program (2 semesters, full-time)
- Early Childhood Education (3 semesters, full-time)
- Course work included: Communications I and II, Minorities, American Indian, Human Relations

Northern Virginia Community College, Fairfax, Virginia
- Liberal Arts Program (1 semester, full-time)
- Course work included: English Composition, History/Western Civilization II

Colorado Mountain College, Glenwood Springs, Colorado
- Liberal Arts Program (1 semester, full-time)
- Course work included: Introduction to Psychology, Physical Science

I am often asked whether or not to list GPAs on a résumé. My reply is, "If you have a GPA of 3.5 or above, it could help you. From 3.0 to 3.5 neither helps nor hurts you, in most cases. Anything from 2.9 or below can actually hurt your chances of getting an interview." I recommend that you list your GPA if you are a recent graduate whose résumé will be competing against the résumés of fellow students, provided it's a good GPA. Otherwise, leave it off.

As I've already mentioned, there is an exception to every rule in the résumé business, so use common sense. If nearly every résumé you see for your industry has GPAs listed, then you should list yours, too. For instance, in academic circles, a GPA is often important on a curriculum vitae.

Technical and Occupational Training

When you attend a trade school, you receive either a diploma or certificate. This type of schooling can be listed under the "Education" heading or under a separate heading called "Training" or "Technical Training." Following are some examples of various training sections.

MICROSOFT COMPUTER SYSTEM ENGINEER (MCSE) COURSE (2007)
Knowledge Alliance and Executrain, Colorado Springs, Colorado
- Networking Essentials, Administering Windows NT 4.0, Windows NT Core Technologies, Internet-working Microsoft NT using TCP/IP, Enterprise Technologies, Internet Information Systems

HEWLETT-PACKARD TRAINING (2005 – 2007)
- MBTI Business Assessment/Application, Understanding Team Development, Interpersonal Communications, Quality Systems, Conflict Management, Peer Appraisal, Applied One-on-One Task Analysis

ACADEMY GRAPHICS (2007)
- Introduction to CADD Systems for PCB Layout and Program File Editing

LICENSED MASSAGE THERAPIST (2007)
Colorado Institute of Massage Therapy, Colorado Springs, Colorado

EMT CERTIFICATION PROGRAM (2006 to 2007)
Memorial Hospital, Colorado Springs, Colorado

- *General Medicine:* Infants and Children, Chest/Abdomen Injuries, Eye/Face/Neck Injuries, Injuries to the Head and Spine, Musculoskeletal Injuries, Burns, Soft Tissue Injuries, OB/GYN, Allergies, Diabetes, Seizures, Syncope, CPR, Defibrillation, Pharmacology, Patient Assessment/Documentation, Geriatrics, Communication, History and Physical Exam, Medical/Legal/Ethical Issues
- *Emergency Medicine:* Multiple Casualty Incidents, Aeromedical Resources, Extrication and Immobilization, Hazardous Materials, Ambulance Operations, Moving Patients, Trauma Skills, Agricultural and Industrial Emergencies, Splinting, Bandaging and Dressings, Bleeding, Shock, PASG, Drowning, Near Drowning, Diving Emergencies, Environmental Emergencies, Poisoning, Respiratory Emergencies, Airway/Ventilation/Oxygen, Cardiac Emergencies
- *Psychiatric:* Behavioral Emergencies, Violent Patients, Drugs and Alcohol

Continuing Education

Continuing education, or professional development, shows that you care about lifelong learning and self-development, so think about any relevant training since your formal education was completed.

Relevant is the key word here. Always look at your résumé from the perspective of a potential employer. Don't waste space by listing training that is not directly or indirectly related to your target job.

EMT CONTINUING EDUCATION (2000 to present)
American Medical Response, Colorado Springs, Colorado
- EMT Refresher Course (2000)
- CPR First Responder (2001)
- EKG Recognition and Interpretation (2000)
- Basic Trauma Life Support (2000)
- EMT Basic IV Course (2000)

INGERSOLL-RAND TRAINING PROGRAMS

Quality: Six Sigma, ASQ-CQM Refresher Course (Pareto charts, flow charts, cause and effect tools, checklists, control charts, histograms, scatter diagrams, activity network diagrams, affinity diagrams, interrelationships diagraphs, matrix diagrams, priorities matrices, process decision program charts, and tree diagrams), Management by Fact

Business: Quality of Leadership, Designing High-Performance Organizations, Project Management, Microsoft Project

CHEM NUCLEAR SYSTEMS TRAINING PROGRAMS
Computers: Global Information Systems (ARC INFO)
Business: Communications, Leadership
Environmental: OSHA Hazardous Materials (40 hours), CPR, Radworker II

GENERAL ELECTRIC TRAINING PROGRAMS
Manufacturing: Manufacturing Management Program (MMP), Manufacturing Studies
Quality: NQA-1 Lead Auditor, KT, Root-Cause Analysis, QC Course, TQM, SPC, WorkOut
Engineering: Verification, Design Files, Change Control, Interchangeability

PROFESSIONAL DEVELOPMENT (Education Career)
- Coaching and Team Building Skills for Manager and Supervisor, SkillPath (March 2007)
- Creating Writers through Assessment and Instruction, Six-Trait Writing, Northwest Regional Educational Laboratory, Portland, Oregon (December 1997, April 1999, and February 2007)
- Reproducibles for Beginning Writers, Read-Write Connection (February 2007)
- Getting the Most from Microsoft Office (February 2007)
- Formats and Frameworks, Guided Reading and Writing, National Literacy Coalition (November 2006)
- TOP: Creating Writers, Portland State University, Portland, Oregon (Winter 2005)
- Creating Writers through Assessment and Instruction, Six-Trait Writing (December 2005)
- International Institute of Assessment Leadership, Center for Performance Assessment (35 contact hours, July 2004)
- Teaching to the Standards (Summer 2003)
- Our Future: Expect the Best (Fall 2002)
- Interactive Volleyball Coaching (Summers 2001, 2002)
- Issues Affecting Change, Special Topics Education, Brigham Young University (Summer 2002)
- Volleyball Coaches Clinic, Brigham Young University (August 2002)
- Goals 2000: Performance Assessment (Spring 2002)
- Implementing Standards and Assessments (Fall 2001)
- Curriculum Development and Assessment (Fall 2001)
- Fellow, Colorado Writing Project, Level 1 (Summer 2001)
- Beginning WordPerfect, Northeastern Junior College (Spring 2000)

PROFESSIONAL DEVELOPMENT (Project Management)

- **Management Courses**: Project Management, Sexual Harassment, Security Awareness, Diversity, Team Leader Training, Working I and III, A–Z in Problem Solving, Infoman Change Management, Microsoft Managing Reports and Forms, Electronic Purchase Requisition, Introduction to Telecommunications

- **Technical Courses**: CA-7 Operational Workshop, Enterprise Systems 102 (Midrange), Storage Management Fundamentals (Mainframe/Midrange), TSO/ISPF, CA-7 and CA-11 Job Scheduling Software, Using JCL Effectively, NDM, Lotus 1-2-3, Introduction to LANs, Introduction to OS/2, Lotus Basic Notes Concepts, Microsoft Windows, Microsoft Project, Microsoft Word, Microsoft Access, TCP/IP Introduction

- **Personal Development**: Negotiation/Assertiveness Skills, Seven Habits of Highly Effective People

PROFESSIONAL DEVELOPMENT (Nursing Career)
- Completed yearly accredited continuous education and monthly in-service workshops taught by doctors, drug companies, and equipment manufacturers.
- Received Category I credit for attending the Transcatheter Cardiovascular Therapeutics Symposium (TCT) (2005, 2007)
- Attended numerous conferences approved by the American Nurses Association
- Completed two years of classroom and clinical experience in non-invasive vascular testing from Cevenar Vascular, Hartford, Connecticut

PROFESSIONAL DEVELOPMENT (Benefits Management Career)
- Completed three parts of the Defined Contribution Course (PA, C1, C2), sponsored by the American Society of Pension Actuaries (ASPA) (2007)
- Attended the annual ASPA conferences and workshops (1998 – present)
- Certified in flexible compensation instruction by the Employers Council on Flexible Compensation (ECFC), requiring five years of experience and a proficiency examination
- Participated in annual ECFC conferences and workshops (2003 – present)
- Completed 40 hours of continuing education per year required by the ASPA and Baird, Kurtz & Dobson (1998 – present)

COLLEGE EDUCATION

Use this form to collect information on your formal college education. Write down everything you can think of, regardless of whether you use it on the final résumé. You will narrow the list later. There is a separate page included in this section for each degree.

DEGREE _____

SCHOOL _____

CITY AND STATE _____

YEARS ATTENDED _____

YEAR GRADUATED _____ GPA _____

MAJOR _____

MINOR _____

THESIS/DISSERTATION _____

_____

~ ~

SIGNIFICANT PROJECTS _____

_____

_____

_____

HONORS, AWARDS, SCHOLARSHIPS, ETC. _____

_____

_____

_____

ACTIVITIES (volunteer, leadership, sports, social groups, etc.) _____

_____

_____

_____

STUDY ABROAD (program, school, country, special areas of study) _____

_____

_____

COLLEGE EDUCATION

Use this form to collect information on your formal college education. Write down everything you can think of, regardless of whether you use it on the final résumé. You will narrow the list later. There is a separate page included in this section for each degree.

DEGREE _____

SCHOOL _____

CITY AND STATE _____

YEARS ATTENDED _____

YEAR GRADUATED _____ GPA _____

MAJOR _____

MINOR _____

THESIS/DISSERTATION _____

_____

~ ~

SIGNIFICANT PROJECTS _____

_____

_____

_____

HONORS, AWARDS, SCHOLARSHIPS, ETC. _____

_____

_____

_____

ACTIVITIES (volunteer, leadership, sports, social groups, etc.) _____

_____

_____

_____

STUDY ABROAD (program, school, country, special areas of study) _____

_____

_____

COLLEGE EDUCATION

Use this form to collect information on your formal college education. Write down everything you can think of, regardless of whether you use it on the final résumé. You will narrow the list later. There is a separate page included in this section for each degree.

DEGREE _____

SCHOOL _____

CITY AND STATE _____

YEARS ATTENDED _____

YEAR GRADUATED _____ GPA _____

MAJOR _____

MINOR _____

THESIS/DISSERTATION _____

_____

~ ~

SIGNIFICANT PROJECTS _____

_____

_____

_____

HONORS, AWARDS, SCHOLARSHIPS, ETC. _____

_____

_____

_____

ACTIVITIES (volunteer, leadership, sports, social groups, etc.) _____

_____

_____

_____

STUDY ABROAD (program, school, country, special areas of study) _____

_____

_____

COLLEGE EDUCATION

Use this form to collect information on your formal college education. Write down everything you can think of, regardless of whether you use it on the final résumé. You will narrow the list later. There is a separate page included in this section for each degree.

DEGREE _____

SCHOOL _____

CITY AND STATE _____

YEARS ATTENDED _____

YEAR GRADUATED _____ GPA _____

MAJOR _____

MINOR _____

THESIS/DISSERTATION _____

_____

~ ~

SIGNIFICANT PROJECTS _____

_____

_____

_____

HONORS, AWARDS, SCHOLARSHIPS, ETC. _____

_____

_____

_____

ACTIVITIES (volunteer, leadership, sports, social groups, etc.) _____

_____

_____

STUDY ABROAD (program, school, country, special areas of study) _____

_____

_____

COLLEGE EDUCATION

Use this form to collect information on your formal college education. Write down everything you can think of, regardless of whether you use it on the final résumé. You will narrow the list later. There is a separate page included in this section for each degree.

DEGREE _____

SCHOOL _____

CITY AND STATE _____

YEARS ATTENDED _____

YEAR GRADUATED _____ GPA _____

MAJOR _____

MINOR _____

THESIS/DISSERTATION _____

_____

~ ~

SIGNIFICANT PROJECTS _____

_____

_____

_____

HONORS, AWARDS, SCHOLARSHIPS, ETC. _____

_____

_____

_____

ACTIVITIES (volunteer, leadership, sports, social groups, etc.) _____

_____

_____

_____

STUDY ABROAD (program, school, country, special areas of study) _____

_____

_____

VOCATIONAL/TECHNICAL TRAINING

Use this form to collect information on your vocational, technical, occupational, and military training. Write down everything you can think of, regardless of whether it relates to your job goal. You will narrow the list later.

NAME OF COURSE _____

PRESENTED BY (company, school, etc.) _____

RESULT (certification, diploma, etc.) _____

DATES ATTENDED _____

~ ~

NAME OF COURSE _____

PRESENTED BY (company, school, etc.) _____

RESULT (certification, diploma, etc.) _____

DATES ATTENDED _____

~ ~

NAME OF COURSE _____

PRESENTED BY (company, school, etc.) _____

RESULT (certification, diploma, etc.) _____

DATES ATTENDED _____

~ ~

NAME OF COURSE _____

PRESENTED BY (company, school, etc.) _____

RESULT (certification, diploma, etc.) _____

DATES ATTENDED _____

~ ~

NAME OF COURSE _____

PRESENTED BY (company, school, etc.) _____

RESULT (certification, diploma, etc.) _____

DATES ATTENDED _____

~ ~

VOCATIONAL/TECHNICAL TRAINING

Use this form to collect information on your vocational, technical, and occupational training. Write down everything you can think of, regardless of whether it relates to your job goal. You will narrow the list later.

NAME OF COURSE _____

PRESENTED BY (company, school, etc.) _____

RESULT (certification, diploma, etc.) _____

DATES ATTENDED _____

~ ~

NAME OF COURSE _____

PRESENTED BY (company, school, etc.) _____

RESULT (certification, diploma, etc.) _____

DATES ATTENDED _____

~ ~

NAME OF COURSE _____

PRESENTED BY (company, school, etc.) _____

RESULT (certification, diploma, etc.) _____

DATES ATTENDED _____

~ ~

NAME OF COURSE _____

PRESENTED BY (company, school, etc.) _____

RESULT (certification, diploma, etc.) _____

DATES ATTENDED _____

~ ~

NAME OF COURSE _____

PRESENTED BY (company, school, etc.) _____

RESULT (certification, diploma, etc.) _____

DATES ATTENDED _____

~ ~

PROFESSIONAL DEVELOPMENT

Use this form to collect information on your professional development and continuing education, including in-services, workshops, seminars, corporate training programs, conferences, conventions, etc. Write down everything you can think of, regardless of whether it relates to your job goal. You will narrow the list later.

NAME OF COURSE _____

PRESENTED BY (company, school, etc.) _____

DATES ATTENDED _____

~ ~

NAME OF COURSE _____

PRESENTED BY (company, school, etc.) _____

DATES ATTENDED _____

~ ~

NAME OF COURSE _____

PRESENTED BY (company, school, etc.) _____

DATES ATTENDED _____

~ ~

NAME OF COURSE _____

PRESENTED BY (company, school, etc.) _____

DATES ATTENDED _____

~ ~

NAME OF COURSE _____

PRESENTED BY (company, school, etc.) _____

DATES ATTENDED _____

~ ~

NAME OF COURSE _____

PRESENTED BY (company, school, etc.) _____

DATES ATTENDED _____

~ ~

NAME OF COURSE _____

PRESENTED BY (company, school, etc.) _____

DATES ATTENDED _____

~ ~

PROFESSIONAL DEVELOPMENT

Use this form to collect information on your professional development and continuing education, including in-services, workshops, seminars, corporate training programs, conferences, conventions, etc. Write down everything you can think of, regardless of whether it relates to your job goal. You will narrow the list later.

NAME OF COURSE _____

PRESENTED BY (company, school, etc.) _____

DATES ATTENDED _____

~ ~

NAME OF COURSE _____

PRESENTED BY (company, school, etc.) _____

DATES ATTENDED _____

~ ~

NAME OF COURSE _____

PRESENTED BY (company, school, etc.) _____

DATES ATTENDED _____

~ ~

NAME OF COURSE _____

PRESENTED BY (company, school, etc.) _____

DATES ATTENDED _____

~ ~

NAME OF COURSE _____

PRESENTED BY (company, school, etc.) _____

DATES ATTENDED _____

~ ~

NAME OF COURSE _____

PRESENTED BY (company, school, etc.) _____

DATES ATTENDED _____

~ ~

NAME OF COURSE _____

PRESENTED BY (company, school, etc.) _____

DATES ATTENDED _____

~ ~

Chapter 4

What if it has been years since you worked at a job and you can't remember what you did? What if it was just yesterday and you can't remember what you did?! Don't worry. You're not getting old. Most of us forget what we did yesterday, so now we need to come up with some strategies for finding ways to describe your work history.

This chapter will talk about resources for finding job descriptions. The next few chapters will then show you how to use them.

First, get your hands on a written description of the job you wish to obtain and for any jobs you have held in the past, as well as for your current job. If you are presently employed, your human resource department is the first place to look. If not, then go to your local library and ask for a copy of *The Dictionary of Occupational Titles* or the *Occupational Outlook Handbook*. These industry standard reference guides offer volumes of occupational titles and job descriptions for everything from abalone divers to zoo veterinarians (and thousands in between). You can also find them on the Internet (see next page). Other places to look for job descriptions include:

- Local government job service agencies
- Professional and technical organizations
- Headhunters (i.e., recruiters)
- Associates who work in the same field
- Newspaper advertisements for similar jobs
- Online job postings (which tend to have longer job descriptions than print ads)

If you have access to the Internet, you will find some great resources at the Web sites on the next page.

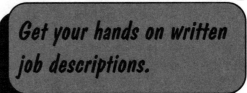

Get your hands on written job descriptions.

- America's Career InfoNet, *www.acinet.org*
- Career Guide to Industries, *www.bls.gov/oco/cg/*
- Careers Online Virtual Careers Show, *www.careersonline.com.au/show/menu.html*
- Dictionary of Occupational Titles, *www.oalj.dol.gov/libdot.htm*
- Exploring Occupations from the University of Manitoba, *www.umanitoba.ca/counselling/careers.html*
- JobProfiles.com, *www.jobprofiles.org*
- Occupational Outlook Handbook, *www.bls.gov/oco/home.htm*
- Occupational Outlook Quarterly, *www.bls.gov/opub/ooq/ooqhome.htm*

Performance evaluations, depending on how well they are written, generally list a description of your major responsibilities, a breakdown of individual tasks, and highlights of your accomplishments. You should *always* keep a folder at home of performance evaluations from every job you have ever held. If you haven't kept them up until now, please start.

Now, make copies of these performance evaluations so you can highlight them as you write your résumé. Use a different colored pen to highlight accomplishments, the things you did above and beyond the call of duty.

Also make copies of the job descriptions you discovered and mark the sentences that describe anything you have done in your past or present jobs. These job descriptions are important sources of keywords, so pay particular attention to nouns and phrases that you can incorporate into your own résumé.

Set these papers aside until Chapter 6 when it will be time to write everything down.

Chapter 5

In today's world of electronic résumés, make sure you know the buzzwords of your industry and incorporate them into the sentences you are about to write. Keywords are the nouns, adjectives, or short phrases that describe any experience and education that might be used to find your résumé in a keyword search of an electronic résumé database, either on the Internet or in a company's own system. They reflect the essential knowledge, skills, and abilities (KSAs) required to do your job.

Since you will find a requirement to define your KSAs for many government jobs, let's stop here for a minute and talk about what KSAs really are. Your *knowledge* is information you have learned from both your work and personal life, including your education, special training, and experience. *Skills* are things you "do"—typing, computer programming, cooking, among many others. *Abilities* are related to your unique talents and natural aptitudes. Abilities are the foundation of your passion, although your skills and knowledge play a part as well. You are the only person in the world who has your unique set of knowledge, skills, and abilities.

Now back to keywords. They are generally concrete descriptions such as:

- C++
- UNIX
- fiber optic cable
- network
- project management
- Spanish
- international
- business development
- Internet
- customer retention
- cost reduction
- long-range planning
- organizational design

> *Keywords reflect the essential knowledge, skills, and abilities required to do your job.*

Even well-known company names (AT&T, IBM, Hewlett-Packard) and universities (Harvard, Yale, Princeton, SMU, Stanford, Tulane, Columbia, etc.) are sometimes used as keywords, especially when it is necessary to narrow down an initial search that calls up hundreds of résumés from a résumé database.

Acronyms and abbreviations here can either hurt you or help you, depending on how you use them. One example given to me by an engineer at a software development company was the abbreviation IN. Think about it. IN could stand for *intelligent networks, Indiana,* or the word *in.* It is better to spell out the abbreviation if there could be any possible confusion.

However, if a series of initials is so well known that it would be recognized by nearly everyone in your industry and would not likely be confused with a real word, then the keyword search will probably use those initials (i.e., IBM, CPA, UNIX). When in doubt, always spell it out at least one time on your résumé. A computer only needs to see the combination one time for it to be considered a "hit" in a keyword search.

Soft skills are sometimes included in search criteria, except for very technical positions where you should concentrate more on your hard skills. I have interviewed some companies that use soft skills extensively for the initial selection of résumés for management positions. A recent survey by CareerBuilder.com listed the most frequently searched soft skills as *oral and written communication, problem solving, leadership, team building, performance, productivity,* and *strategic planning,* among others.

At the end of this chapter, you will find more examples of keywords for specific industries, although there is no such thing as a comprehensive listing of keywords for any single job. Computerized applicant tracking applications allow a recruiter or hiring manager to personalize his or her list for each job opening, so it is an evolving process. You will never know whether you have listed absolutely every keyword possible, so focus instead on getting on paper as many related skills as possible, remembering to be absolutely honest and accurate.

The job descriptions and performance evaluations you found in Step 3 are some of the most important sources for keywords. You can also be certain that nearly every noun, and some adjectives, in a job posting or advertisement will be keywords, so make sure you use those words somewhere in your résumé, using synonyms wherever you can. Just make sure you can justify every word on your résumé—don't exaggerate. If you don't have the experience or skill, don't use the keyword.

The form at the end of this chapter will help you to make a list of the keywords you have determined are important for your particular job search. Also list common synonyms for those words when you can. As you incorporate these words into the sentences of your résumé, check them off.

One caution. Always tell the truth. The minute a hiring manager speaks with you on the telephone or begins an interview, any exaggeration of the truth will become immediately apparent.

It is a bad idea to say, "I don't have experience with MS Word computer software" just to get the words *MS Word* or *computer software* on paper so your résumé will pop up in a keyword search.

In a cover letter, it might be appropriate to say, "I don't have five years of experience in marketing but can add two years of university training in the subject to three years of in-depth experience as a marketing assistant with Hewlett-Packard." That is legitimate reasoning, but anything more manipulative can be hazardous to your job search.

According to an article at CareerJournal.com, it is getting harder for job seekers to game the systems that recruiters use to identify potential candidates. Some candidates have tried to hide keywords so they can't be seen by the naked eye by using white text on a white background, typing so small that it looks like a solid horizontal line, and even inserting Web coding in online résumés that's hidden from plain view. Newer applicant tracking and résumé database software are able to detect these tricks, discrediting the applicant. Some technology even penalizes job seekers who use keywords out of context by placing their résumé at the bottom of the search results.

Keywords in Electronic Résumés

Using the right keywords for your particular experience and education is critical to the success of your electronic résumé. Without the right keywords, your résumé will float in cyberspace forever waiting for a hiring manager to find it. If your résumé contains all the right keywords, then you will be among the first candidates whose résumés are reviewed. If you lack only one of the keywords, then your résumé will be next in line after résumés that have them all, and so on.

Remember, your keywords are the specific terminology used in your job that reflect your experience and skills. For instance, *operating room* and *ICU* immediately classify the experience of a nurse, but *pediatric ICU* narrows it down even further.

Don't try to limit your résumé by using fewer words. If your information is longer than one page, a reader looking at a computer screen won't be able to tell, but the computer doing a keyword search will know if a word is not there. Recall, however, that you only need to use a word one time for it to be considered a "hit" in a keyword search. Try to use synonyms wherever possible to broaden your chances of being selected.

You should also understand the difference between a simple keyword search and a concept search. When a recruiter brings an e-mailed résumé onto the screen and sends the computer on a search for a single word like *marketing*—which one can do in any word processing program with a few clicks of a mouse or function key—he or she is performing a keyword search.

You are also performing a keyword search when you type a word or combination of words into the command line of a search engine like Yahoo! or Google (see example below). In that case, sometimes the computer searches entire documents for matches and other times it looks only at headers or extracts from the files.

Screen shot used with permission of Google.

A concept search, on the other hand, can bridge the gap between words by reading entire phrases and then using sophisticated artificial intelligence to interpret what is being said, translating the phrase into a single word, like *network*, or a combination of words, like *project management*.

For example, in a simple keyword search on *Manager of Product Sales,* ordinary software would return a match on a candidate's résumé that reads "worked for a Manager of Product Sales." A concept search can distinguish between this résumé and another candidate's résumé that indicated "served as a Manager of Product Sales."

The various software packages that extract data from electronic résumés are incredibly sophisticated. They can read the grammar of noun, verb, and adjective combinations and extract the information for placement on the form that will become your entry in a résumé database. Expert system extraction engines use a complex knowledge base of more than 200,000 rules and over ten million résumé terms. They recognize grammatical structure variations, including synonyms and context within natural language text.

They even know the difference between words by their placement on the page and their relationship to the header that precedes it—Experience, Education, or Computer Skills.

Because of this complicated logic, and because each company and each hiring manager has the ability to personalize the search criteria for each job opening, it is impossible to give you a concrete list of the thousands of possible keywords that could be used to search for any one job.

For instance, Sun StorageTek, a high-tech company in Louisville, Colorado, graciously conducted a keyword search of their résumé database for me and brought up the following criteria from two different hiring managers for the same job title. These are keywords extracted from real job requisitions written by hiring managers.

FINANCIAL ANALYST/SENIOR ACCOUNTANT

REQUIRED
- BS in finance or accounting with 4 years of experience or
- MBA in related field with 2 years of relevant experience
- certified public accountant
- forecasting

DESIRED
- accounting
- financial
- trend analysis
- financial statement
- results analysis
- trends
- strategic planning
- develop trends
- financial modeling
- personal computer
- microcomputers
- DCF
- presentation skills
- team player

REQUIRED	DESIRED
• BS in finance or accounting with 4 years of experience or	• ability
	• customer
• MBA in related field with 2 years of relevant experience	• new business
	• financial analysis
• accounting	• financial
• financial reporting	• forecasting
• financial statement	• process improvement
• Excel	• policy development
	• business policies
	• PowerPoint
	• Microsoft Word
	• analytical ability

Sample Keywords

You can see why it is so difficult to give definitive lists of keywords and concepts. However, it is possible to give you samples of actual keyword searches used by the recruiters at Sun StorageTek to give you some ideas.

Let me emphasize again that you should list only experience you actually have gained. Do not include the keywords on the following pages in your résumé just because they are listed here.

ACCOUNT EXECUTIVE

REQUIRED
• BS degree
• 3 years technical selling experience
• Fortune 500 account management experience
• sales
• storage industry
• solution selling

DESIRED
• Siebel
• quota levels
• Value-Added Dealers (VAD)
• Value-Added Resellers (VAR)

ACCOUNTING ANALYST

REQUIRED
• BA or MBA
• 2–4 years of experience
• asset management
• SAP
• accounting

DESIRED

- fixed assets
- capital assets
- corporate tax
- US GAAP

BASE SALES REPRESENTATIVE

REQUIRED

- 2–4 years of sales or contract management experience
- 2+ years of telemarketing or telesales experience

DESIRED

- Siebel
- storage industry

BUSINESS MANAGER, CENTRAL ARCHIVE MANAGEMENT

REQUIRED

- BS in engineering or computer science
- 10 years of related engineering and/or manufacturing experience
- strategic planning
- network
- product management
- program management

DESIRED

- business plan
- line management
- pricing
- team player
- CAM
- marketing
- product strategy
- vendor
- general management
- OEM
- profit and loss

BUSINESS OPERATIONS SPECIALIST

REQUIRED

- bachelor's degree
- 4 years of directly related experience
- production schedule
- project planning

DESIRED

- ability to implement
- CList
- data analysis
- off-shift
- team player
- automation
- ability to plan
- customer interaction
- VM
- JCL
- MVS
- UNIX
- analytical ability
- customer interface
- network
- skills analysis
- automatic tools

DEVELOPMENT ENGINEER, ADVISORY

REQUIRED

- BS/BA, Masters desired
- 5–10 years mechanical engineering experience
- 10+ years experience in hardware design
- EMC/EMI debug
- mechanical design
- tape drive

DESIRED

- DFSS (Design for Six Sigma)
- ANSYS or Metlab
- mechanisms design
- shock
- vibration
- NARTE
- tape library
- data storage

FINANCIAL ANALYST, STAFF

REQUIRED

- BS in Finance or Accounting
- 1–2 years related experience
- customer-focused experience

- excellent written communication skills
- collection
- financial forecast
- financial modeling
- financial reporting
- financial consolidation
- reconciliation

DESIRED
- international finance
- Hyperion consolidation software
- channel experience

ORDER SPECIALIST

REQUIRED
- BS degree
- 1–3 years experience
- order administration
- order fulfillment
- invoice processing
- Microsoft Word
- Excel

DESIRED
- database

PROJECT MANAGER, HUMAN RESOURCES

REQUIRED
- bachelor's degree in human resources, business, or related field
- 6 years broad experience

DESIRED
- communication
- project management
- milestone development
- time management
- benchmarking
- recruiting
- long-range planning
- sourcing
- vendor management
- recruitment processing outsourcing (RPO)

SECRETARY III

REQUIRED
- high school education or equivalent
- 5 years of experience
- typing skill of 55–60 wpm
- interpersonal skills
- oral communication

DESIRED
- administrative assistance
- clerical
- data analysis
- file maintenance
- material repair
- PowerPoint
- project planning
- reports
- screen calls
- troubleshoot
- answer phones
- communication skills
- document distribution
- mail sorting
- Microsoft Word
- presentation
- publication
- schedule calendar
- secretarial
- appointments
- confidential
- edit
- material
- policies and procedures
- problem solving
- records management
- schedule conference
- telephone interview

SOFTWARE ENGINEER—EMBEDDED, ADVISORY LEVEL

REQUIRED
- BS or MS degree in one of the computer sciences or engineering
- 12–14 years of experience minimum
- controller-architecture design experience
- disk controller
- fiber channel

- software/hardware integration
- embedded systems
- system level debugging
- object-oriented design
- script building

DESIRED
- open systems
- product development

SOFTWARE ENGINEER, SENIOR

REQUIRED
- BS/MS in engineering, computer science, or closely related field
- 8–9 years of experience

DESIRED
- C++
- customer
- hiring/firing
- prototype
- structured design
- code development
- methodology
- real time
- supervision
- communication skills
- experiment design
- problem solving
- software design
- testing

SYSTEMS ENGINEER, SENIOR

REQUIRED
- BS degree in related field
- 8–10 years of experience
- pre-sales
- systems engineering
- z/OS
- data storage

DESIRED
- systems configuration
- capacity planning
- data facility hierarchical storage manager (DFHSM)
- hierarchical storage controller (HSC)
- presentation skills

Sample Résumés with Keywords Highlighted

Let me show you how keywords can be extracted from an actual résumé. In the example on the following pages, the résumé has possible keywords highlighted using bold and italic letters. Résumés for different industries generate completely different keywords. The only keywords that might be the same are ones for "soft" skills.

Just because I've highlighted all possible keywords in a résumé doesn't mean that the hiring manager will write each one of them in a job requisition. Instead, this exercise is meant to help you become more aware of the nouns, adjectives, and sometimes verbs that *might* become keywords in a résumé database search, whether it is at Careerbuilder.com or in a company's private database of résumés.

You will also notice that I've only highlighted the word the first time it appears. To applicant tracking software, the number of times a word appears in a résumé or its position at the top, middle, or bottom of a résumé doesn't increase its importance. Relevance is more important than keyword density to these applications. For instance, your résumé will rank higher if you have more years of experience than the other candidates. The software extracts that information using the "from" and "to" dates on your job titles.

NOTE: Do not highlight keywords on your own résumé! They are highlighted on these examples solely as a tool to help you understand the concept of which words become keywords in a search.

MARGARET DeVITO

NONPROFIT ORGANIZATIONAL DEVELOPMENT

e-Commerce • Customer Relationship Management • Organizational Development • Program Management
Aligning information technology with business to create innovative solutions that drive change.

Accomplished business strategist with more than 12 years enhancing **operational efficiencies**, developing innovative solutions, and providing **organizational leadership** in **nonprofit** settings. Able to provide vision and direction for key technology development while aligning client needs with organizational goals. Strong ability to translate business needs into **technological requirements**. Skilled **program manager**, analytical **problem solver**, and organizational **leader** with extensive experience in:

- *Nonprofit Client Relationship*
- *Strategic Planning*
- *Client Experience Analysis*
- *Organizational Development / Change*

- *Process Re-engineering*
- *Team Building*
- *Vision Planning*
- *Community Needs Analysis*

EDUCATION

MASTER OF ARTS, ORGANIZATIONAL LEADERSHIP (2006)
Chapman University, Roseville, California
- Relevant course work: ***Organizational Behavior***, Organizational Development, Organizational **Research**, Team Development, Self / Systems / Leadership, Storytelling in Leadership, Democracy / Ethics / Leadership.

BACHELOR OF SCIENCE, APPAREL AND MERCHANDISING (1988)
Colorado State University, Fort Collins, Colorado

NONPROFIT EXPERIENCE

SENIOR E-COMMERCE MARKETING SPECIALIST
Focus on the Family (nonprofit 501(c)(3)), Colorado Springs, Colorado (2007 – present)
Provide leadership and expertise for the development of e-commerce solutions for the Focus on the Family **Web site**. Considered a super-user of the site's **software.** Currently analyzing top sellers by category and developing strategies for **cross-selling, upselling**, and **product merchandising.**
- Developed and implemented ongoing enhancement / **optimization strategies**, which increased revenue from the e-commerce site by $200,000 in three months.
- Analyzed and reviewed **site user data**, and identified areas of opportunity for increasing revenue.
- Trained others on **best practices** and implemented merchandising and technology strategies for the site.

VOLUNTEER / BOARD OF DIRECTORS
Crossroads Diversified Services, Sacramento, California (2003 – 2007)
Wellspring Women's Center, Oak Park, California (2004 – 2006)
Sacramento Sirens, Sacramento, California (2006)
Volunteered to help nonprofit organizations close the growing digital divide between business and nonprofit entities. Introduced **technological capabilities** and created organizational **visions, missions,** and business strategies.
- Served as the secretary of the board of directors for Crossroads, a $3.0 million nonprofit entity providing job opportunities for persons with disabilities or other barriers to getting work.
- Created a process and **operations manual** for the for-profit Sacramento Sirens women's professional football team, and helped to provide guidelines for their **501(c)(3) nonprofit foundation.**

BUSINESS EXPERIENCE

BUSINESS ESCALATION PROGRAM MANAGER
Hewlett-Packard / Compaq, Roseville, California (2001 – 2003)
Promoted to identify and implement plans to improve IT problem resolution for HP's global customers. Ensured that HP **storage products** met or exceeded **customer expectations** regarding availability and operability.
- Selected as one of the few HP / Compaq employees (6,000 out of 165,000) granted stock options and asked to stay during the merger.
- Created documentation to resolve **implementation issues** for a Fortune 500 retailer, ensuring the customer purchased additional **new products** after reviewing only the **prototypes.**

**BUSINESS
EXPERIENCE**

Business Escalation Program Manager (continued)
- Resolved and closed 66% of *global escalations* on or ahead of schedule.
- Retained a major client (an $80 billion healthcare organization) after successfully resolving an escalation affecting 150 hospitals throughout the U.S. The client ordered an additional product with greater *enterprise storage capacity* at a price point of more than $5 million per order.
- Identified the needs of the combined HP / Compaq Enterprise Storage organizations *for knowledge management* to incorporate *organizational changes* and *process re-engineering.*
- Streamlined *shipping* escalation processes after 9/11 for the Roseville *manufacturing* site.

PROJECT MANAGER
Agilent (a former HP division), Colorado Springs, Colorado (2000)
Developed *project plans* to integrate Fort Collins IT teams into Agilent's centralized *help desk.*
- Provided improved support for customers and reduced IT *cost-of-delivery* for *customer support.*
- Developed *training plans* for the Colorado Springs site administrative assistant customers so they could learn how to effectively utilize the company's *e-mail application*. This information was used to address customer needs on future *application rollouts*.

MESSAGING SUPPORT MANAGER
Agilent (a former HP division), Colorado Springs, Colorado (1999 – 2000)
Managed the Messaging Call Center providing *Level 2 internal support* for *field* and *factory employees*. Provided client and *server support* using *Microsoft Outlook* and *Exchange Server* platforms for employee *e-mail* needs. Supervised up to 30 internal support staff and *contractors* at *distributed sites*.
- Led the IT outsourced e-mail team to reduce *call times* from 4 minutes to an average of 26 seconds within 30 days.
- Successfully managed a crisis caused by the large-scale Love Bug *computer virus* in May 2000.
- Contained call center *costs* for internal IT support by identifying and repairing a problem with *support tools*.

TEAM LEAD
Hewlett-Packard, Colorado Springs, Colorado (1998 – 1999)
Led the Colorado Springs IT help desk team (~1,800 employees) in providing first- and *second-level support*. Planned and monitored *delivery of services* to employees to ensure that *system* and *application business needs* were met.
- Ranked number one in *customer satisfaction* out of all U.S. HP internal site IT teams.

CUSTOMER SUPPORT ENGINEER
Hewlett-Packard (formerly Colorado Memory Systems), Loveland, Colorado (1991 – 1998)
Managed the Customer Care Center *Level 1 Agent tape backup systems* on *PCs* and *UNIX workstations* in the U.S. and Europe—lived four months in England. Worked on *Level 1 NT* and *UNIX servers*. Served as the HP *liaison* to Customer Care Center agents in England and The Netherlands.
- Received three awards from co-workers for outstanding *teamwork.*
- Key member of the Loveland Site United Way Campaign Team. Increased corporate contributions from 41% to 86%.

**PROFESSIONAL
DEVELOPMENT**

MARKETLIVE SUMMIT (2007)
- Attended a three-day *e-commerce* application seminar presented by MarketLive, Inc.

UNIX SYSTEM ADMINISTRATION, LEVELS 1 AND 2 (2002)
Sierra Community College, Rocklin, California

NT ADMINISTRATION CERTIFICATION (1998)
Front Range Community College, Fort Collins, Colorado
- Selected as one of 80 students out of 900 applicants for the term.

KEYWORDS

❏ Keyword:_____
   ❏ Synonym:_____
   ❏ Synonym:_____

❏ Keyword:_____
   ❏ Synonym:_____
   ❏ Synonym:_____

❏ Keyword:_____
   ❏ Synonym:_____
   ❏ Synonym:_____

❏ Keyword:_____
   ❏ Synonym:_____
   ❏ Synonym:_____

❏ Keyword:_____
   ❏ Synonym:_____
   ❏ Synonym:_____

❏ Keyword:_____
   ❏ Synonym:_____
   ❏ Synonym:_____

❏ Keyword:_____
   ❏ Synonym:_____
   ❏ Synonym:_____

❏ Keyword:_____
   ❏ Synonym:_____
   ❏ Synonym:_____

❏ Keyword:_____
   ❏ Synonym:_____
   ❏ Synonym:_____

❏ Keyword:_____
   ❏ Synonym:_____
   ❏ Synonym:_____

❏ Keyword:_____
   ❏ Synonym:_____
   ❏ Synonym:_____

❏ Keyword:_____
   ❏ Synonym:_____
   ❏ Synonym:_____

❏ Keyword:_____
   ❏ Synonym:_____
   ❏ Synonym:_____

❏ Keyword:_____
   ❏ Synonym:_____
   ❏ Synonym:_____

❏ Keyword:_____
   ❏ Synonym:_____
   ❏ Synonym:_____

❏ Keyword:_____
   ❏ Synonym:_____
   ❏ Synonym:_____

❏ Keyword:_____
   ❏ Synonym:_____
   ❏ Synonym:_____

❏ Keyword:_____
   ❏ Synonym:_____
   ❏ Synonym:_____

❏ Keyword:_____
   ❏ Synonym:_____
   ❏ Synonym:_____

❏ Keyword:_____
   ❏ Synonym:_____
   ❏ Synonym:_____

❏ Keyword:_____
   ❏ Synonym:_____
   ❏ Synonym:_____

❏ Keyword:_____
   ❏ Synonym:_____
   ❏ Synonym:_____

❏ Keyword:_____
   ❏ Synonym:_____
   ❏ Synonym:_____

❏ Keyword:_____
   ❏ Synonym:_____
   ❏ Synonym:_____

KEYWORDS

❑ Keyword:_____
   ❑ Synonym:_____
   ❑ Synonym:_____

❑ Keyword:_____
   ❑ Synonym:_____
   ❑ Synonym:_____

❑ Keyword:_____
   ❑ Synonym:_____
   ❑ Synonym:_____

❑ Keyword:_____
   ❑ Synonym:_____
   ❑ Synonym:_____

❑ Keyword:_____
   ❑ Synonym:_____
   ❑ Synonym:_____

❑ Keyword:_____
   ❑ Synonym:_____
   ❑ Synonym:_____

❑ Keyword:_____
   ❑ Synonym:_____
   ❑ Synonym:_____

❑ Keyword:_____
   ❑ Synonym:_____
   ❑ Synonym:_____

❑ Keyword:_____
   ❑ Synonym:_____
   ❑ Synonym:_____

❑ Keyword:_____
   ❑ Synonym:_____
   ❑ Synonym:_____

❑ Keyword:_____
   ❑ Synonym:_____
   ❑ Synonym:_____

❑ Keyword:_____
   ❑ Synonym:_____
   ❑ Synonym:_____

Chapter 6

Now that you have the basic information gathered for your résumé, you need to create a list of your jobs and write basic sentences to describe your duties. Start by using a separate page at the end of this chapter for each of the jobs you have held for the past 10 or 15 years. You can generally stop there unless there is something in your previous work history that is particularly relevant to the new job you are seeking.

Starting with your present position, list the title of every job you have held, along with the name of the company, the city and state, and the years you worked there. You don't need to list full addresses and zip codes, although you will need to know that information when it comes time to fill out an application. You should use a separate page for each job title even if you worked for the same company in more than one capacity.

By the way, you *can* use a computer. I've had people assume that they had to write this all out in longhand simply because I suggest a separate piece of paper for each job. You can download MS Word, WordPerfect, and PDF files of all the forms in this book by going to my Web site at *www.patcriscito.com*.

You can list years only (2006 – present) or months and years (May 2006 – present), depending on your personality. People who are detail oriented are usually more comfortable with a full accounting of their time. Listing years alone covers some gaps if you have worked in a position for less than a full year while the time period spans more than one calendar year. For instance, if you worked from December 2006 through May 2007, saying 2006 – 2007 certainly looks better. If you are concerned about gaps in your work history, then listing years only is to your advantage.

From the perspective of recruiters and hiring managers, most don't care whether you list the months and years or list the years only. However, regardless of which method you choose, be consistent throughout your résumé,

Consistency of style is important on a résumé.

especially within sections. For instance, don't use months some of the time and years alone within the same section. Consistency of style is important on a résumé, since it is that consistency that makes your résumé neat, clean, and easy to read.

Under each job on its separate page, make a list of your duties, incorporating phrases from the job descriptions wherever they apply. You don't have to worry about making great sentences yet or narrowing down your list. Just get the information down on paper.

This is the most time-consuming part of the résumé writing process. Depending on how quickly you write/type, it could take an entire day just for this step. Anything worth doing, however, is worth doing right, so you will want to take the time to do this step right.

Unpaid Experience

Don't forget internships, practicums, and unpaid volunteer work in your experience section. Experience is experience whether you are paid for it or not. If the position or the knowledge you gained is relevant to your current job search, then list it on your résumé.

You can either include unpaid experience along with your paid experience, or you can create a separate section just for your volunteer history, like this:

VOLUNTEER HISTORY

Junior League of Colorado Springs, Colorado Springs, Colorado (2003 – 2007)
Developed goals and action plans, promoted projects to the community, and recruited members. Provided information and training to other league members and educated members on placement opportunities and policies. Attended court hearings and made recommendations to social caseworkers to improve the quality of legal representation for abused children. Raised $30,000 in funds for community projects, reconciled financial statements, and arranged publicity.
- Court Appointed Special Advocate (CASA) Program (August 2003 – May 2007)
- Placement Advisor, Committee Member (June 2005 – May 2007)
- Historian Committee, Chairperson (June 2006 – February 2007)
- Membership Development Committee (August 2005 – May 2006)
- Community Service Corps Committee (January 2003 – May 2004)

Cheyenne Mountain Newcomers Club, Colorado Springs, Colorado (2003 – 2007)
Planned, organized, and coordinated activities for more than 300 members. Maintained membership records and coordinated printing and mailing of directories. Presided at all general and executive board meetings in president's absence.
- First Vice President (December 2006 – May 2007)
- Second Vice President (July 2005 – May 2006)
- General Meetings Chairperson (August 2004 – May 2005)

EXPERIENCE—JOB NO. 1

JOB TITLE _____

NAME OF EMPLOYER _____

CITY AND STATE _____

DATE STARTED _____ DATE ENDED _____

SUMMARY SENTENCE (The overall scope of your responsibility, overview of your essential role in the company, kind of products or services for which you were responsible) _____

_____

_____

_____

_____

NUMBER OF PEOPLE SUPERVISED AND THEIR TITLES OR FUNCTIONS _____

_____

_____

_____

DESCRIPTION OF RESPONSIBILITIES (Don't forget budget, hiring, training, operations, strategic planning, new business development, production, customer service, sales, marketing, advertising, etc.) _____

_____

_____

_____

_____

_____

_____

_____

_____

_____

_____

_____

_____

_____

_____

ACCOMPLISHMENTS (Leave this section blank until Step 6 in Chapter 7) _____

_____

_____

_____

_____

_____

_____

_____

_____

_____

_____

_____

_____

EXPERIENCE—JOB NO. 2

JOB TITLE _____

NAME OF EMPLOYER _____

CITY AND STATE _____

DATE STARTED _____ DATE ENDED _____

SUMMARY SENTENCE (The overall scope of your responsibility, overview of your essential role in the company, kind of products or services for which you were responsible) _____

_____

_____

_____

_____

NUMBER OF PEOPLE SUPERVISED AND THEIR TITLES OR FUNCTIONS _____

_____

_____

_____

_____

DESCRIPTION OF RESPONSIBILITIES (Don't forget budget, hiring, training, operations, strategic planning, new business development, production, customer service, sales, marketing, advertising, etc.) _____

_____

_____

_____

_____

_____

_____

_____

_____

_____

_____

_____

_____

_____

_____

ACCOMPLISHMENTS (Leave this section blank until Step 6 in Chapter 7) _____

_____

_____

_____

_____

_____

_____

_____

_____

_____

_____

_____

EXPERIENCE—JOB NO. 3

JOB TITLE _____

NAME OF EMPLOYER _____

CITY AND STATE _____

DATE STARTED _____ DATE ENDED _____

SUMMARY SENTENCE (The overall scope of your responsibility, overview of your essential role in the company, kind of products or services for which you were responsible) _____

_____

_____

_____

_____

NUMBER OF PEOPLE SUPERVISED AND THEIR TITLES OR FUNCTIONS _____

_____

_____

_____

_____

DESCRIPTION OF RESPONSIBILITIES (Don't forget budget, hiring, training, operations, strategic planning, new business development, production, customer service, sales, marketing, advertising, etc.) _____

_____

_____

_____

_____

_____

_____

_____

_____

_____

_____

_____

_____

_____

_____

ACCOMPLISHMENTS (Leave this section blank until Step 6 in Chapter 7) _____

_____

_____

_____

_____

_____

_____

_____

_____

_____

_____

_____

_____

EXPERIENCE—JOB NO. 4

JOB TITLE _____

NAME OF EMPLOYER _____

CITY AND STATE _____

DATE STARTED _____ DATE ENDED _____

SUMMARY SENTENCE (The overall scope of your responsibility, overview of your essential role in the company, kind of products or services for which you were responsible) _____

_____

_____

_____

_____

NUMBER OF PEOPLE SUPERVISED AND THEIR TITLES OR FUNCTIONS _____

_____

_____

_____

_____

DESCRIPTION OF RESPONSIBILITIES (Don't forget budget, hiring, training, operations, strategic planning, new business development, production, customer service, sales, marketing, advertising, etc.) _____

_____

_____

_____

_____

_____

_____

_____

_____

_____

_____

_____

_____

_____

_____

ACCOMPLISHMENTS (Leave this section blank until Step 6 in Chapter 7) _____

_____

_____

_____

_____

_____

_____

_____

_____

_____

_____

_____

EXPERIENCE—JOB NO. 5

JOB TITLE _____

NAME OF EMPLOYER _____

CITY AND STATE _____

DATE STARTED _____ DATE ENDED _____

SUMMARY SENTENCE (The overall scope of your responsibility, overview of your essential role in the company, kind of products or services for which you were responsible) _____

_____

_____

_____

_____

NUMBER OF PEOPLE SUPERVISED AND THEIR TITLES OR FUNCTIONS _____

_____

_____

_____

_____

DESCRIPTION OF RESPONSIBILITIES (Don't forget budget, hiring, training, operations, strategic planning, new business development, production, customer service, sales, marketing, advertising, etc.) _____

_____

_____

_____

_____

_____

_____

_____

_____

_____

_____

_____

_____

_____

_____

ACCOMPLISHMENTS (Leave this section blank until Step 6 in Chapter 7) _____

_____

_____

_____

_____

_____

_____

_____

_____

_____

_____

_____

_____

EXPERIENCE—JOB NO. 6

JOB TITLE _____

NAME OF EMPLOYER _____

CITY AND STATE _____

DATE STARTED _____ DATE ENDED _____

SUMMARY SENTENCE (The overall scope of your responsibility, overview of your essential role in the company, kind of products or services for which you were responsible) _____

_____

_____

_____

_____

NUMBER OF PEOPLE SUPERVISED AND THEIR TITLES OR FUNCTIONS _____

_____

_____

_____

_____

DESCRIPTION OF RESPONSIBILITIES (Don't forget budget, hiring, training, operations, strategic planning, new business development, production, customer service, sales, marketing, advertising, etc.) _____

_____

_____

_____

_____

_____

_____

_____

_____

_____

_____

_____

_____

_____

_____

ACCOMPLISHMENTS (Leave this section blank until Step 6 in Chapter 7) _____

_____

_____

_____

_____

_____

_____

_____

_____

_____

_____

_____

EXPERIENCE—JOB NO. 7

JOB TITLE _____

NAME OF EMPLOYER _____

CITY AND STATE _____

DATE STARTED _____ DATE ENDED _____

SUMMARY SENTENCE (The overall scope of your responsibility, overview of your essential role in the company, kind of products or services for which you were responsible) _____
_____
_____
_____
_____

NUMBER OF PEOPLE SUPERVISED AND THEIR TITLES OR FUNCTIONS _____
_____
_____
_____
_____

DESCRIPTION OF RESPONSIBILITIES (Don't forget budget, hiring, training, operations, strategic planning, new business development, production, customer service, sales, marketing, advertising, etc.) _____
_____
_____
_____
_____
_____
_____
_____
_____
_____
_____
_____
_____
_____
_____

ACCOMPLISHMENTS (Leave this section blank until Step 6 in Chapter 7) _____
_____
_____
_____
_____
_____
_____
_____
_____
_____
_____
_____
_____

EXPERIENCE—JOB NO. 8

JOB TITLE _____

NAME OF EMPLOYER _____

CITY AND STATE _____

DATE STARTED _____ DATE ENDED _____

SUMMARY SENTENCE (The overall scope of your responsibility, overview of your essential role in the company, kind of products or
services for which you were responsible) _____

_____

_____

_____

_____

NUMBER OF PEOPLE SUPERVISED AND THEIR TITLES OR FUNCTIONS _____

_____

_____

_____

_____

DESCRIPTION OF RESPONSIBILITIES (Don't forget budget, hiring, training, operations, strategic planning, new business development,
production, customer service, sales, marketing, advertising, etc.) _____

_____

_____

_____

_____

_____

_____

_____

_____

_____

_____

_____

_____

ACCOMPLISHMENTS (Leave this section blank until Step 6 in Chapter 7) _____

_____

_____

_____

_____

_____

_____

_____

_____

_____

_____

EXPERIENCE—JOB NO. 9

JOB TITLE _____

NAME OF EMPLOYER _____

CITY AND STATE _____

DATE STARTED _____ DATE ENDED _____

SUMMARY SENTENCE (The overall scope of your responsibility, overview of your essential role in the company, kind of products or services for which you were responsible) _____

_____

_____

_____

_____

NUMBER OF PEOPLE SUPERVISED AND THEIR TITLES OR FUNCTIONS _____

_____

_____

_____

DESCRIPTION OF RESPONSIBILITIES (Don't forget budget, hiring, training, operations, strategic planning, new business development, production, customer service, sales, marketing, advertising, etc.) _____

_____

_____

_____

_____

_____

_____

_____

_____

_____

_____

_____

_____

_____

ACCOMPLISHMENTS (Leave this section blank until Step 6 in Chapter 7) _____

_____

_____

_____

_____

_____

_____

_____

_____

_____

_____

_____

EXPERIENCE—JOB NO. 10

JOB TITLE _____

NAME OF EMPLOYER _____

CITY AND STATE _____

DATE STARTED _____ DATE ENDED _____

SUMMARY SENTENCE (The overall scope of your responsibility, overview of your essential role in the company, kind of products or services for which you were responsible) _____

_____

_____

_____

_____

NUMBER OF PEOPLE SUPERVISED AND THEIR TITLES OR FUNCTIONS _____

_____

_____

_____

_____

DESCRIPTION OF RESPONSIBILITIES (Don't forget budget, hiring, training, operations, strategic planning, new business development, production, customer service, sales, marketing, advertising, etc.) _____

_____

_____

_____

_____

_____

_____

_____

_____

_____

_____

_____

_____

_____

_____

_____

_____

ACCOMPLISHMENTS (Leave this section blank until Step 6 in Chapter 7) _____

_____

_____

_____

_____

_____

_____

_____

_____

_____

_____

_____

_____

Chapter 7

When you are finished with your work history, go back to each job and think about what you might have done above and beyond the call of duty. What did you contribute to each of your jobs? How did you measure your success? What were you most proud of? What made you feel good at the end of the day? Did you:

- Exceed sales quotas each month?
- Save the company money by developing a new procedure?
- Generate new product publicity in trade press?
- Control expenses or cut overhead?
- Expand business or attract/retain customers?
- Restore lost accounts?
- Improve customer satisfaction ratings?
- Improve the company's image or build new relationships?
- Improve the quality of a product?
- Do something that made the company more competitive?
- Make money? Was it a record?
- Save money or time without compromising the company's products or services?
- Introduce new and better policies, procedures, processes, or systems?
- Increase efficiency or make work easier?
- Lower the company's debt?
- Increase productivity?
- Improve workplace safety?
- Solve a problem?
- Create a business partnership?
- Improve recruiting systems?

Overused words lose their effectiveness, like a song played on the radio again and again.

65

- Train/mentor any personnel who were promoted?
- Lower employee turnover or improve morale?
- Bring new vision or direction to the company?
- Rate above average on performance evaluations?

Or were you

- Selected for a significant project(s)?
- Considered a subject matter expert?
- Recruited especially to solve a major problem?
- Up against significant competition in the market?

Go back to the experience forms at the end of Chapter 6 and write down any accomplishments that show potential employers what you have done in the past, which translates into what you might be able to do for them in the future.

Quantify whenever possible. Numbers are always impressive. But don't duplicate wording throughout the résumé. If you use dollars in one case, use percentages in another. Overused words lose their effectiveness, like a song played on the radio again and again.

Remember, you are trying to motivate the potential employer to buy . . . you! Convince your reader that you will be able to generate a significant return on their investment in you.

Sample Accomplishment Sentences

Following are some real accomplishments used by real people on real résumés. They are extracted from many different résumés, so don't be surprised if the bullets jump around within the sections. Each bullet is a separate accomplishment. They aren't used in a résumé as they are listed here.

Your achievements won't be identical, but you can use these sentences as a foundation for your own words. Many of the phrases can cross over various industries, but some are specific to a particular job or company.

AVIATION
- Successfully set the standard for safe operations throughout the organization.
- Commended by upper management for mentoring and training junior pilots to improve their technical, tactical, and leadership skills.
- Designated to bring safety operations up to standard only two months before major inspections.
- Twice chosen to perform mid-level management responsibilities while only a junior officer.
- Hand picked to fly local general officers and visiting dignitaries.
- Developed and implemented improvement programs to correct flightline operating deficiencies.

ACCOUNTING

- Developed and implemented numerous improvements to financial reporting, budgeting, and internal controls that supported sales growth of 200%.
- Reduced charge-offs from .2% to .1% and receivables turnover from 50 to 42 days during this period.
- Over a five-year period, lowered overall borrowing costs by 1%.
- Identified $3.5 million in misused funds for return to the USOC.
- Personally recovered $1.423 million in 1997 out of a department total of $1.642 million.
- Audited $10 million in Olympic Games tickets, identifying opportunities to strengthen internal controls, improve operational efficiencies, and save hundreds of thousands of dollars.
- Conducted an analytical review of a $5 million inventory and spearheaded actions to revalue the inventory with material adjustments.
- Succeeded in delivering 25 complete systems to users, including the automation of a formerly paper-based order entry system that increased billing efficiency by 25%.
- Selected to serve on a statewide task force to develop a comprehensive internal controls program.

BAKERY MANAGEMENT

- Evaluated and changed the production schedule of the bakery department to introduce new products, which increased profits and better met customer needs.

BANKING

- Implemented the training rollout for the automated profiling system, a computer-based contact management system that allows bankers to add value to their customer relationships and sell additional business lines.
- Created an inspection process to drive usage of the profiling system by bankers, achieving 45% system use for all customers purchasing product in the first year of implementation.
- Recommended, implemented, and managed an alternative delivery strategy known as dedicated bankers, which increased the percentage of mortgage customers buying additional products from 20% to 40% in only one year.
- Successfully managed a targeted census tract location with high burden ratios and processing costs (ranked second in transaction volume compared to size).
- Increased assets from $60 million to $99.5 million in five years; led the city in annuity sales.
- Determined that small business customers were being underserved and developed a strategic plan to bring commercial banking back to the branch.

COMMUNICATION

- Established the division's quarterly newsletter for distribution to the staff and volunteers of the Olympic sports organizations, which significantly improved communication and compliance with grant guidelines.
- Facilitated communication between developers and users; improved relationships by prioritizing IT changes and setting realistic user expectations.

COMPUTERS

- As a system administrator, improved SMU's computer network efficiency by identifying areas requiring change and developing, testing, and implementing new practices and procedures.
- Streamlined an automated network-based database that maintained records in excess of $1.3 million within the External Relations Office.

- Created and maintained Web pages to improve executive relationships for the Dean's Council.
- Championed the first-generation informational Web site linked to major vendors and industry trade associations. Instrumental in the creation of the second-generation Web site offering an e-commerce component—the first in the textile converting industry *(www.tapetex.com)*.
- Maintained computer network support levels despite a $1.2 million budget cut.
- Decreased paperwork 50% by completely reviewing the circuit provisioning program.
- Opened an interactive CAD-CAM design studio used by customers to develop custom patterns and designs—the only one of its kind in the industry.

CONSTRUCTION
- Executed take-offs from blueprints, estimated costs, and bid jobs to ensure profitability.

CUSTOMER SERVICE
- Boosted customer retention rates from 85% to 99% by developing a Customer First program that was implemented in the field as well as in the call center.
- Interviewed all company departments and created a process flow map for service delivery that eliminated redundancies and improved overall efficiency.
- Provided a high level of customer service to patients and their families.
- Proactively maintained client relationships with 300+ corporate accounts.
- Created a quick response customer service team equipped with contact management software.
- Developed a new specialist concept for providing customer technical service and provisioning of MCI's services that increased revenue by 40%.

EDUCATION ADMINISTRATION
- Selected to turn around a high school with declining enrollment, low teacher morale, a high dropout rate, deteriorating building, and poor academic reputation.
- Succeeded in revitalizing the staff and building consensus among teachers, the community, and students.
- Created a safe, productive, caring, and positive school climate through effective leadership that included modeling, rewards, communication, increased visibility, and appreciation for diversity.
- Developed and implemented innovative programs that have made Mitchell High School a magnet in the district.
- Implemented a variety of intervention programs to promote student achievement and retention.
- Improved attendance three percentage points by increasing the visibility of security personnel and creating an Attendance Committee that revised policies and improved parental involvement.
- Established an emphasis on instruction and ensured that all students were academically challenged and individually successful.
- Developed better programs and course offerings that resulted in the highest ACT improvement of any large high school on the Front Range.
- Improved writing scores on the DWA state assessments by an entire grade level.
- Achieved the highest scholarship dollar amount per graduate of any school in the district for 2006 – 2007.
- Recognized twice by the Chamber of Commerce for excellence in community partnerships.
- Partnered with Booz-Allen Hamilton, ARINC, MCI, and the Citadel Mall to adopt classes. Employees followed the students through all four years of high school, providing mentoring, career exploration, and training opportunities. Received the Colorado CAPE Award for the Booz-Allen Hamilton partnership.

- Developed a unique partnership with Peterson Air Force Base to enhance the Career Technology Center.
- Created an award-winning mentorship program with the Colorado Springs Firefighters Association that involves local firefighters mentoring at-risk students.
- Developed community partnerships to rehabilitate the physical plant using volunteer help and donated materials, which has generated a new sense of pride among students.
- Led the development of a courtroom building that provides classroom space for pre-law courses, mock trial competitions, and simulations of actual court cases.
- Implemented a pilot mentorship program called "Choices" to teach junior and senior student leaders how to mentor freshmen classmates toward improved performance.
- Developed a partnership with the El Paso County building and construction industry to provide hands-on experience for students interested in the trade.
- Approached the El Paso County Contractors Association for grants and sponsorships for the Wheels of Learning program, which prepares students for careers in the building trades.

EVENT PLANNING
- Developed a wide network of vendors, facilities, speakers, and caterers to meet specific needs.
- Revitalized underperforming programs and achieved significant profitability.
- As an Executive Officer to an Army General, managed more than 35 worldwide trips in 12 months.
- Assisted the director of development with special events, notably the 25th Anniversary Gala, which was the single most profitable event in the organization's history.

FIELD ENGINEER
- Technical expert called in to resolve the most difficult problems.
- Improved efficiency and lowered labor/job costs, significantly improving profitability.
- Implemented an engineering approach to problem identification and achieved a defect density rating of 1.9 when the industry standard is 1.4 and perfection is 2.0.

FINANCE
- Successfully guided the company through a lengthy period of extreme financial distress.
- Represented the company during the preparation of the first registered Internet public venture capital offering as well as several private placements.
- Conceived a stabilization plan to reduce deficits inherited from previous management and negotiated forgiveness of significant vendor debt.

FUND-RAISING
- Raised $45,000 in three weeks for a heart transplant patient through newspaper, television, and radio promotion; set up bank accounts and coordinated special events.
- Provided information that helped one client reduce fund-raising costs by 65%.
- Founded a successful consulting business that provided fund-raising and development services to high-profile nonprofit organizations in New York and Colorado for more than twelve years.
- Developed a results-oriented reputation that ensured frequent referrals and repeat business from satisfied clients.
- One of three founders of a nonprofit theater venture that produced a three-week Equity showcase on Theatre Row, a premier Off-Broadway venue.
- Wrote and negotiated an umbrella agreement with an existing nonprofit organization to facilitate fund-raising.

- Succeeded in raising enough funds to meet budget requirements when the norm in the industry is a loss.
- Solicited government, foundation, corporate, and individual contributions accounting for 32% of the $1.2 million operating budget.
- Formalized the fund-raising program that is still used today. This established a sound financial foundation and provided the means for the organization to redefine itself amongst its peers as a premier instrument for promoting new playwrights.
- Created an all-purpose appeal that articulated the organization's history, mission, and programs.
- Part of a development team that raised $670,000—an 11% increase over the previous year—and exceeded corporate, foundation, and individual contribution goals.
- Researched and wrote grant proposals for foundation and corporate donors, generating an average of 20 grants per month to identified prospects.

GREENSKEEPER

- Gained extensive experience in growing and managing cool-season grasses, including knowledge of bentgrass greens, microclimatic conditions, and winterization.
- Enhanced turf grass quality and course playability using both current and innovative methods and technologies.

HEALTHCARE

- Part of the team responsible for the preparations that earned a score of 94 on the September 2007 JCAHO survey.
- Expanded the client base to include other Mercy subsidiaries, other hospitals, and various physician practices.

HOSPITALITY/TOURISM

- Built the hotel into a strong competitor for the city's business market and ranked in the top 10% for customer service out of 1,140 Hampton hotels.
- Developed housekeeping policies and procedures that resulted in a hotel cleanliness yield that exceeded corporate averages by as much as 23 points.
- Analyzed sales trends, developed forecasts and budgets, and set up rate structures that increased the average daily rate by $2.00 and occupancy by 1.7%.
- Promoted through the ranks from busboy to head waiter; developed a reputation for reliability and hard work; worked 35–40 hours per week while in college full-time.
- Inherited mother's restaurant specializing in casual lunch and catering; succeeded in growing the corporate client base and sold the business at a profit two years later.
- Maintained expenses below budget through accurate planning, purchasing, and waste reduction controls.
- Implemented operating efficiencies that kept the business profitable in spite of tight margins.
- Managed a restaurant and lounge recognized as first out of 54 in a five-state region.

HUMAN RESOURCES

- Designed and managed the company's self-funded hospitalization program, with resulting per-employee costs significantly below national averages.
- Created and implemented a progressive operations manual that significantly improved operating efficiency and, ultimately, profitability.
- Studied problematic behavioral trends, developed crisis intervention strategies and emergency responses, and made recommendations for changes to senior management.

- Conceptualized, developed, and co-facilitated The Silent Retreat, an award-winning experiential weekend for students and staff.
- Transformed the organizational culture and improved operating efficiency through cross-functional coaching/training and tactical restructuring that decentralized operations and brought the employees closer to their tasks and clients.
- Instituted a sales group compensation program that was completely performance based, motivating a 10% increase in sales.
- Developed a measurement process to analyze on-time and complete delivery performance, which permitted rapid corrective actions and improved response rates.
- Provided behavioral feedback as an executive coach to the group leaders and regional presidents.
- Created an atmosphere that valued continual learning, risk taking, and personal accountability among employees.
- Improved productivity and morale by initiating systems for accountability, formalizing job duties, and instituting training programs.
- Decreased recruiting costs 25% by implementing an employee referral system and using Web sites more effectively.

INVENTORY MANAGEMENT AND LOGISTICS
- Achieved a 98.8% service goal with 17.9 inventory turns in the grocery warehouse, where the corporate benchmark is 97% with 18 turns.
- Collaborated with category managers, marketing department, 113 vendors, and transportation providers to create supply and logistics cost-saving opportunities and to coordinate direct store deliveries.
- Helped save the Lane & Edson account by providing support for a critical shipping problem.
- Authored new interim and year-end physical inventory procedures for increased efficiency in the annual external audit.
- Improved warehouse requisition and receipt processing to less than one day; location accuracy to 98%; inventory accuracy to 97%; demand satisfaction rates to 90%; and zero balance rates to 3.6% (reduced from 36%).
- Re-engineered existing supply processes to save limited resources, recovering $26 million.
- Received the Joint Service Commendation Award for improving inventory stock levels, accountability, consumption tracking, restocking, and customs procedures for the joint U.S. task force of Army, Navy, Air Force, and Marines.
- Honored with two Meritorious Service Medals for innovations in logistical support.

JOINT VENTURES
- Approached a Belgian mill and formed a partnership that permits CTM to serve as their agent in the U.S., generating $2 million in new annual revenue.
- Created a strategic alliance with a major distributor of raw materials to the footwear industry, opening new Asian markets for the company and creating significant additional profit centers.
- Established a strategic distribution partnership in Latin America with Glen Raven Mexicana that expanded the market globally.
- Negotiated exclusive North American distribution agreements with two European mills, resulting in an annual sales increase of approximately $3 million.
- Developed a strategic partnership with Milliken, Inc., and Duro Industries to better serve one of the company's largest customers, W. L. Gore, resulting in a 350% increase in revenue over three years.

LAW

- Successfully negotiated individual product liability settlements of up to $250,000.
- Member of a three-attorney panel appointed by the New Mexico Court of Appeals to issue advisory decisions in pending civil appeals.
- Wrote the advisory decision in the appeal of *Miller v. NM Dept. of Transportation,* the essence of which was adopted by the New Mexico Supreme Court.
- Selected twice in fifteen months as an arbitrator for the New Mexico trial-level court to arbitrate cases with damage claims less than $15,000, using procedures similar to those governing American Arbitration Association proceedings.
- Lead counsel or sole counsel for the injured plaintiff / worker in at least 30 jury trials with a minimum trial length of three days, plus another 50 non-jury trials of at least two days.
- Since 1990, have prepared and prosecuted to conclusion, either by trial or settlement, over 650 workers' compensation cases involving both physical and economic injuries.
- Met deadlines for pretrial procedures, trials, and appellate briefings by effectively utilizing attorney associates and support staff.
- Designed a complete set of recurring forms to manage a typical workers' compensation claim from initial client interview through requested findings and conclusions.

MARKETING

- Developed a vital network of business and industry contacts instrumental to the rapid growth of the company.
- Successfully gained new customers through effective marketing, sales presentations, and follow-up.
- As marketing director for a retirement home, increased occupancy rates from 20% to 90%.
- Changed the company's perception in the marketplace by creating innovative marketing materials and making it more visible.
- Managed the company's transition to a global marketing focus through targeted sales planning, re-engineering of operations, and sound financial management, leading to sales diversification and enhanced opportunities for future growth in a shrinking market.
- Developed proprietary products for customers that strengthened their brand name equity and increased the company's profit margins.
- Enhanced domestic representation and diversified the product lines, increasing sales by 40% to $36 million.
- Developed and conducted quarterly focus groups with up to 150 management users; provided executive management with formal feedback that included solution-driven results.
- Developed effective sales and marketing programs that included direct mail campaigns, print advertising, promotions, and free delivery services.
- Wrote a strategic operating plan to improve profitability by more effectively allocating resources to key market segments and deploying technology to increase efficiency.

MANUFACTURING

- Increased equipment availability from 78% to 94% within the first month by reducing down time through the implementation of a quality improvement strategy.
- Reduced maintenance work-in-process to less than 90 days with a production index of >1.0.
- Designed and implemented new floor layout to improve efficiencies and work flow.
- Reduced labor standards by an average of 25% on all product lines.
- Reduced rework rate by 50% by detailed in-process inspection.
- Reduced monthly failure rate from 2.5 units to .30 units.
- Implemented quick responses to assembly line accidents and other emergencies.

MERGERS & ACQUISITIONS
- Member of the Wells Fargo corporate steering committee responsible for merging the operations of the two banks (Norwest and Wells Fargo) into a functional sales tracking system.
- Coordinated the merger of a bank into one location and assumed the management of a new bank gained in the acquisition.

MILITARY
- Consistently promoted ahead of peers; selected for Technical Sergeant under the Stripes for Exceptional Performers (STEP) program.
- Selected for the 2006 Noncommissioned Officer of the Year Award at the command level for service above and beyond the expected.
- Successfully managed the maintenance of automotive equipment returning from Desert Storm, taking on twice the normal workload with no additional assets.

NURSING
- Member of the Access collaborative department team; helped to coordinate changes that improved patient satisfaction by allowing patients immediate access to the provider of their choice at times convenient for them.
- Ensured laboratory protocol was in compliance with Clinical Laboratory Improvement Amendment (CLIA).
- Coordinated a full 80-victim disaster drill and then rewrote the entire disaster plan in collaboration with the staff development RN.
- Furnished high-quality nursing care in the emergency room of a regional hospital seeing 4,000 patients per month, 600 requiring pediatric care.
- Instituted a Braslowe Tape System of acute pediatric assessment and treatment, as well as a geriatric fall prevention and risk assessment program.
- Designed and implemented a tool to identify victims of domestic violence who presented to the ER, which ensured proper care and follow-up.
- Ensured optimum patient care in spite of often adversarial relationships between private and public emergency services.
- Initiated and participated in staff and interdisciplinary team conferences to improve the quality of care delivered to residents.
- Served as a role model for county public health nurses and other providers.
- Acted as a resource person to new nursing staff and facilitated team cohesion.

QUALITY ASSURANCE
- Investigated and resolved quality and service complaints, promoting repeat business and improving profitability.
- Honored for a commitment to 100% customer satisfaction and zero defects.
- Improved response to system outages by streamlining procedures and keeping leadership informed.

SALES
- Referred more than $15 million in new placements annually.
- Recognized by Lanier's Atlanta headquarters for generating the highest yearly sales volume in the Western Region during the first six months on the job; eight-time recipient of the monthly top production award.
- Hired geographically dispersed sales executives and developed a team-based environment that communicates horizontally and not just vertically.

- Researched and implemented a Web-based software tool (salesforce.com) to enhance sales reporting from the field.
- Expanded the sales force to facilitate the development of high-profile key accounts, growing sales from $35 to $54 million.
- Designed sales management processes to promote sales effectiveness and achieve long-term revenue growth and increase customer loyalty across multiple channels.
- Created solid working relationships with internal and external partners to improve opportunity identification and sales closings.
- Selected for several corporate task forces, including retail job descriptions, retail incentives, and go-forward sales training curriculum initiatives.
- Selected as a statewide sales trainer to introduce and implement an innovative sales process long before the industry moved in that direction.
- Increased gross sales from $1,500 to $80,000 per month in one year.
- Interfaced with vendors, customer service representatives, and medical personnel to streamline product delivery and maintained effective working relationships.
- Utilized negotiation and persuasion skills to gain a continually higher percentage of sales per account.
- Influenced the group's senior leadership to support and participate in a defined sales management accountability matrix that promoted active supervision of operations that drive results.
- Completed month-long corporate training program in Manhattan and succeeded in developing 200 clients in the first year with $4.3 million in assets.

SECRETARY, CLERK
- Displayed a professional demeanor with a cheerful, positive attitude.
- Took reservations for a private beach and minimized conflicts in the schedule.
- Improved access to treatment options by developing a resource information sheet for drug treatment centers, respite options, and other resources in Colorado Springs and Denver, which was adopted by multiple centers statewide.

TEACHER
- Prepared a master plan for student accountability as chairperson of the Proficiency Committee.
- Selected to assist in the evaluation, modification, and organization of Cheraw Elementary School's math, science, reading, and writing curriculum.
- Developed a successful classroom motivational tool that included special shirts for students.
- Wrote multiple grants and received funding for special programs.
- Awarded "Outstanding American History Teacher of the Year" for Southeast Colorado by the Daughters of the American Revolution (2007).
- Appointed to the Master Teacher Advisory Group for the U.S. Space Foundation (2007).
- Selected for the national "Time Magazine Award" for developing and implementing a mock presidential election for all of the schools in the Cheraw District (2005).
- Recipient of a Colorado Endowment for the Humanities (2005).

TELECOMMUNICATION
- Identified 180 leased communication circuits for removal, saving $2.1 million in annual leased line costs.
- Researched and developed a communications network strategy for U.S. locations in the Netherlands, saving $480,000 in international leased line costs and ensuring survivability of communications services.

TRAINING

- Coached training staff to improve the quality of seminar presentations.
- Taught six weeks of initial management training and three weeks of continued management training at The Management Training Center; personally responsible for launching the careers of 400 management employees.
- Redesigned and implemented a new training model based on the Mager Method for the annual ten-day resident advisor training program, which is still in use today.
- Introduced a sales training program that included 18 months of in-house experience prior to being assigned to a designated territory.
- Developed cross-training programs that improved the morale and the efficiency of operations and lowered turnover rates.

Awards and Honors

In a research study of corporate hiring practices sponsored by the Career Management Alliance *(www.careermanagementalliance.com),* the researcher found that decision makers weren't much interested in awards even if they applied to the job they were trying to fill.

The study concluded, "Hiring managers don't know how to judge the value of awards. For example, a résumé that just mentions the name of the award might not provide enough information. However, readers would learn more if they knew this award went only to the top five performers in a sales force numbering more than five hundred."

The key, then, is to focus on the accomplishment more than the award itself. Naming the honor or award is secondary to the return on investment the hiring manager perceives from the sentence. For example:

- Received the National Sales Excellence Award in 2007 by becoming one of the top five producers of mutual fund sales within the peer group.

- Selected by United Technologies Sikorsky Aircraft Company to receive their Igor I. Sikorsky Helicopter Rescue Award for a successful high-risk mountain rescue.

- Won two quarterly superior customer service awards in two years by competing with 18 bakeries in the district.

- Selected for the Service Excellence Award (4th quarter of 2000) for personal customer service excellence.

- Received a monetary award for improving the working relationship between couriers and service agents.

- Achieved Best-in-Class customer service scores based on quarterly client surveys.

- Recipient of the Gold Level Reward for exceptional performance during 2007.

- Received Gold Star award for exceptional performance during a crisis call.

Remember the rule that there is an exception to every rule in the résumé business? Well, here's another one. If the award is so self-explanatory in your industry that explaining it would be insulting to your reader, then list those awards or honors in a separate section at the bottom of your résumé, like this for a teacher:

- High Plains Educator Award (2007)
- Who's Who Among America's Teachers (2006, 2007)
- Outstanding Young Woman of America (2006)

. . . or like this for an Olympic medalist in Taekwondo:

- Awarded the USOC Developmental Coach of the Year, Taekwondo (2006)
- Olympic Games, Bronze Medal (2006), selected as captain of the team
- Taekwondo Times Hall of Fame (2006)
- Pan American Games, Bronze Medal (2005)
- Pan Am Taekwondo championships, Gold Medal (1998, 2004)
- U.S. Olympic Festival, Gold Medal (2004)
- World Games, Silver Medal (2003), U.S. World Team Member (8 times)
- World Championships, Bronze Medal (2001, 2003, 2005)
- Selected as an International Referee by the World Taekwondo Federation
- Captain, U.S. National Team (2001 – 2006)
- President's Best Player Award (2001)

Chapter 8

Now that you have the words on paper, go back to each list and think about which items are relevant to your current job target. Cross out those things that don't relate, including entire jobs (like flipping hamburgers back in high school if you are now an electrical engineer with ten years of experience).

Remember, your résumé is just an enticer, a way to get your foot in the door. It isn't intended to be all-inclusive. You can choose to go back only as far as your jobs relate to your present objective. Be careful not to delete sentences that contain the most important keywords you identified in Step 4 (Chapter 5).

Change Is Inevitable

You know the old saying, "The only constant is change." Perhaps you should make a copy of the pages before you begin marking them up. They are a great record of your work history, and you never know when you might want to change careers, which means you would need some of that information.

According to the U.S. Department of Labor, the average worker today will change jobs 15 times in his or her career and hold 9.2 jobs between the ages of eighteen and thirty-four. Today, workers are much more free to change not just jobs but careers.

I have been writing résumés since 1980, and the biggest change I've seen since the early 1990s is the number of clients who have decided to, for example, leave computer programming for acting or to change from nursing to pharmaceutical sales.

Part of the reason for this transition is social and part is the result of the modern workplace. According to William Hine, Dean of the School of Adult and Continuing Education at Eastern Illinois University, "The half-life of a college degree is three to five years." There was a time when you could graduate from college and stay in the

> **The average worker today will change jobs 15 times.**

same job for thirty years and then retire with a gold watch. Not so today. You must be committed to lifelong learning or your career will leave you behind.

That means you can also make the choice to retool, get a new degree, and start a new career in mid-life. It's perfectly acceptable.

It also means that being a packrat can pay off when you decide to change careers! So, store the original sheets in the same file you created for your performance evaluations and job descriptions, and use the copies for this step.

Take the copies and decide which jobs are relevant to today's job search. You only need to use about ten to fifteen years of those jobs, unless there is something very powerful in your early career that will help you get a job. Now, set aside the jobs that are too old or irrelevant. Try to limit your list of final jobs to no more than six, although you can list more if they are truly relevant or contain valuable experience.

Focus on the sentences in the relevant experience summaries.

- Which ones are the most powerful?
- Which ones summarize your experience the best?
- Which ones contain the keywords of your industry?
- Which ones highlight your accomplishments the best?

Delete Education

Next, do the same for your education and training worksheets. Copy them, file away the originals, and cross out anything that doesn't relate to your current job goal.

That does not apply to your formal education, however. Even if you have a graduate degree in your career field and your undergraduate degree is unrelated, leave them both on your résumé. Your reader will need to see the progression of your formal education.

If you have a bachelor's degree and an associate degree, you don't need to list them both unless there is something about the major of your associate degree that you don't have in your bachelor's degree. Remember, it is okay to list almost anything on your résumé as long as it is relevant to your job search.

Chapter

Step 8
Dynamic
Sentences

It's time to do some serious writing now. You must make dynamic, attention-getting sentences of the duties and accomplishments you have listed under each job, combining related items to avoid short choppy phrases. Here are the secrets to great résumé sentences:

- In résumés, you never use personal pronouns (I, my, me). Instead of saying, *"I planned, organized, and directed the timely and accurate production of code products with estimated annual revenues of $1 million"* you should say: *"Planned, organized, and directed. . . ."* Writing in the first person makes your sentences more powerful and attention grabbing, but using personal pronouns throughout a résumé is awkward. Your reader will assume that you are referring to yourself, so the personal pronouns can be avoided.

- Make your sentences positive, brief, and accurate. Since your ultimate goal is to get a human being to read your résumé, remember to structure the sentences so they are interesting to read.

- Use verbs at the beginning of each sentence (designed, supervised, managed, developed, formulated, and so on) to make them more powerful (see the list at the end of this chapter).

- Incorporate keywords from the list you made in Step 4 (Chapter 5).

- Make certain each word means something and contributes to the quality of the sentence.

Finding Help

If it is difficult for you to write clear, concise sentences, take the information you have just listed to a professional writer who can help you turn it into a winning résumé. Choose someone who is a Nationally Certified Résumé Writer

> *Make certain each word means something and contributes to the quality of the sentence.*

(NCRW), Master Résumé Writer (MRW), or Certified Professional Résumé Writer (CPRW). That way you can be assured that the person has passed the strictest tests of résumé writing and design in the country, including peer review, administered by the National Résumé Writers' Association (NRWA), Career Management Alliance, and Professional Association of Résumé Writers and Career Coaches (PARW/CC), respectively. The expense of a professional written résumé is a small investment when compared to the advantages it provides for your career.

To find certified résumé writers, visit these Web sites:

- National Résumé Writers' Association, *www.nrwaweb.com*
- Career Management Alliance, *www.careermanagementalliance.com*
- Professional Association of Résumé Writers and Career Coaches, *www.parw.com*
- Career Directors International, *www.careerdirectors.com*

What are the benefits of partnering with a professional résumé writer? According to the NRWA, you will gain access to:

- Expert résumé writing, editing, and design skills.

- Needed objectivity and expertise to play up your strengths, downplay your weaknesses, and position yourself for interview success.

- The precise know-how to target your career and industry correctly.

- Winning résumé, job search, interviewing, and salary negotiation strategies from recognized experts.

- Experienced professionals who have passed rigorous résumé industry exams and demonstrated their commitment to the profession by obtaining ongoing training.

- Writers who are dedicated to providing the highest quality service and a superior finished product.

Résumé writers work in one of three ways: 1) they gather all of the information they need from you in a personal interview, 2) they require that you complete a long questionnaire before they begin working on your résumé, or 3) they use a combination of both methods. In any case, you have already done most of the data collection if you have followed Steps 1 through 6 and Steps 10 and 11 in this book. This preparation sometimes makes the résumé easier to write and many professional résumé writers will pass on that savings to you in the form of lower fees.

If you are going to proceed from here and finish the résumé on your own, let me show you how to rewrite sentences so they are more powerful. The original sentences in these examples were on real résumés. The rewrites are my fine-tuning based on interviews with each client, which gathered more information and clarified the original intent of the writer.

Original Sentence: Responsible for leading team of application engineers, delivery consultants, and technical trainers in pre-sales and post-sales activities.

Rewrite: Led a team of 20 application engineers, delivery consultants, and technical trainers in the development of customized enterprise software solutions.

Original Sentence: Generation of accurate and meaningful client proposals based on initial client needs and assessment.

Rewrite: Generated effective client proposals based on a comprehensive assessment of client requirements.

Original Sentence: Telecommunication sales associate who achieved quota each month after training phase.

Rewrite: Successfully sold telecommunication services, achieving sales goals each month and generated more than $1 million in annual revenue.

Original Sentence: Responsible to ensure that time is spent on being pro-active about the future financial needs of the district.

Rewrite: Proactive in ensuring that the future financial needs of the district were met.

Original Sentence: Helped the district make assessment and accountability that accompanies data not an event but rather a practice that we seek and value.

Rewrite: Assured that assessment and accountability became part of the district's culture and not a simple event.

Original Sentence: Marketing Coordinator; for all internal and external marketing for Club Sports six up-scale fitness clubs and a hotel and fitness resort.

Rewrite: Coordinated all of the internal and external marketing for six upscale fitness clubs and the Renaissance ClubSport hotel and fitness resort.

Original Sentence: Inside sale support responsible for aftermarket parts and equipment sales for over 200 municipalities as well as expediting and tracking purchase orders, sales generated yearly were approximately $100,000.

Rewrite: Provided inside sales support for aftermarket parts and equipment sales to 200+ municipalities, personally generating annual sales of more than $100,000.

Original Sentence: Processed and reviewed applications for residency.

Rewrite: Reviewed applications for residency, checked credit and personal references, and approved new occupants.

Original Sentence: Sold and achieved sales goals.

Rewrite: Integral member of the teller team responsible for exceeding sales goals for credit card accounts, ATM cards, instant cash cards, and new account referrals.

Original Sentence: Coordinating with the local printer, all collateral for the club.

Rewrite: Developed collateral materials and ensured that all clubs had the most recent sales aids.

Power Verbs

Now that you have some samples of good writing, let's look at the words that made it possible. Power verbs at the beginning of sentences make them more interesting and, well, "powerful." Try to use a variety of these words. It's easy to choose the same one to begin every sentence, but there are synonyms buried within this list that will make your writing better.

A

abated
abbreviated
abolished
abridged
absolved
absorbed
accelerated
accentuated
accommodated
accompanied
accomplished
accounted for
accrued
accumulated
achieved
acquired
acted
activated
actuated
adapted
added
addressed
adhered to
adjusted
administered
adopted
advanced
advertised
advised
advocated
affirmed
aided
alerted
aligned
allayed
alleviated
allocated
allotted
altered
amassed
amended
amplified
analyzed
answered
anticipated
appeased
applied
appointed
appraised
approached
appropriated
approved
arbitrated
aroused
arranged
articulated
ascertained
aspired
assembled
assessed
assigned
assimilated
assisted
assumed
assured
attained
attended
attracted
audited
augmented
authored
authorized
automated
averted
avoided
awarded

B

balanced
bargained
began
benchmarked
benefitted
bid
billed
blended
blocked
bolstered
boosted
bought
branded
bridged
broadened
brought
budgeted
built

C

calculated
calibrated
canvassed
capitalized
captured
cared for
carried
carried out
carved
catalogued
categorized
caught
cautioned
cemented
centralized
certified
chaired
challenged
championed
changed
channeled
charged
charted
checked
chose
chronicled
circulated
circumvented
cited
clarified
classified

cleaned
cleared
closed
coached
co-authored
coded
cold called
collaborated
collated
collected
combined
commanded
commenced
commended
commissioned
communicated
compared
competed
compiled
complemented
completed
complied
composed
compounded
computed
conceived
concentrated
conceptualized
concluded
condensed
conducted
conferred
configured
confirmed
confronted
connected
conserved
considered
consolidated
constructed
consulted
consummated
contacted
continued

contracted
contributed
controlled
converted
conveyed
convinced
cooperated
coordinated
copied
corrected
correlated
corresponded
counseled
counted
created
credited with
critiqued
cultivated
customized
cut

D

dealt
debated
debugged
decentralized
decided
decoded
decreased
dedicated
deferred
defined
delegated
deleted
delineated
delivered
demonstrated
deployed
depreciated
derived
described
designated
designed

detailed
detected
determined
developed
devised
devoted
diagnosed
diagrammed
differentiated
diffused
directed
disbursed
disclosed
discounted
discovered
discussed
dispatched
dispensed
dispersed
displayed
disposed
disproved
dissected
disseminated
dissolved
distinguished
distributed
diversified
diverted
divested
divided
documented
doubled
drafted
dramatized
drew up
drove

E

earned
eased
economized
edited

educated
effected
elaborated
elected
elevated
elicited
eliminated
embraced
emphasized
employed
empowered
enabled
encountered
encouraged
ended
endorsed
enforced
engaged
engineered
enhanced
enlarged
enlisted
enriched
enrolled
ensured
entered
entertained
enticed
equipped
established
estimated
evaluated
examined
exceeded
exchanged
executed
exercised
exhibited
expanded
expedited
experienced
experimented
explained
explored

exposed
expressed
extended
extracted
extrapolated

F

fabricated
facilitated
factored
familiarized
fashioned
fielded
filed
filled
finalized
financed
fine-tuned
finished
fixed
focused
followed
forecasted
forged
formalized
formatted
formed
formulated
fortified
forwarded
fostered
fought
found
founded
framed
fulfilled
functioned as
funded
furnished
furthered

G

gained
garnered
gathered

gauged
gave
generated
governed
graded
graduated
granted
graphed
grasped
greeted
grew
grouped
guaranteed
guided

H

halted
halved
handled
headed
heightened
held
helped
hired
honed
hosted
hypnotized
hypothesized

I

identified
ignited
illuminated
illustrated
implemented
imported
improved
improvised
inaugurated
incited
included
incorporated
increased

incurred
indicated
individualized
indoctrinated
induced
influenced
informed
infused
initialized
initiated
innovated
inspected
inspired
installed
instigated
instilled
instituted
instructed
insured
integrated
intensified
interacted
interceded
interfaced
interpreted
intervened
interviewed
introduced
invented
inventoried
invested
investigated
invigorated
invited
involved
isolated
issued
itemized

J

joined
judged
justified

L

launched
learned
leased
lectured
led
lessened
leveraged
licensed
lifted
lightened
limited
linked
liquidated
listened
litigated
loaded
lobbied
localized
located
logged

M

made
maintained
managed
mandated
maneuvered
manipulated
manufactured
mapped
marked
marketed
mastered
maximized
measured
mediated
memorized
mentored
merchandised
merged
merited
met

minimized
mobilized
modeled
moderated
modernized
modified
molded
monitored
monopolized
motivated
mounted
moved
multiplied

N

named
narrated
navigated
negotiated
netted
networked
neutralized
nominated
normalized
noticed
notified
nurtured

O

observed
obtained
offered
officiated
offset
opened
operated
optimized
orchestrated
ordered
organized
oriented

originated
outdistanced
outlined
outperformed
overcame
overhauled
oversaw
owned

P

paced
packaged
packed
paid
pared
participated
partnered
passed
patterned
penalized
penetrated
perceived
perfected
performed
permitted
persuaded
phased out
photographed
piloted
pinpointed
pioneered
placed
planned
played
polled
posted
praised
predicted
prepared
prescribed
presented
preserved

presided
prevailed
prevented
priced
printed
prioritized
probed
processed
procured
produced
profiled
programmed
progressed
projected
promoted
prompted
proofread
proposed
protected
proved
provided
pruned
publicized
published
purchased
pursued

Q

quadrupled
qualified
quantified
queried
questioned
quoted

R

raised
rallied
ranked
rated
reached

reacted
read
realigned
realized
rearranged
reasoned
rebuilt
received
reclaimed
recognized
recommended
reconciled
reconstructed
recorded
recovered
recruited
rectified
redesigned
redirected
reduced
re-engineered
referred
refined
refocused
regained
registered
regulated
rehabilitated
reinforced
reinstated
reiterated
rejected
related
released
relied
relieved
remained
remediated
remodeled
rendered
renegotiated
renewed
reorganized

repaired
replaced
replicated
replied
reported
represented
reproduced
requested
required
requisitioned
researched
reserved
reshaped
resolved
responded
restored
restructured
retained
retooled
retrieved
returned
revamped
revealed
reversed
reviewed
revised
revitalized
revolutionized
rewarded
risked
rotated
routed

S

safeguarded
salvaged
saved
scanned
scheduled
screened
sculptured
searched

secured
segmented
seized
selected
sent
separated
sequenced
served as
serviced
settled
set up
shaped
shared
sharpened
shipped
shortened
showed
shrank
signed
simplified
simulated
sketched
skilled
slashed
smoothed
sold
solicited
solidified
solved
sorted
sourced
sparked
spearheaded
specialized
specified
speculated
spent
spoke
sponsored
spread
spurred
stabilized
staffed

staged
standardized
started
steered
stimulated
strategized
streamlined
strengthened
stressed
stretched
structured
studied
subcontracted
submitted
substantiated
substituted
succeeded
suggested
summarized
superceded
supervised
supplied
supported
surpassed
surveyed
swayed
swept
symbolized
synchronized
synthesized
systemized

T

tabulated
tackled
tailored
talked
tallied
targeted
tasted
taught
teamed

tempered
tended
terminated
tested
testified
tied
tightened
took
topped
totaled
traced
tracked
traded
trained
transacted
transcribed
transferred
transformed
transitioned
translated
transmitted
transported
traveled
treated
trimmed
tripled
troubleshot
turned
tutored
typed

U

uncovered
underlined
underscored
undertook
underwrote
unearthed
unified
united
updated
upgraded

upheld
urged
used
utilized

validated
valued
vaulted
verbalized
verified

viewed
visited
visualized
voiced
volunteered

weathered
weighed
welcomed
widened

withstood
witnessed
won
worked
wove
wrote

yielded

Chapter 10

Y ou are almost done! Now, go back to the sentences you have written and think about their order of presentation. Put a number 1 by the most important description of what you did for each job. Then place a number 2 by the next most important duty or accomplishment, and so on until you have numbered each sentence.

Again, think logically and from the perspective of a potential employer. Keep related items together so the reader doesn't jump from one concept to another. Make the thoughts flow smoothly.

The first sentence in a job description is usually an overall statement of the position's major responsibilities. The rest of the sentences should begin with your most important duties and accomplishments and proceed to lesser ones.

Let me give you an example of a job description in rough draft format and one that has been rearranged, and I'm sure you will see what I mean.

JOHNSON UNIVERSITY HOSPITAL, New Brunswick, New Jersey (2000 – 2003)
Director, Pediatric Emergency Department
- Recently developed and implemented an expansion of the department into a new children's hospital.
- Hired and managed a staff of 40 employees, directed performance improvement initiatives, and implemented departmental standards of care.
- Analyzed trends for key indicators to improve subsequent code responses.
- Member of the Performance Improvement Committee.
- Analyzed 72-hour readmission trends to find problems with practice patterns.
- Selected for the Code Response Team: Developed a new performance improvement form.
- Redesigned resuscitation guidelines for residents and nursing staff.
- Directed clinical and administrative operations of a 12,000-visit-per-year pediatric emergency department.

> *The first sentence in a job description is usually an overall statement of the job's major responsibilities.*

- Developed and managed an operating budget of $1.3 million.
- Developed staffing standards and evaluated the qualifications/competence of department personnel to provide appropriate levels of patient care.
- Member of the Health Policy and Strategic Planning Committee responsible for preparing the hospital and staff for JCAHO accreditation reviews.
- Implemented a pain initiative.

After numbering and rearranging the sentences, the section reads much stronger and has a better flow. I like to use a paragraph format for duties and bullets for accomplishments, like in the sample below.

JOHNSON UNIVERSITY HOSPITAL, New Brunswick, New Jersey (2000 – 2003)
Director, Pediatric Emergency Department
Directed clinical and administrative operations of a 12,000-visit-per-year pediatric emergency department. Developed and managed an operating budget of $1.3 million. Hired and managed a staff of 40 employees, directed performance improvement initiatives, and implemented departmental standards of care. Developed staffing standards and evaluated the qualifications/competence of department personnel to provide appropriate levels of patient care. Served as a member of the Health Policy and Strategic Planning Committee responsible for preparing the hospital and staff for JCAHO accreditation reviews.

Key Accomplishments
- Recently developed and implemented an expansion of the department into a new children's hospital.
- Member of the Performance Improvement Committee: Analyzed 72-hour readmission trends to find problems with practice patterns. Implemented a pain initiative. Redesigned resuscitation guidelines for residents and nursing staff.
- Selected for the Code Response Team: Developed a new performance improvement form. Analyzed trends for key indicators to improve subsequent code responses.

Here is my reasoning for rearranging the sentences:

1. The first sentence was selected because it was a good overall statement of the job's major responsibility.

2. The second sentence added a further sense of scope by describing the size of the director's.

3. The third sentence also increased the scope by discussing the number of employees managed and other supervisory responsibilities.

4. The next two sentences are secondary job duties and special assignments.

5. In order to emphasize achievements, key accomplishments were pulled out into a separate section.

6. The first bullet was the most important accomplishment and the most recent.

7. All of the bullets that applied to the Performance Improvement Committee were listed together in a separate paragraph.

8. The last accomplishment was the least important.

Before and After Sample

Perhaps it would help to see a sample of a résumé before it had been rewritten and rearranged. The résumé on the next two pages was a first attempt without following the instructions in this book. The final version is shown on the last two pages of this chapter.

Pay special attention to the way bullets were expanded and rearranged to make them more powerful and compelling. The computer skills and education sections were moved to the top of the résumé because they were Paul's strongest qualifications for his new job goal (Web site design).

PAUL O. JONES
1234 North Tejon Street
Denver, CO 80210

303.123.4567
Jones1234@pcisys.net

Objective

A challenging technical position at an excelling high tech company.

Education

University of Colorado, Colorado Springs
Bachelor of Arts in Fine Arts Studio, December 2002
- Primary Emphasis: Digital Imaging, Sculpture

Professional Courses

- Intermediate HTML
- Advanced HTML
- Windows NT 4.0 Administration
- UNIX Fundamentals

Qualifications

Very attentive to accuracy and detail, as well as efficiency and organization. Excellent written, verbal, and interpersonal skills.

- Programming Languages: HTML, exposure to JavaScript.
- OS Platforms: Windows (9x/NT/2000/XP), exposure to MacOS and UNIX.
- Software: Adobe Photoshop, Adobe Image Ready, Microsoft Internet Information Server, WebTrends Analysis Suite, and Microsoft Office.

Experience

WorldCom, Inc.   **May 1998 – June 2002**
2424 Garden of the Gods Road • Colorado Springs, Colorado 80919

Software Development (Applications Developer II)
- Responsible for the design, development, and maintenance of several WorldCom intranet and internet web sites.
- Redesigned existing intranet and internet web sites inherited from other groups/organizations within WorldCom to provide users with a fresh browsing experience and enhanced organization of the web site content.

System Administrator (Software Systems Engineer I)
- Responsible for the implementation, monitoring, and maintenance of several WorldCom intranet and internet web sites and web servers within both Windows and UNIX environments.
- Provided weekly web traffic and usage analysis reports for many of the sites hosted within the Windows and UNIX web server environments using WebTrends Analysis Suite.

Best Buy Stores, Inc.   **August 1992 – April 1998**
801 North Academy Boulevard • Colorado Springs, Colorado 80909

Customer Service, Service Technician, and Sales
- Performed sales and return/exchange transactions, handled customer issues, and placed service orders.
- Performed testing/troubleshooting and minor repairs on consumer electronics, handled shipping, receiving, and inventory of repair units.
- Made sales in Media (software & music), Computer hardware and accessories, Cellular Phones, and Digital Satellite Systems.

| **Other Experience** | *The Mercury Cougar Collector's Page* | **Sep 1995 – Feb 1999** |

Conception, design, and maintenance of an automotive web site, in which enthusiasts of the 1967-73 Mercury Cougar could display photos of their cars and obtain information.

Exhibitions and Awards

Student Art Exhibition

Gallery of Contemporary Art • University of Colorado, Colorado Springs

May 1998 – Sculpture
May 1997 – Sculpture
May 1996 – Digital Image

Aardvark-Zymurgy: The works of the '97-98 UCCS Art Graduates
December 1997

The Warehouse Gallery, Colorado Springs, Colorado

Display of two sculptures and a digital image.

Purchase Prize, Student Art Exhibition   May 1996

Gallery of Contemporary Art • University of Colorado, Colorado Springs

Digital image, *Message from the Gods*, was purchased by the university for display in the University Center.

PAUL O. JONES

QUALIFICATIONS	• Creative Web Developer with a strong background in the design, development, and administration of large corporate Intranet and Internet Web sites.
	• Detail-oriented professional who gains great satisfaction from knowing that a project was done right.
	• Enthusiastic team player with an outgoing, friendly communication style.

COMPUTER SKILLS

Programming Languages: HTML, MS Visual InterDev, JavaScript

Operating Systems: Windows (9x/NT/2000/XP), Macintosh, and UNIX

Design Software: Adobe Photoshop, Adobe Image Ready, Adobe Live Motion, Lightwave 3-D

Business Applications: MS Word, Excel, Access, PowerPoint, Outlook, Internet Explorer, Microsoft Internet Information Server, WebTrends Analysis Suite

EDUCATION

BACHELOR OF ARTS (December 2002)
University of Colorado, Colorado Springs, Colorado
- Major in Fine Arts Studio with an emphasis on digital imaging and sculpture
- Computer course work: Electronic Imaging, Advanced Project in Electronic Imaging, Web Art, Advanced Computer Art, Introduction to Computer Art
- Design course work: Independent Study in Fine Arts, Photography, 20th Century Sculpture, Advanced Drawing, Art History, Color Drawing, Advanced Studio Problems, Studio 3-D, Beginning Studio 2-D
- 3-D Topics: Form, Wood, Wood Sculpture, Advanced Sculpture, Advanced Figure Sculpture
- Business course work: Conflict Management, Macroeconomics, Interpersonal Communications, Political Science, Quantitative and Qualitative Reasoning Skills

PROFESSIONAL DEVELOPMENT
- Intermediate and Advanced HTML, WorldCom, Colorado Springs, Colorado
- Windows NT 4.0 Administration, WorldCom, Colorado Springs, Colorado
- UNIX Fundamentals, WorldCom, Colorado Springs, Colorado
- Lightwave 3-D Modeling Software, Washburn University, Denver, Colorado

EXPERIENCE

FREELANCE WEB DESIGNER (1995 – present)
Paul White Consulting, Colorado Springs, Colorado
- Designed a Web site for High West Siding and Windows—*www.highwestsiding.com.* (2003)
- Conceived, designed and maintained a Web site for enthusiasts of the 1967–1973 Mercury Cougar called The Mercury Cougar Collector's Page. The site allowed interested people to display photos of their classic cars and obtain information. (1995 – 1999)

APPLICATIONS DEVELOPER II (Software Developer) (1999 – 2002)
WorldCom, Colorado Springs, Colorado
- Designed, developed, and maintained several WorldCom Intranet and Internet Web sites.
- Met with internal customers to determine their requirements, brainstormed with the development team, and designed the look and feel of each site.
- Redesigned existing Web sites inherited from other groups and organizations within WorldCom to provide users with a fresh browsing experience and enhanced organization of content.
- Recognized for reliability, initiative, customer service skills, and ability to meet tight deadlines.
- Discovered a virus attack on the servers and recovered data quickly to minimize downtime.

ADDRESS

1234 N. Tejon Street • Denver, Colorado 80210
Phone: (303) 123-4567 • E-mail: jones1234@pcisys.net

EXPERIENCE (continued)	**SOFTWARE SYSTEMS ENGINEER I (System Administrator)** (1998 – 1999)

WorldCom, Colorado Springs, Colorado
- Served as primary systems administrator for 20 Windows NT servers and backup administrator for the UNIX servers, together hosting up to 150 Web sites.
- Backed up the systems weekly to ensure that data was available for recovery purposes.
- Configured and managed Web server software, including MS Internet Information Server and Netscape Enterprise Server.
- Monitored and maintained Intranet and Internet Web sites and provided weekly Web traffic and usage analysis reports using WebTrends Analysis Suite.
- Served as team lead on various server installation projects.
- Customized Web site configuration to provide user-friendly development environments and convenient access for content management.

CUSTOMER SERVICE REPRESENTATIVE, TECHNICAL SERVICE TECHNICIAN (1992 – 1998)
Best Buy Stores, Inc., Colorado Springs, Colorado
- Successfully sold computer hardware and accessories, cellular telephones, digital satellite systems, software, and music in a retail setting.
- Won numerous sales awards for consistently meeting or exceeding revenue goals and selling value-added services.
- Handled returns and exchanges, placed service orders, and ensured customer satisfaction.
- Performed testing, troubleshooting, and minor repairs on consumer electronics.
- Managed shipping, receiving, and inventory of repair units.

ART EXHIBITIONS

STUDENT ART EXHIBITION (1996 – 1998)
Gallery of Contemporary Art, University of Colorado, Colorado Springs, Colorado
- Displayed a digital image and two sculptures.
- Won a Purchase Prize for a digital image entitled *Message from the Gods.* The image was purchased by the University for display in the University Center.

AARDVARK–ZYMURGY: THE WORKS OF UCCS ART GRADUATES (1997 – 1998)
The Warehouse Gallery, Colorado Springs, Colorado
- Displayed two sculptures and a digital image.

Chapter 11

At the bottom of your résumé (or sometimes toward the top), you can add anything else that might qualify you for your job objective. This includes licenses, certifications, special skills, publications, speeches, presentations, exhibits, grants, special projects, research, affiliations, and sometimes even interests if they truly relate. See the form at the end of this chapter to collect this information.

People often ask me what should NOT be included in a résumé. Well, there are very few times when photographs or personal information are appropriate on a résumé. Usually such facts only take up valuable white space, especially details such as age, sex, race, health, or marital status, and other information that potential employers are not allowed to ask anyway. If such information is included on a résumé, there is always the possibility a hiring manager will unintentionally discriminate against you during the hiring process.

As I said before, however, there are exceptions to every rule in the résumé business! Here are some of them:

- Submitting a résumé to a U.S. company doing business in certain foreign countries is one example. On such a résumé, an "Interests" section would show a prospective employer that your hobbies are compatible with the host country.

- Students, or those who have recently graduated, often have a difficult time coming up with enough paid experience to demonstrate their qualifications. But, if they have held leadership positions in campus organizations or have supervised groups of people and organized activities on a volunteer basis, then an "Activities" section could strengthen those qualifications.

- A list of sporting interests would be helpful for a person looking for a sports marketing position.

> Use your judgment. Only you know best what qualifications are important in your field.

• International résumés in almost all cases require date of birth, place of birth, citizenship, marital status, sex, and often a photograph.

And the list goes on. It is important to use your judgment, since only you know best what qualifications are important in your field. For instance, several of my clients are ministers. In their line of work, it is very important to list a great deal of personal information that most employers would not need to know or even be allowed by law to request. In their case, the information they provide relates directly to bona fide occupational qualifications for the jobs they are seeking.

Photographs

Photographs on a résumé are required by many foreign companies requesting a curriculum vitae. However, in the United States, photographs are discouraged in all but a few industries. For instance, if you are trying for a job as an actor, model, newscaster, or in some other field where your appearance is, again, a bona fide occupational qualification, then a photograph is appropriate.

References

References are not usually presented on a résumé since most employers will not take the time to check references until after an interview. By then, they will have your completed application with a list of references. You also don't want to impose on your friends, associates, or former employers unnecessarily or too frequently. There is nothing wrong with taking a nicely printed list of professional (not personal) references with you to an interview, however. The form at the end of this chapter will help you prepare that list.

Here's one of those exceptions to the rule again. If an advertisement requests that a list of references be sent with the résumé and cover letter, then by all means supply the list. You don't want to be accused of not following directions!

Avoid that needless line at the bottom of the résumé that says, "References available upon request." It takes up valuable white space that you need to define the sections of your résumé in order to draw the reader's eyes logically down the page.

Pretend you are an interviewer. You ask, "Will you provide references?" The interviewee replies, "Sorry, no, I can't do that." Will you even think twice about continuing to consider this candidate? I think not. It is assumed that you will provide references when requested.

Samples

Here are some samples of additional information included in real résumés. Remember, each one had a bona fide reason for including this information. In other words, the information strengthened their qualifications in some way.

TECHNOLOGY SKILLS (when the goal is a network system administrator job in military telecom)

Networking

- Served as System Administrator for an AT&T UNIX-based mainframe computer system supporting national consumers on four workstations tied into a global network of 14 servers and 16 clients.
- Evaluated information management requirements and identified organizational IT needs.
- Maintained consistent, reliable, and secure information by establishing policies, procedures, methods, and standards for system access and disaster recovery.
- Performed systems analysis and programming tasks to maintain computers and control their use.
- Created new user accounts, logon scripts, network directory shares, and password resets.
- Installed and upgraded software and tested programs to ensure functionality.
- Maintained and troubleshot printer servers, configured printers, and created new printer shares.
- Proficient in real-time system integration and troubleshooting techniques, process flow, and equipment requirements.

Telecommunications

- Seventeen years of experience in the operation, installation, activation, and maintenance of telecommunications systems for the U.S. Navy, including HF, UHF, VHF, FDM, TDM, and satellite voice and data communications circuitry, call routing, and translations.
- Supported commands over a 3,000 mile area with telephony, digital/analog voice, data, and video systems.
- Coordinated with commercial carriers to restore high- and low-speed circuits: cross-connects, CODEX modems, troubleshooting using frequency and time division multiplexing, and repairs/basic maintenance of telecommunications equipment.
- Performed daily quality control checks on hundreds of voice, data, and video circuits, coordinating usage and outages with commercial carriers, other worldwide commands, and in-house users.
- Reported circuit outages to various local and national authorities, made restoration recommendations, and kept senior management informed of problems.
- Tested telecommunications systems, modems, PC hardware, and associated terminals, cabling, and switching equipment/facilities.
- Experienced in the operation and troubleshooting of FCC-100, Racal 9600, and SDD 1900 modems, CV-8448 and CV-2048 NRZ-CDI converters, multiplexers, key switching units, and Voxtel PBX.

Security

- Managed the operation, installation, maintenance, and troubleshooting of Communications Security (COMSEC) equipment, including KG-84A/C, KG-75 FASTLANE, KG-175 TACLANE, KG-96, KYV-5, KY-57/58, KIV-19, KYK-13, KOI-18, CZY-10, STU-III secure phone cryptography equipment.

- As Communications Security Material (CSM) System Controller, managed a COMSEC account with more than 1,000 highly classified, extremely sensitive items.
- Issued, destroyed, and documented COMSEC materials. Inventoried and tracked each piece of CMS using an automated tracking system. Issued receipts and destroyed CMS material, maintaining two-person integrity at all times.

Hardware
- Mainframe Computer Systems and Architecture: Tellabs DAX, Alcatel 600E, MUSIC, Streamliner, Newsdealer, TACINTEL, VAX 6000, DECstations, DEC PDP-11/70, GTE IS-1000.
- Storage Devices: magnetic tape drives, optical disk drives.
- RF Equipment: antennas, satellites, transmitters, receivers.
- Imagery Systems: FIST, DVITS, JDISS.
- Test Equipment: Data Sentry 10, ADC Patch Panels, Firebird 6000, Logitech Test Generator, Halcyon Test Set, Sage 930 and 950, T-Com, T-Berd, oscilloscopes, multimeters, signal analyzers.

Business Applications
- Proficient in Microsoft Word, Excel, PowerPoint, Outlook, and Internet Explorer.
- Extensive experience working in Windows and SCO UNIX environments.
- Working knowledge of various Defense Information Systems Agency (DISA) circulars.
- Experienced in statistical analysis and data processing.

TECHNOLOGY SKILLS (for network/system administration)

Certifications
- Microsoft Certified Professional (MCP), 2001 – present
- A+ Certification, 2001 – present
- Security+ Certification, in process

Networking
- Hands-on experience with the configuration and networking of Windows NT/2000/XP workstations, including upgrades from earlier versions, installation of Windows Server 2000/2003, and installation of network hardware.
- Extensive training in Microsoft Windows 2000/XP (both the Professional and Server versions), including network and operating system essentials, supporting a network infrastructure, implementing and administrating Directory and Server, and designing a directory services infrastructure.
- Supported a 12-server network, which required making and updating a network diagram of servers and peripheral equipment. Developed the migration strategy from Server 2000 to 2003. Rebuilt three servers to Server 2003.
- Use Stat Scanner 6.0 to scan the network and apply security patches on 12 servers and multiple workstations.
- Previously Cisco certified to install, configure, and operate LAN, WAN, and dial-up access services for networks, including IP, IGRP, IPX, serial, AppleTalk, frame relay, IP RIP, VLANs, RIP, Ethernet, Access Lists.

Software/Hardware

- Installed and configured software and hardware for networks, workstations, and PCs.
- Partitioned hard drives, set up Windows NT/2000/XP, and backed up servers using HP Data Protector.
- Used Stat Scanner 6.0 and Retina Scanner to secure the network, Smart Draw Suite to update and maintain network diagrams, and Norton Ghost to create and apply software images.
- Proficient in MS Word, Excel, PowerPoint, Exchange, Netscape, and Internet Explorer.

PRESENTATIONS (for nursing administration)

- *Pediatric Emergency Department Product Line Implementation,* Organization of Nurse Executives, New Jersey, March 2007.
- *Pediatric Education for Prehospital Professionals,* National Course Roll Out, Robert Wood Johnson University Hospital, New Brunswick, New Jersey, September 2006.
- *Financial Awareness of Hospital Nurses,* Robert Wood Johnson University Hospital, New Brunswick, New Jersey, May 2006.
- *Initiatives in Pediatric Emergency Services,* Board of Directors, Robert Wood Johnson University Hospital, New Brunswick, New Jersey, May 2006.
- *Hypothermia: Emergency Care of the Complex Patient,* Nursing Grand Rounds, CentraState Medical Center, Freehold, New Jersey, September 2004.
- *Newborn Care: Basic Assessment to Resuscitation,* Paramedic Curriculum, Robert Wood Johnson University Hospital, Emergency Medical Services Program, New Brunswick, New Jersey, June 2004, 2005, 2006, 2007.
- *Introduction to Pediatric Emergency Care,* Robert Wood Johnson University Hospital, New Brunswick, New Jersey, October 2004.
- Course Instructor for the Neonatal Resuscitation Program, Robert Wood Johnson University Hospital, New Brunswick, New Jersey, quarterly since January 2004.
- Course Instructor for Pediatric Advanced Life Support classes, Robert Wood Johnson University Hospital, New Brunswick, New Jersey, quarterly since January 2004.

AFFILIATIONS (for nursing administration)

- Executive Board Member, Seton Hall University Nursing Alumni (2005 – present)
- Member, American Nurses Association (ANA) (2006 – present)
- Member, New Jersey State Nurses Association (NJSNA) (2006 – present)
- Member, American Association of Nurse Executives (AONE) (2006 – present)
- Member, Gamma Nu Chapter, Nursing Honor Society (2005 – present)
- Member, Chair's Council of the College of Nursing (2003 – 2004)
- Peer Mentor, Sophomore and Junior Nursing Students (2003 – 2004)
- Member, Student Nurses Association, Seton Hall University (2001 – 2004)
  - President (2003 – 2004)
  - Delegate to the 2004 NSNA Convention, Pittsburgh, Pennsylvania
  - Delegate to the 2004 NJSNA Convention, Atlantic City, New Jersey
  - Publicity Chairperson (2002 – 2003)

AFFILIATIONS (for tourism management)

- Appointed to the Rules Committee of the Colorado Passenger Tramway Safety Board; created guidelines for funicular railway rules that were adopted nationwide (2003 – 2006).
- Member, Board of Directors, Pikes Peak Country Attractions Association (2000 – present); Executive Board Member (2002 – 2004), Vice President (2005 – 2006), and President (2006 – 2007).
- Member, Trees Committee, Pikes Peak Hospice (1992 – 2005); coordinated the installation of lighting on all trees for an annual fund-raising event that generates $135,000 a year.

CERTIFICATIONS (for nursing)

- Instructor, Pediatric Advanced Life Support (PALS)
- Instructor, Neonatal Resuscitation Program
- Instructor, Pediatric Emergency for Prehospital Providers
- Provider, Basic Life Support (BLS)
- Licensed Registered Nurse in Illinois and New Jersey

KEY CONTACTS (for public relations)

Print Media

- Newspapers: Sports editors, national sports columnists, and NBA columnists from the top 40 major newspapers and wire services, including *USA Today, The New York Times, Chicago Tribune, Los Angeles Times, The Wall Street Journal,* Associated Press, Bloomberg, Reuters, among others. Beat writers covering NBA teams in all 29 NBA markets, representing 100 major newspapers.
- Magazines: Top NBA and sports columnists from leading sports publications (*Sports Illustrated, The Sporting News, ESPN Magazine,* etc.) and mainstream news and business writers from *Time, Newsweek, Fortune, Business Week,* and others.

Television

- Network sports executives and on-air announcers and correspondents for major network and cable stations, including NBC, ESPN, HBO, TNT, Fox Sports, CNN, MSG Network, and others.
- A variety of contacts among on-air correspondents and producers from network television news departments, including NBC's *Meet the Press,* the *CBS Evening News,* and ABC's *20/20,* among others.

Sports

- Comprehensive working relationships with executives in the legal, marketing, and communications departments of professional sports leagues, unions, and teams.
- Broad contacts with a significant number of influential sports agents and many other player representatives concentrating in areas such as marketing, public relations, and financial planning.
- Extensive interaction with NBA players serving on the NBPA Executive and Negotiating Committees, and each NBA player serving as a team player representative over the past three years.

COMMUNITY SERVICE (for law enforcement)

- Member, Colorado Springs Workforce Management Council (2000 – present); Chairperson of the Recruitment Subcommittee for all city employees
- Board of Directors, National Alliance of the Mentally Ill (NAMI)
- Member, El Paso County Justice Advisory Council responsible for allocating resources for the jail population and addressing issues affecting law enforcement in the community
- Member, National Organization for Black Law Enforcement Executives (NOBLE)
- Member, International Association of Chiefs of Police (IACP)
- Member, 4th Judicial District Domestic Violence Recertification Board for health care providers (1999 – 2002)
- Member, School District 20 Principal Selection Committee (1998 – present)
- Served as liaison between the Police Department and the NAACP
- Worked with the Care Coalition Community Network to develop prevention programs for high-risk youth
- Member, Martin Luther King Jr. Holiday Committee
- Public Information Chairman for the Cinco de Mayo Committee
- Liaison to the Armed Forces Disciplinary Control Board
- Member, Consortium for the Developmentally Disabled
- Director and Past President of the Colorado Springs Police Athletic League
- Regional Chairman, National Police Athletic League

LEADERSHIP (for sports management)

U.S. Olympic Committee
- Member, Audit Committee (2005 – 2006)
- Appointed to the CEO Transition Team (2004 – 2005)
- Athletes Advisory Committee (1989 – 1997)

World Taekwondo Federation
- Vice Chair, Junior Committee (2005 – present)
- Member, Collegiate Committee (2002 – 2004)

U.S. Taekwondo Union
- Member, Executive Committee (1989 – 2002)
- Member, Coaching Science Committee (1999 – 2002)
- Member, National Tournament Committee (1989 – 2002)
- Member, Board of Directors (1988 – 2001)
- Chairman, Athletes Advisory Council (1989 – 1996)

Taekwondo Associations
- President, Big Sky Taekwondo Academy (1984 – 1995)
- President, Montana State Taekwondo Association (1988 – 1995)
- Chief Instructor, Montana State University (1984 – 1995)

Community Organizations
- Board of Directors, Citrus Heights Chamber of Commerce (1998 – 2001)
- Director of Workforce San Juan, a guidance program for at-risk youth (1998 – 2001)

VOLUNTEER EXPERIENCE (for admission to law school)

- Volunteered more than 130 hours to the Peterson Outdoor Adventure Program; served as a guide for all-terrain vehicle, water skiing, sailing, and canoe trips (2006 – 2008).
- Organized numerous community activities as a member of Beta Sigma Phi; donated baked goods monthly for the Center for Domestic Violence; raised more than $500 for the Circle of Hope Foundation; delivered holiday baskets for needy families (2005 – 2006).
- Fed homeless and needy families during the holidays; organized the entire military unit to assist for two years, feeding 500+ homeless at each event (2003 – 2006).
- Led neighbors in developing a local Neighborhood Watch program; collaborated with local Sheriff's deputies to provide signs and organize meetings to deter violence and crime (2005).
- Raised more than $500 in food, clothing, and toys for the needy at Christmas (2002 – 2005).
- Represented the military at the Colorado State Fair to provide the public with information about Cheyenne Mountain Air Force Base (2004).
- Organized a class at the Airman Leadership School to refurbish the Colorado Springs Ronald McDonald House (2004).
- Coordinated two very successful base-wide cookie drives to provide treats for military members stationed in the Middle East during the holiday season (2003 – 2004).
- Organized two holiday parties for residents of Laurel Manor Nursing Home (2002, 2004).
- Volunteered with Special Olympics; motivated participants during relay activities (1997).
- Raised hundreds of dollars for local charities by organizing the 21st Operation Group's annual "Slip-n-Slide" charity softball tournament (2003).

CERTIFICATIONS (for quality assurance)

Certified Quality Manager, American Society for Quality (2001 – present)
Certified RAB Quality System Auditor, RAB 16-hour Lead Auditor Course (1997)
Certified Quality Auditor, American Society for Quality (1996 – present)
Certificate of Quality Auditing, Pennsylvania State University (1996)
Certificate of Environmental Management System, Pennsylvania State University (1995)

LANGUAGES (for international jobs)

Spanish: Native tongue
English: Highly proficient, writing and speaking (PET, FIST Certificate, TOEFL, TSE, TWE)
Portuguese: Fluent speaking, proficient writing
French: Working knowledge (5 years Alliance Française)

CREDENTIALS FILE (for a recent graduate)

A credentials file is available from the University of Kansas upon request.

CREDENTIALS (for a teacher)

Colorado Professional Principal License (2002 – 2007)
Colorado Professional Administrator License (2002 – 2003)
- K–12 Director of Special Education Endorsement

Colorado Professional Teacher License (2002 – 2007)
- K–12 Aurally Handicapped Endorsement

LICENSES AND CERTIFICATIONS (for a nurse)

- Registered Nurse, State of Connecticut, E-34102
- Registered Nurse, State of Florida, RN-1932832
- Certified, Advanced Cardiac Life Support (ACLS)
- Certified, Basic Life Support (BLS)

RELATED QUALIFICATIONS

AFFILIATIONS (professional associations, chambers of commerce, Toastmasters, etc.) _____

_____

_____

_____

_____

_____

LANGUAGES (with levels of proficiency*) _____

_____

_____

*Fluent (absolute ability, native), Highly Proficient (three to five years of usage in the country), Proficient (able to understand the subtleties of
the language), Working Knowledge (can conduct everyday business), Knowledge (exposure to the language, courtesy phrases)

LICENSES _____

_____

_____

_____

CERTIFICATIONS _____

_____

_____

_____

CREDENTIALS _____

_____

_____

_____

PRESENTATIONS/SPEECHES (title, meeting, sponsoring organization, city, state, date) _____

_____

_____

_____

EXHIBITS _____

_____

_____

_____

PUBLICATIONS (authors, article title, publication title, volume, issue, page numbers, date) _____

_____

_____

_____

GRANTS _____

_____

_____

_____

RELATED QUALIFICATIONS

SPECIAL PROJECTS _____
_____
_____
_____

RESEARCH _____
_____
_____
_____

UNIQUE SKILLS _____
_____
_____
_____

VOLUNTEER ACTIVITIES, CIVIC CONTRIBUTIONS _____
_____
_____
_____
_____
_____
_____

HONORS, AWARDS, DISTINCTIONS, PROFESSIONAL RECOGNITION _____
_____
_____
_____

COMPUTERS _____
_____

Applications (MS Word, Excel, PowerPoint, etc.) _____
Operating Systems (Windows, Macintosh, UNIX, etc.) _____
Databases (Access, Oracle, etc.) _____
Programming Languages _____
Networking _____
Communications _____
Hardware _____

OTHER RELEVANT SKILLS _____
_____

Actors (singing, musical instruments, martial arts, etc.) _____
Secretaries (typing speed, shorthand, etc.) _____
Welders (TIG, MIG, ARC, etc.) _____

INTERNATIONAL (travel, living, cross-cultural skills, etc.) _____
_____
_____
_____

OTHER RELATED QUALIFICATIONS

_____

_____

_____

_____

_____

_____

_____

_____

_____

_____

_____

_____

_____

_____

_____

_____

_____

_____

_____

_____

_____

_____

_____

_____

_____

_____

_____

REFERENCES

Unless an advertisement specifically requests references, don't send them with your résumé. Type a nice list of three to six references on the same letterhead as your résumé to take with you to the interview. Use this form to collect the information for your reference list. Choose people who know how you work and are not just personal friends or family members.

NAME _____
RELATIONSHIP TO YOU _____   NUMBER OF YEARS KNOWN _____
COMPANY _____
MAILING ADDRESS _____
CITY, STATE, ZIP _____
WORK PHONE _____   CELL PHONE _____
HOME PHONE _____   E-MAIL _____

NAME _____
RELATIONSHIP TO YOU _____   NUMBER OF YEARS KNOWN _____
COMPANY _____
MAILING ADDRESS _____
CITY, STATE, ZIP _____
WORK PHONE _____   CELL PHONE _____
HOME PHONE _____   E-MAIL _____

NAME _____
RELATIONSHIP TO YOU _____   NUMBER OF YEARS KNOWN _____
COMPANY _____
MAILING ADDRESS _____
CITY, STATE, ZIP _____
WORK PHONE _____   CELL PHONE _____
HOME PHONE _____   E-MAIL _____

NAME _____
RELATIONSHIP TO YOU _____   NUMBER OF YEARS KNOWN _____
COMPANY _____
MAILING ADDRESS _____
CITY, STATE, ZIP _____
WORK PHONE _____   CELL PHONE _____
HOME PHONE _____   E-MAIL _____

NAME _____
RELATIONSHIP TO YOU _____   NUMBER OF YEARS KNOWN _____
COMPANY _____
MAILING ADDRESS _____
CITY, STATE, ZIP _____
WORK PHONE _____   CELL PHONE _____
HOME PHONE _____   E-MAIL _____

NAME _____
RELATIONSHIP TO YOU _____   NUMBER OF YEARS KNOWN _____
COMPANY _____
MAILING ADDRESS _____
CITY, STATE, ZIP _____
WORK PHONE _____   CELL PHONE _____
HOME PHONE _____   E-MAIL _____

Step 11
Qualifications
Summary

We really are almost done! One last thing before you put it all together. Think about the objective (or focus) that you determined in Step 1 (Chapter 2). Rewrite this objective on the form at the end of this chapter, then write four or five sentences that give an overview of your qualifications.

This profile, or qualifications summary, should be placed at the beginning of your résumé. You can include some of your personal traits or special skills that might have been difficult to get across in your job descriptions. Some HR professionals might disagree with me. They say that they skip over descriptions of unverifiable claims about personal strengths, but there are just as many HR managers who read every word. Besides, you want to make sure you cover your soft skills for electronic résumés where keywords defined in job requisitions often request such strengths.

Here is a sample profile section for a computer systems technician looking for a job with a military contractor:

- Experienced systems/network technician with significant communications and technical control experience in the military sector.
- Focused and hardworking; willing to go the extra mile for the customer.
- Skilled in troubleshooting complex problems by thinking outside the box.
- Possesses a high degree of professionalism and dedication to exceptional quality.
- Current Top Secret security clearance with access to Sensitive Compartmentalized Information.

Avoid using laundry lists of keywords in place of the sentences of a profile section. First of all, they aren't very interesting for a human being to read, and second, keywords used out of context do not have the same impact when processed by electronic résumé processing software. Newer applications use artificial intelligence to determine a keyword's credibility based on the surrounding text.

> *Recruiters spend as little as ten seconds deciding whether to read a résumé from top to bottom.*

For human readers, however, it is okay to pull out a few key bullets that highlight your areas of expertise (see sample below). Just make sure you use the same words somewhere within the body of your résumé.

- Dedicated accountant with thirteen years of diverse experience that includes
  - Public accounting
  - Internal auditing
  - Nonprofit accounting
  - Compliance auditing
  - Tax preparation
  - Reporting
- Certified Public Accountant in California and Colorado; Certified Internal Auditor.
- Analytical and thorough professional with a track record of success managing the toughest assignments.
- Effective team player with exceptional communication, writing, and interpersonal skills.

A new trend in résumé writing allows us to incorporate philosophy statements into the profile of a résumé. The bullets are more accomplishment driven and use fewer soft-skill keywords.

AREAS OF EXPERTISE

P&I Management • Strategic Planning
Transportation/Logistics • Budgeting
Sales/Marketing • Business Development
Supply Chain Management • Outsourcing
Technology Enhancements
Quality Management • Regulatory Affairs
Customer Satisfaction • Vendor Relations

"It's all about the people. The greatest reward of leadership is helping to develop people, which, when handled properly, leads to exceptional organizational results."

SENIOR-LEVEL EXECUTIVE

- Strong record of streamlining operations, reducing costs, and increasing profitability while facilitating quality and operations improvements for both large and small organizations.

- Definitive success in start-up and turnaround situations, as well as stable business environments.

- Domestic and international experience in a broad range of industries.

- Recent Executive MBA with a concentration in Finance, International Business, and Corporate Strategy.

A similar idea creates a section for quotes from performance evaluations, letters of reference, customer comments, and other positive comments that are difficult to weave into the body of a résumé. You can put the quotes in the margins of the résumé, in pull-out boxes, in a separate section, or worked individually at the end of a relevant bullet. Here is a sample of customer comments in a separate section:

CUSTOMER COMMENTS

"Allan has proven to be extremely knowledgeable and professional in executing my local Cable TV media campaigns. Having worked in cable advertising sales myself for six years, I can appreciate when a media salesperson does a great job from the initial schedule planning stage to the final invoice." Mike Smith, Champion

"His thorough knowledge of his product and the sales process are evidence of his many years of success in media sales. I enthusiastically recommend Allen for any sales position and am confident that his competency and positive attitude would make him a valuable asset." Christin Jones, Academy Agency & Advisors

"As a representative for Adelphia Cable, Allan was one of the few who understood the true meaning of the word 'service.'" Robert Smith, Adams Advertising Agency

"Allan has the four traits that make him a great sales rep: friendly, responsible, efficient, and fun. If Allan is applying for a job with your company, I suggest hiring him immediately!" Brian Jones, Hanson Marketing & Advertising

Now, back to the profile section. It must be relevant to the type of job for which you are applying, so customize it for each application if possible. It might be true that you are "compassionate," but will it help you get a job as a high-pressure salesperson? Write this profile from the perspective of a potential employer. What will convince this person to call you instead of someone else?

Busy recruiters spend as little as ten seconds deciding whether to read a résumé from top to bottom. You will be lucky if the first third of your résumé gets read, so make sure the information at the top entices the reader to read it all.

Samples

Let's look at some sample profiles for various industries. You will notice some significantly different styles of presenting the information. Choose the style that best presents your information.

ARTIST

- Creative graphic artist with experience in pen-and-ink illustration, watercolor, and oil mediums.
- Background in magazine/book, children's book, graphic novel, and comic book illustration.
- Hardworking, loyal artist with definitive leadership and sales abilities.
- Self-starter; able to motivate others to perform to their maximum potential.

ATTORNEY

- Licensed attorney in private practice since 1979 (Colorado and New Mexico).
- Board Certified Civil Trial Specialist, National Board of Trial Advocacy, with extensive litigation experience (initially certified 1990, recertified 1995, 2000, and 2005).
- Recognized specialist in workers' compensation law by the New Mexico Legal Specialization Board.
- Admitted to practice before the U.S. Court of Appeals, 10th Circuit; U.S. District Court for the District of New Mexico; U.S. District Court for the Western District of Texas; District Courts of the State Colorado; and all courts in the State of New Mexico.
- Successful Federal Administrative Law Judge applicant (awaiting placement).

- Extensive experience in the preparation and trial of injury claims resulting from both workers' compensation and off-the-job injuries.
- Exceptional knowledge of administrative procedures, rules of evidence, and trial practices.
- Able to communicate in a clear, concise manner with people of diverse backgrounds and levels of authority.

BOOKKEEPER

- Experienced bookkeeper and administrator with twenty years of diverse experience.
- Background in management, general ledger, financial statements, accounts payable, accounts receivable, and payroll.
- Computer literate in Windows, QuickBooks Pro, One-Write, MS Word, Excel, and Business Works.
- Dependable, accurate, and well organized; able to handle multiple tasks simultaneously.

BUYER

- Dependable, efficient procurement professional with thirteen years of experience in the grocery business.
- Quick learner who is able to troubleshoot complex problems and multitask effectively.
- Self-motivated team player with exceptional communication and interpersonal skills.
- Proven leader who enjoys finding better ways of doing things and making value-added improvements.

CERTIFIED PUBLIC ACCOUNTANT, FINANCIAL EXECUTIVE

- Experienced Financial Executive and Certified Public Accountant with a strong background in:

– Accounting	– MIS	– Acquisitions
– Budgeting	– Administration	– Banking Relationships
– Credit Management	– HR Management	– Environmental Compliance
– Reporting	– Benefits	– Legal Issues

- CFO at the time of an initial public offering; supervised SEC reporting and investor relations.
- Managed preparation of the first registered Internet public venture capital offering and several private placements to accredited investors.
- Negotiated a variety of long-term and short-term loan syndications and developed cash management functions.
- Licensed CPA in Arizona and Ohio (inactive); won the Silver Award for the second highest exam grade in Ohio.

CHILD CARE PROVIDER

- Dedicated child care provider with more than eleven years of experience.
- Fair and just with a commitment to setting a good example.
- Patient instructor who enjoys working with children.
- Effective team player with strong interpersonal and communication skills.

CONSTRUCTION PROFESSIONAL

- Experienced construction professional with a background in residential and commercial roofing and general contracting.
- Quality oriented with a dedication to getting the job done right the first time.
- Well-organized with a natural aptitude for math; skilled in analyzing tasks and breaking them down into manageable pieces.

CONSULTANT

- Detail-oriented consultant with a strong entrepreneurial spirit and a background in consultative selling and MIS.
- Experience with e-business, competitive strategy development, strategic business planning, re-engineering, custom development, data-driven models, process assessment/improvement, and information technology.
- Extensive background in international marketing, importing, advertising design, and new business development.
- Proven history of building new business by identifying, calling on, and driving business decisions at the executive level.
- High-energy team player with exceptional leadership, analytical, problem solving, communication, and presentation skills.

CRIMINAL INVESTIGATOR

- Experienced criminal investigator with eighteen years as a Deputy U.S. Marshal with full law enforcement authority and a background in management, investigative, and supervisory positions.
- Dedicated manager who welcomes a challenge.
- Team player who is willing to work long hours to get the job done.
- Proven reputation for working well with others and serving as a role model/mentor.

EDITOR, BOOK PUBLISHING

- Experienced editor with a strong book publishing background, including:
  - Math
  - Science
  - Test Preparation
  - Medical
  - Nursing
  - Allied Health
  - Business
  - Art
  - Gardening
  - Juvenile
  - Parenting
  - Child Care
- Skilled wordsmith with the ability to transform a rough draft into a marketable finished product.
- Effective team player with outstanding communication and interpersonal skills.
- Knowledge of Windows, MS Word, Excel, WordPerfect, Internet browsers, and e-mail.

EMT/FIREFIGHTER

- Experienced EMT and registered firefighter with a strong desire to help people.
- Quick thinker who enjoys a fast pace and the challenge of a job's physical demands.
- Adept at working under pressure and managing multiple tasks simultaneously.
- Effective team player with a positive attitude and strong interpersonal skills.
- Proven problem solver who enjoys getting to the root of a challenge.

ELECTRONICS TECHNICIAN

- Experienced electronics technician with a strong background in test and engineering.
- Detail-oriented and analytical; able to manage the details while seeing the whole picture.
- Respected for the ability to solve problems and get things done when others give up.
- Effective team player with exceptional communication and interpersonal skills.

ENGINEER

- Experienced engineering professional with a strong background in:
  - Quality control/quality assurance
  - Electrical/mechanical systems
  - Precision-process maintenance
  - Analysis and problem solving
  - Equipment fabrication
  - Test equipment operation
  - Electronic principles and theories
  - Computer-controlled devices
- Proven expertise in engineering enhancements to fabrication tools, chemical mechanical polishing, vacuum systems, pneumatic systems, diffusion, and gas delivery systems.
- Skilled in reading and interpreting blueprints, engineering prints, and other schematic drawings.

EXECUTIVE SECRETARY

- Experienced executive secretary with a strong work ethic and proven customer service skills.
- Quick learner who enjoys the challenge of new responsibilities.
- Effective team player who is dependable, cooperative, and able to work under tight deadlines.
- Strong communication and interpersonal skills; tactful when working with difficult people.

FACILITY MAINTENANCE

- Experienced technician with a diverse background in industrial and commercial facility maintenance.
- Nationally Certified Apartment Maintenance Technician (CAMT) since 2000.
- HVAC Certified (Universal), Esco Institute since 1993; EPA Certified since 1996.
- Dependable, loyal worker who can fix just about anything and learns quickly.
- Personable and courteous; proven track record of exceptional customer service.
- Good listener with a quick sense of humor and the ability to work well with all types of people.
- Exceptional attendance record; never missed a page call in eight years of 24-hour-a-day availability.

FIELD ENGINEER, TELECOM

- Experienced field engineer, cable splicer, communications technician, and supervisor.
- Background in the installation, testing, and maintenance of analog/digital telephone and central office equipment.
- Self-motivated team player who works well independently and manages time efficiently.
- Long track record of perfect attendance with no on-the-job accidents.
- Flexible worker with the ability to analyze and prioritize project assignments.
- Proven reputation for providing exceptional customer service.

FINANCIAL PLANNER

- Experienced financial planner with proven expertise in retirement planning, investments, insurance, and asset management.
- Hold current Series 7, 63, 65, 31, life, health, and accident insurance licenses.
- Committed to the highest levels of integrity and professional ethics.
- Team leader with exceptional communication skills and an engaging interpersonal style.
- Able to work effectively with people from diverse backgrounds and levels of authority.
- Knowledge of Windows, MS Word, WordPerfect, Outlook, e-mail, and the Internet.

FINANCE PROFESSIONAL

- Seasoned finance professional with extensive experience in:
  - Venture capital
  - Business valuation
  - Operations management
  - Mergers/acquisitions
  - Due diligence
  - Strategic planning
  - Business plan analysis
  - Financial modeling
  - New business development
- Multi-disciplinary executive with a diverse background in marketing/sales, finance, accounting loan origination and servicing, and public accounting.
- Able to effectively motivate both management and operating personnel to achieve maximum results.
- Skilled in applying logical but creative approaches to problem resolution.

HIGH TECH or CORPORATE TRAINING

- Eight years of experience as an **Instruction Designer** and **Trainer** in both the corporate and public sectors.
- Strong background in developing company training programs, computer-based instruction, and corporate university programs.
- Skilled in organization, leadership, project management, team building, and problem solving.
- Effective team player with proven interpersonal, communication, presentation, and writing skills.

INFORMATION ANALYST

- Dedicated information analyst with more than eighteen years of programming/data processing experience in the telecommunications, banking, and government sectors.
- Certified Xenix Systems Administrator.
- Skilled in analysis, construction, implementation, troubleshooting, production support, operations support, help desk, testing (unit, regression, integration, and systems), training, and maintenance.
- Detail oriented and organized; comfortable taking the initiative and working independently.

LAW ENFORCEMENT

- Proven leader with more than twenty years of law enforcement experience and expertise in program development, project management, team motivation, and public relations.
- Service-oriented professional with the ability to promote positive organizational values.

- Personally dedicated to ensuring the delivery of quality service.
- Experienced public speaker with strong communication and presentation skills.

LOGISTICIAN, MATERIALS MANAGER

HIGHLIGHTS OF QUALIFICATIONS

Experienced materials manager and gifted logistician with a proven background in:
Administration • Operations • Contract Negotiations • Cost Control • Budgeting
Forecasting • Purchasing • Automated Inventory Tracking Systems • Transportation • Distribution
Self-motivated leader with strong interpersonal, communication, and motivation skills.
Able to organize and prioritize multiple projects with divergent needs.
Holds a current Secret security clearance.

MANAGER, GENERAL

- Forward-thinking manager with diverse experience in:
  - Business development
  - Change management
  - Process re-engineering
  - Strategic planning
  - Consultative selling
  - Marketing
  - Employee development
  - Training and facilitation
  - Supervision
- Skilled in applying logical but creative approaches to problem resolution.
- Self-motivated; comfortable working independently and taking the initiative.
- Effective team player with exceptional communication and presentation skills.

MANAGER, GENERAL

- Experienced manager with a proven track record of improving productivity and profitability.
- Resourceful at finding innovative solutions to complex problems.
- Able to work outside the job description and to manage crises with ease.
- Personable team player with strong communication and interpersonal skills.

MANAGER, HEALTHCARE

- Self-motivated healthcare manager with a passion for taking on new responsibilities.
- Proven supervisor with the ability to motivate workers and lead by example.
- Skilled in applying logical but creative approaches to problem resolution.
- Open to re-evaluating traditional methods and finding better ways to get the job done.
- Personable team player with strong communication and presentation skills.

MANAGER, HUMAN RESOURCES

Well-rounded human resource management professional offering
more than five years of experience in:
Recruiting • Interviewing • Employee Selection • Placement • Job Descriptions
Position Evaluation • Training • Discipline • Workers' Compensation • Pay
EEOC Compliance • Labor Relations • ADA • FMLA

MANAGER, TOURISM/HOSPITALITY

- Adaptable manager with nine years of experience in the tourism/hospitality industry, including:
  - Strategic planning
  - Multi-property management
  - Budgeting and operations
  - Marketing and promotion
  - Personnel development
  - Public/guest relations
  - Reservation sales
  - Revenue maximization
  - New property construction
- Confident leader who is able to motivate employees to excel in customer service.
- Effective team player with excellent communication and interpersonal skills.
- Self-motivated professional with a strong work ethic and proven problem-solving skills.

MANUFACTURING

- Sixteen years of manufacturing experience from research and development phase to high-volume production requirements.
- Skilled in the development of documentation and procedures to meet regulatory requirements.
- Able to work equally well on an independent basis or as a cooperative team member.
- Excellent leadership and organizational skills; strong oral and written communication abilities.

MEDICAL ASSISTANT

- Registered Medical Assistant with an Associate Degree in medical assisting.
- Experienced in recordkeeping, filing, typing (55 wpm), scheduling, phone etiquette, dictation, and most office machines.
- Knowledge of computers; experienced with WordPerfect and MEDISOFT; familiar with many other Windows and MS-DOS applications.
- Responsible and dependable professional with a strong medical ethic.
- Excellent organizer who is able to work independently and as part of a team.

MENTAL HEALTH PROFESSIONAL

- Experienced mental health professional with a diverse background in inpatient and medical psychiatric assessment and therapy, including
  - Social work
  - Individual therapy
  - Group therapy
  - Evaluation
  - Disposition
  - Domestic violence
  - Crisis intervention
  - Suicide prevention
  - Chemical dependency
- Certified Alcohol Counselor I (CACI) in the state of Colorado.
- Innovative, highly energetic worker with demonstrated organizational and social skills.
- Able to accept and appreciate differences in others; nonjudgmental and impartial.
- Sensitive and empathetic team player with finely tuned communication and interpersonal abilities.

NURSE

- Dedicated Interventional Cardiology Nurse with a reputation for astute clinical judgment.
- Respected professional with a strong background in critical care nursing and pharmacology.

- Compassionate caregiver who quickly establishes and maintains rapport with patients.
- Detail-oriented and precise; dedicated to providing excellence in patient care.
- Adept at managing multiple tasks simultaneously and working under pressure.
- Knowledge of Windows, computerized charting, and electronic cardiac systems.

NURSE ADMINISTRATOR

- Dedicated nurse administrator who enjoys new challenges and works well in high-pressure environments demanding hard work and self-motivation.
- Licensed Registered Nurse (New Jersey 120960) with graduate education in health systems administration and business management.
- Effective team leader with proven communication, interpersonal, and presentation skills.
- Detail-oriented professional with strong problem-solving abilities.
- Compassionate caregiver who is able to quickly establish and maintain rapport with patients and other healthcare providers.

NURSING

- Registered Nurse, Washington, RN 00100096
- Registered Nurse, California, RN 289035
- Certified Emergency Nurse, 9606587
- National Registry Paramedic, PO 856139
- Certified Emergency Medical Technician, Washington
- PADI Dive Master and Rescue Diver, 23415
- Advanced Cardiac Life Support (ACLS)
- Pediatric Advanced Life Support (PALS)
- Certified PALS Instructor
- Prehospital Trauma Life Support (PHTLS)

OCCUPATIONAL THERAPIST

- Compassionate occupational therapist with an enthusiasm for helping others.
- Persuasive motivator with an inherent understanding of people and a genuine caring attitude.
- Effective team player who works well with others and strives to create win-win relationships.
- Able to collaborate with other healthcare professionals to develop productive treatment plans.

OFFICE WORKER

- Dependable office worker with more than five years of hands-on experience.
- Able to thrive in a fast-paced environment, managing multiple tasks simultaneously.
- Versatile, quick learner who loves challenge and adapts well to new situations.
- Self-motivated; works well with little or no supervision.
- Knowledge of Windows, MS Word, Excel, Access, and SQL computer software.
- Skills: typing, ten-key, fax, copiers, laser printers, and multiple phone lines.

PILOT

- Experienced leader with a proven track record in aviation operations and safety management.
- Diverse background as a pilot with strong technical and training skills.
- Current FAA Commercial Pilot License with rotorcraft and instrument ratings.
- Ambitious professional who adapts quickly to changing conditions.

PROJECT MANAGER

- Experienced project manager with a proven background in the development and implementation of complex computer and communication networks.
- Dedicated professional who is skilled at identifying process improvements and developing quality solutions that are faster, cheaper, and better.
- Effective team leader with strong communication and interpersonal skills.
- Current top secret security clearance with special background investigation (TS/SBI), SCI reinstatable.

PUBLIC RELATIONS

- Seasoned public relations expert with a vast range of industry and media contacts.
- Nationally recognized spokesman, commentator, and expert on the business and law of sports.
- Strong background in sports journalism with major newspapers, radio stations, and television networks.
- Quick thinker who is skilled at applying logical but creative approaches to challenges.

PUBLIC RELATIONS

- Creative and versatile public relations professional with a strong desire to succeed.
- Self-motivated, articulate team player with exceptional speaking and writing skills.
- Proficient researcher with proven experience using MediaMap, Lexis-Nexis, databases, the Internet, search engines, Windows, and PowerPoint.
- Quick learner who is committed to keeping abreast of advancements in his field and who derives satisfaction from a hard day's work.

SALES AND MARKETING POSITION

- Demonstrated success in sales and management positions for more than seventeen years.
- Proven ability to develop new markets and maintain profitable client relationships.
- Consistent high achiever recognized for exceptional sales accomplishments with fiercely competitive products in a shrinking marketplace.
- Respected for powerful negotiating and closing abilities.
- Self-motivated and focused; comfortable working independently with little supervision.

SENIOR EXECUTIVE

- High-energy senior executive with a demonstrated track record of success in:
  - Sales/marketing
  - Finance
  - Strategic planning
  - Technical innovations
  - Business development
  - Negotiations
  - Operations management
  - International business
  - Staff development
- Proven ability to combine high-caliber analytical and strategic planning skills with outstanding business development and marketing expertise in both domestic and global business arenas.
- Fast-track professional who thrives on challenges and takes a hands-on leadership role to position the company for growth in a changing environment.
- Recognized for ingenuity, integrity, and the ability to negotiate win/win scenarios.

SOCIAL WORKER

- Empathetic medical social worker with experience in:
  - Special needs children
  - Counseling/advocacy
  - Part C funding
  - Case management
  - Training
  - Service coordination
  - Abuse and neglect
  - Team building
  - Facilitation
- Self-motivated with a commitment to providing quality care.
- Creative professional who enjoys a challenge and sees the big picture.
- Excellent knowledge of IFSP and IEP processes, best practices in early intervention, legal rights of the special education population, and the health problems and medical needs of children.
- Extensive network of community resources on the Front Range in education, mental health, pediatric services, healthcare, and human services.

SUPERINTENDENT, GOLF COURSE

- Experienced golf course superintendent focused on efficient operations, exceptional attention to detail, and the highest level of course conditioning and playability for the perfect golf experience.
- Ten years of experience in greenskeeping and golf course management.
- Skilled administrator who leads by example and promotes a strong team work ethic.
- Extensive knowledge of horticulture, including an undergraduate degree in landscape horticulture/turf management.

TEACHER

- Dedicated teacher with the desire to instill in children the passion to be lifelong learners.
- Able to set and maintain high expectations with the belief that children will rise to them and be reliable, respectful, responsible, and ready to learn.
- Outgoing and patient instructor who enjoys working with children.
- Effective team player with strong communication and interpersonal skills.

TECHNICIAN, TELECOMMUNICATIONS

- Self-motivated telecommunications technician with fourteen years of diverse experience.
- Expertise in the installation, troubleshooting, and repair of digital and analog communications, teleconferencing, video, and computer network equipment.
- Respected for the ability to solve complex problems and to get things done when others give up.
- Thrives in fast-paced, challenging environments; holds a current secret security clearance.

TRAINER, INSTRUCTIONAL DESIGNER

- Experienced trainer, instructional designer, manager, and change agent with a background in both corporate and academic environments.
- **Training:** Creative presenter, facilitator, and coach with strong communication and inter-personal skills. Proven ability to use innovative delivery methods and group dynamics to improve the quality of the training experience. Adept at teaching across a wide variety of cultural differences.
- **Problem Solving:** Conceptual thinker who enjoys the challenge of analyzing systems and making them more effective. Experienced organizational developer who has conducted focus groups and sensing interviews to design departmental improvements.
- **Teamwork:** Collaborative team player with the ability to motivate others and build strong teams that can work together to accomplish an organization's goals.
- **Certifications:** Ropes Course Trainer. Mager Criterion Referenced Instructor. Train the Trainer. Myers-Briggs Type Indicator, FIRO-B, Strong, and Campbell instruments.

CONTACT INFORMATION

This final stage of information gathering will provide you with all the information you need to begin your résumé. For the contact information, you can use your full name, first and last name only, or shortened names (Pat Criscito instead of Patricia K. Criscito).

Do not use work telephone numbers or a work e-mail address on your résumé. Potential employers tend to consider that an abuse of company resources, which implies you might do the same if you are working for them. Listing a cellular telephone number on your résumé gives a hiring manager a way to reach you during working hours. Today, people often have only a cell phone, which is fine. It is also okay to keep a cell phone with an area code that is different from the area code where you live. That is becoming so common that hiring managers don't even question it anymore.

Avoid the use of "cutesy" e-mail addresses on a résumé. If you use *babycakes@aol.com* for your personal e-mail, create a second e-mail address under your account that will be more professional. If your only access to the Internet is at work, then create a free-mail account at any of the more than 1,000 free e-mail providers, including *hotmail.com, aol.com, juno.com, yahoo.com, mail.com, excite.com, netscape.com,* or *netzero.com.* Check *www.refdesk.com* for a list of even more free e-mail services.

NAME _____

ADDRESS _____

CITY/STATE/ZIP _____

COUNTRY (if applying outside the country where you live)_____

HOME PHONE _____   CELL PHONE _____

E-MAIL _____

WEB SITE _____

QUALIFICATIONS PROFILE

Keep the qualifications profile short, sweet, and to the point. I tend to limit them to five or six bullets, although there are exceptions to this rule when creating a curriculum vitae or other types of professional résumés. I'll give you a few extra places to list that information if you need a longer profile, but try to use no more than six of the blanks.

You can title this section with any of the following headlines: Profile, Qualifications, Highlights of Qualifications, Expertise, Strengths, Summary, Synopsis, Background, Professional Background, Executive Summary, Highlights, Overview, Professional Overview, Capsule, or Keyword Profile.

OBJECTIVE/FOCUS (this can become the first sentence of your profile or stand alone) _____
_____
_____
_____

SECOND SENTENCE (areas of expertise) _____
_____
_____
_____

STRENGTHS _____
_____
_____
_____

STRENGTHS _____
_____
_____
_____

STRENGTHS _____
_____
_____
_____

STRENGTHS _____
_____
_____
_____

STRENGTHS _____
_____
_____
_____

STRENGTHS _____
_____
_____
_____

Chapter 13

Step 12
Putting It
All Together

Now it's time to put this all together into the perfect résumé. You have a qualifications summary, your education, experience, and other relevant information. How do you decide which section goes first, second, third, and last? That depends . . . everything in the résumé business depends!

Start with the section that contains your strongest qualifications for your target job. If you have had little experience in your prospective field but have a degree that qualifies you for a starting position in the industry, then by all means list your education first. Most people eventually move their education below their experience as they get further from their school days. If you change your career and go back to school, then the education will move to the top again and begin to gravitate to the bottom as you gain relevant experience.

The same idea goes for information within each section. For instance, if your job title is more impressive than where you worked, then list it first.

VICE PRESIDENT OF MARKETING
Little Known Company, Boulder, Colorado

IBM CORPORATION, Boulder, Colorado
Assistant Export Coordinator

Functional or Chronological

There are three basic types of résumés—reverse chronological, functional, and a combination of the two. There are fad styles that come and go, but the three I've just mentioned are the classics.

A reverse-chronological résumé arranges your experience and education in chronological order with the most recent dates first. This style is the most popular résumé with recruiters and hiring managers. It showcases your jobs one at a time and shows a clear chronology of your work history. Use it:

Everything in the résumé business depends.

1. When your last job is a strong foundation for your current objective.

2. When you are staying in the same field as your past job(s).

3. When you have a strong history of promotion or development in your career.

4. When your prior titles or company names are an asset to your current job search.

5. When you are in a highly traditional field (education, banking, government, etc.).

6. When you are working with an executive recruiter.

Most of the résumés I write are reverse-chronological, but that doesn't mean a different type of résumé might not fit your needs better. A functional résumé organizes your work experience by the functions you performed regardless of date. The functional résumé highlights your skills and potential instead of your work history. Use it:

1. When you want to play down gaps in your experience.

2. When you are entering the job market for the first time.

3. When you are reentering the job market, for example after raising children.

4. When you want to change careers.

5. When you have changed jobs too many times or have lots of jobs to show because you have been doing consulting, freelance, or temporary work.

6. When you have done the same things in every job and don't want to use the same descriptions over and over again.

7. When you need to de-emphasize your age but exploit older experience.

8. When you need to list volunteer experience and community or school activities to strengthen your qualifications.

List your functional paragraphs in their order of importance, with the items listed first that will help you get the particular job you are targeting. Refer to Step 9 (Chapter 10) of this book for ideas on how to rearrange your résumé sentences to better capture your reader's attention.

You should know that there are very rare instances when I would recommend a purely functional résumé, however. In the 1980s, true functional résumés developed a bad reputation because applicants were not listing where they gained their experience. It made recruiters suspicious that the applicant was trying to hide something. A combination functional/chronological résumé will avoid this problem. Always list a brief synopsis of your actual work experience at the bottom of your functional résumé with each title, employer, and the dates worked.

Here are some sample functional/chronological combination résumés that might help you decide if this style is right for you.

Leesa A. Murphy

PROFILE
- Dedicated administrative assistant with 7+ years experience in the judicial court system.
- Self-starter with strong problem solving and organizational abilities.
- Demonstrated ability to handle difficult situations with tact.
- Skilled in analyzing a task and breaking it down into manageable pieces.
- Team player with exceptional communication and interpersonal skills.
- Knowledge of MS Word, Windows, Excel, and proprietary systems.

EXPERIENCE

LEGAL EXPERIENCE
- Coordinated and set court dockets and dates, prepared juries for trial, and assisted pro se individuals.
- Created new files, maintained filing system, and typed judge's directives, orders, and letters.
- Collected traffic fines, managed collections registry for criminal/juvenile cases, and assisted in the collections process by turning cases over to State Collections.
- Worked closely with the Department of Labor in the investigation of employment status and wage garnishments; met with 20 to 30 people per day.
- Maintained the personnel expense reimbursement program (COFORS).
- Set appointments for 30 probation officers.
- Performed intake and input new cases in the computer system.
- Routed mail and copied files for the District Attorney's office.
- Entered data for child support and domestic cases.

ADMINISTRATION/MANAGEMENT
- Developed and implemented all office procedures for the recovery center.
- Accountable for the establishment and preparation of financial statements, insurance billings, monthly and daily accounting reports.
- Reviewed all deposits, accounts receivable, and insurance payments.
- Analyzed, negotiated, and resolved problem accounts.
- Supervised and evaluated office personnel.
- Issued demand letters, negotiated repayments/settlements, developed payment plans, and processed collection paperwork.
- Improved monthly accounts receivable status ratings from below standard (a $40,000 deficit) to 98% in less than a year.
- Developed systems for work flow and record keeping that significantly improved efficiency.

OTHER EXPERIENCE
- Extensive public relations and customer service background.
- Excel in dealing with difficult people and situations.
- Provided secretarial support and front desk reception services.
- Processed military personnel paperwork for transitions, issued passports, and maintained records.

WORK HISTORY

Municipal Court Clerk, Municipal Court, Colorado Springs, Colorado		2004 – present
Collections Investigator, 4th Judicial District Court, Colorado Springs, Colorado		2003 – 2004
Assistant Division Clerk, 4th Judicial District Court, Colorado Springs, Colorado		2001 – 2003
Court Clerk II, 4th Judicial District Court, Colorado Springs, Colorado		1999 – 2001
Secretary I, 4th Judicial District Court, Colorado Springs, Colorado		1998 – 1999
Office Manager, Lakeside Recovery Center, Tacoma, Washington		1996 – 1997
Administrative Assistant, United States Army		1990 – 1996

EDUCATION

Pikes Peak Community College, 3-hour course in Psychology
Kansas State University, 12 hours of liberal arts studies
Central Texas College, 6 hours of liberal arts studies

ADDRESS

12345 Anywhere Street, Newtown, Colorado 80907 · (719) 555-1234

129

MICHAEL D. NEWMAN

Phone: (781) 555-1245 ▪ 20 Anywhere Street ▪ Newtown, Massachusetts 02368 ▪ mnewman@protypeltd.com

PROFILE
- Experienced Advertising Director with demonstrated success in:
  - Major accounts
  - Classified advertising
  - Retail accounts
  - Research
  - New product development
  - Sales and training
  - Budgeting
  - Graphic arts and production
  - Planning and scheduling
- Practical problem solver with exceptional analytical, creative, and communication skills.
- Strong background in building new territories and using creative marketing approaches.
- Demonstrated ability to create client loyalty above and beyond the relationship.
- Proficient in Windows 95, MS Word, Excel, PowerPoint, Access, Quark, AIM billing system, and ATEX classified front-end software.

EXPERIENCE
Major Accounts
- Managed the major accounts sales team for *The Gazette,* a Freedom Corporation newspaper with a circulation of 121,000.
- Made sales presentations to senior management of major accounts in cities nationwide.
- Developed a new client base and expanded existing accounts to achieve $17 million in annual sales.

Research and New Product Development
- Directed the development of new products for *The Gazette,* including demographic and psychographic market research, feasibility studies, product design and packaging, budgeting, scheduling, implementation, sales, and P&L.
- Analyzed statistical and other market data and used the results to create sales presentations to advertisers; researched and analyzed competitive information.
- Instrumental in building the online division of the newspaper (coloradosprings.com).
- Developed the *Home in Colorado* magazine that won the 1999 Addy Award for best in-home publication with more than four colors.
- Created a sales and marketing product manual to delineate newspaper sections, ancillary products, and the demographics of the newspaper's core readership.
- Implemented the weekly *Peak Computing Magazine* from the ground up; responsible for product development and design, placement, distribution, setting advertising rates, sales, and creation of a companion Web site.
- Collaborated with sister properties to develop "Living Well," a health tab special feature of the *Patriot Ledger.*
- Created an innovative research program for the *Times Advocate* (Team: Research) that provided the sales team with comprehensive and accurate demographic information to increase the effectiveness of client advertising.

Classified and Retail
- Directed retail sales to major, national, local, and automotive accounts of the *Patriot Ledger*, a daily newspaper with a circulation of 82,000.
- Directly supervised all commercial advertising sales functions for the *News-Chronicle* (a community newspaper with a circulation of 30,000), increasing revenues by 22%.
- Sold *Pennysaver* classified advertisements to commercial account advertisers.
- Increased gross sales by 131%, decreased new territory delinquencies by 40%, and achieved the top 10% of all sales executives.

Management and Supervision
- Developed and managed sales budgets of up to $17 million; accountable for print bids, production costs, and full profit and loss.
- Negotiated dollar volume contracts averaging $400,000, with highest being $1 million.
- Hired, trained, supervised, and mentored up to 5 managers and 45 staff members.
- Developed and negotiated a new commission plan for the *Patriot Ledger* retail department with union leaders.
- Managed production functions for the *Patriot Ledger* through prepress, including graphic design, copy input, page layout, and dispatch.

EXPERIENCE	*Management and Supervision (continued)*

- Contributed to the design and installation of an integrated advertising computer system that provides fully automated order entry, advertisement tracking, production, and pagination.
- Increased revenues for *Peak Computing* by 870% in 13 months and display advertisers by 400%, ultimately achieving $750,000 in annual sales.
- Managed the Porch Plus alternative delivery program for the *Times Advocate,* increasing revenues from $130,000 to $1.5 million.
- Collaborated with *The Orange County Register* to increase the market for Porch Plus.
- Served as co-chair of the San Diego North County Golf Expo, generating significant goodwill and $70,000 in new revenue.

Training

- Developed curriculum for and implemented a complete sales training program for all advertising associates of *The Gazette.*
- Wrote the company training manual for all departments.
- Conducted sales training seminars and created incentive programs.

HISTORY

PATRIOT LEDGER, Quincy, Massachusetts   2004 – present
Retail Advertising Director

THE GAZETTE, Colorado Springs, Colorado   2000 – 2004
Manager of Research and New Products   2004
Major Accounts / New Products Development Manager / Advertising Trainer   2002 – 2004
Sales Manager for Peak Computing Magazine   2000 – 2002

TIMES ADVOCATE, Escondido, California   1999 – 2000
Marketing / Research Coordinator
Retail Sales Manager for Porch Plus (Alternative Delivery Service)

NEWS-CHRONICLE, Encinitas, California   1998 – 1999
Sales Manager (Retail and Classified)

PENNYSAVER, San Diego, California   1995 – 1998
Classified Account Executive and Line Supervisor

EDUCATION

BACHELOR OF ARTS, Material and Logistics Management   1988
Michigan State University, East Lansing, Michigan

CONTINUING EDUCATION
Numerous leadership development training programs, including Legal Issues for Supervisors, Tactical Leadership (Hiring the Best, Performance Management, Documentation and Discipline, and Sexual Harassment), Train the Trainer, among others.

PUBLICATION

Wrote and published an article in *Retail Insights* entitled "Customer Service" directed toward media advertising managers and directors.

TONY PACHECO

12 Anywhere Trail
Newtown, Colorado 81005

Phone: (719) 555-1234
E-mail: pacheco@protypeltd.com

PROFILE

- Experienced human resources manager with a diverse background in both manufacturing and high-tech services industries.
- Self-motivated professional with a strong work ethic and the ability to get the job done.
- Flexible quick learner who enjoys taking on new challenges and learning new processes.
- Known for the ability to bridge philosophies, build mutual trust, and create consensus.
- Bilingual—native English speaker, working knowledge of Spanish.
- Knowledge of Windows, MS Word, Excel, PowerPoint, Access, MS-Works, and e-mail.

AREAS OF EXPERTISE

Human Resource Regulations
- Safety Management/OSHA
- Wage and Hour/Wage Determinations
- State Laws/Federal Laws
- Service Contract/Davis-Bacon
- Employment/Labor Law/NLRB

Salary Administration
- Job Descriptions
- Standard Operating Procedures
- Position Evaluation
- Exempt/Nonexempt Pay
- Rate Ranges and Progression

Recruitment/Selection
- Executive/Administrative
- Nonexempt Hourly Sourcing
- Temporary Employment
- Outside Contractors
- Examination/Placement

Employee Relations
- EEOC/ADA/EEO-1 Reporting
- Affirmative Action Program Report
- Human Resources Auditor
- Corporate Advisor to the VP Services Dept.
- Federal Mediation and Conciliation
- Management Training of Contractual Intent
- Employee Relations Committee
- Negotiations Observer/Advisor
- Chief Contract Negotiator
- Grievance Handling/Steps I-II-III Arbitration
- Mutual Gains Bargaining Negotiations
- Arbitrator Selection
- Collective Bargaining Agreement (CBA)
- Arbitration Hearings (opening statement to end)

Benefits/Compensation
- 401k/Pensions/COBRA/WARN
- Workers' Compensation
- Loss Control

EXPERIENCE

HUMAN RESOURCES/LABOR RELATIONS MANAGER (2002 – present)
Mason and Hanger Corporation, Colorado Springs, Colorado
- Provide advice and counsel to managers and supervisors relating to human resource policies, procedures, and employee benefits for this military contractor with 400 employees in three sites.
- Listen to employee problems and provide feedback to functional managers to ensure that corrective action is taken.
- Discuss employee morale with site and program managers, indicating remedial action to resolve problem areas.
- Motivate and educate supervisors and manager to ensure consistent, equal, and fair treatment of all employees.
- Administer compensation and benefit programs, including insurance and 401k pension plans.
- Audit personnel records and maintain their security and confidentiality.
- Developed policies and procedures for exit interviews and ensured compliance with federal and state laws and regulations.
- Implemented an affirmative action program to meet federal requirements.
- Serve as a liaison between management and three unions.
- Negotiate and administer three collective bargaining agreements.
- Successfully increased trust between the union and the company, resulting in fewer filed grievances; saved more than half a million dollars by settling disputes without arbitration.
- Selected to diffuse a stalled bargaining agreement that had been referred for mediation with the Federal Mediation and Conciliation Board.
- Brought negotiations back on track and succeeded in negotiating a three-year contract in only four hours.

EXPERIENCE **(continued)**	**BUSINESS PROCESS TEAM MEMBER AND BUYER** (2001 – 2002) **Colorado Fuel and Iron Corporation**, Pueblo, Colorado

- Responsible for re-engineering departments and implementing process efficiencies.
- Rewrote job descriptions, combined jobs, and downsized operations of the tube mill, which saved $1 million a year in salaries, benefits, and production costs.
- Reorganized the Human Resources Department by outsourcing benefits administration to contractors, eliminating a vice president position and downsizing the department by two-thirds.
- Conducted task analyses, combined responsibilities for sales people, eliminated outside sales positions with extravagant perquisites, and instituted accountability measures to save more than $1 million per year.
- Made recommendations to hiring managers for staffing levels to meet production needs.
- Conducted performance evaluations of department managers and counseled them on areas needing improvement.
- Screened résumés, interviewed hundreds of workers, and made hiring recommendations to restaff the mill with non-union workers during an extended strike.
- Lowered the rejection rate of the rail mill by 7% through re-engineering of the dock to reduce damaged finished goods.
- As a buyer, sourced vendors and purchased more than $12 million in raw materials per month.
- Negotiated an across-the-board 10% decrease in prices from all vendors.
- Inventoried products received by rail and ensured that raw materials were received in time for production.

HUMAN RESOURCES/SAFETY COORDINATOR (2000)
Colorado Fuel and Iron Corporation, Pueblo, Colorado

- Implemented a $500,000 fall protection program for the steel mill that saved $4 million in noncompliance fines from OSHA.
- Conducted training classes on safety issues; developed drug and alcohol policies and procedures for the human resources department.

PRODUCTION WORKER (1997 – 2000)
Colorado Fuel and Iron Corporation, Pueblo, Colorado

- Financed a full undergraduate and graduate education as a laborer in this steel mill.
- Worked up the ladder to supervisor on the production floor of the Steel Making Department.

EDUCATION

MASTER OF BUSINESS ADMINISTRATION (1998)
Regis University, Denver, Colorado

- Emphasis in international business.
- Graduated in the top 15% of the graduating class.

BACHELOR OF ARTS DEGREE (1991)
Antioch University, George Meany Center for Labor Studies (AFL–CIO) Yellow Springs, Ohio

- Major in labor studies/labor relations.
- Completed 180 credit hours to graduate first in the class.
- Served as class president for two years.

LABOR CERTIFICATE (1989)
University of Colorado, Boulder

- Completed two six-week programs per year for a total of four years.

AFFILIATIONS

Member, Human Resources Association, Pueblo, Colorado
Member, Human Resources Association, Colorado Springs, Colorado
Member, National Society for Human Resource Management

COMMUNITY
SERVICE

Volunteer to teach and tutor adult students at the community college level in adult basic education, reading, literacy, and international business

133

LORETTA SCHWARTZ

PROFILE
- Focused retail manager with twenty years of experience.
- Background in marketing, sales, staff development, merchandising, and customer service.
- Effective team player with strong interpersonal and communication skills.
- Skilled in creating staff loyalty and empowering employees to excel.

EXPERIENCE

MANAGEMENT/ADMINISTRATION
- Directed the operations of 22 retail stores in three states with combined sales volume of $17.1 million.
- Served as a liaison between store management and home office merchandisers and senior managers.
- Approved sales goals and provided direction for floor sets (merchandising).
- Managed the daily operations of a high-volume retail clothing store; responsible for visual merchandising, floor supervision, and resolution of customer complaints and adjustments.
- Promoted from supervisor to manager of a $750,000 volume store and then to manager of a Casual Corner with more than $1 million in annual sales volume.
- Conceptualized and coordinated innovative fashion shows, breakfast clubs, and other promotions to increase sales volume and create customer loyalty.
- Developed new business through community involvement, seminars, and monthly training of sales staff to enhance customer service through the merchandise sales approach.

SUPERVISION/STAFF DEVELOPMENT
- Developed ten staff members for promotion to store manager or assistant store manager positions.
- Recruited, hired, trained, supervised, and evaluated sales associates, store supervisors, assistant managers, and store managers.
- Responsible for staff scheduling, ensuring adequate floor coverage, and overseeing payroll.

ACHIEVEMENTS
- Assumed responsibility for a failing district, closed unprofitable stores, and turned around declining units until all stores were profitable.
- Honored with membership in the Champions Club (1996–1997) for achieving #26 out of 860 stores in the country; Champions Club (1998–1999) achieving #48 out of 860 stores.
- Won numerous suit, dress, and pantyhose promotions by increasing sales over plan.
- Built sales volume through focused productivity training, visual merchandise presentation, and exceptional customer service.
- Voted President (1991–1996) and Vice President (1990) of the Towne East Square Merchants Association.
- President (1990–1994) and Vice President (1997) of Citadel Merchants Association.
- Selected as City Fashion Coordinator for Colorado Springs (1989–1990).
- Miss America Pageant Official (1989); First Runner Up, Miss Colorado Springs (1990).

WORK HISTORY

DISTRICT SALES MANAGER, Casual Corner, Denver, CO	2001 – present
MANAGER, Casual Corner, Citadel Mall, Colorado Springs, CO	1995 – 2001
MANAGER, Casual Corner, Towne East, Wichita, KS	1993 – 1995
MANAGER, Casual Corner, Towne West, Wichita, KS	1990 – 1993

TRAINING

CASUAL CORNER CORPORATE TRAINING: TRAC I-III (Personal Selling, Beyond Customer Service, Driving the Business), MOHR Management Training

1445 Anywhere Court • Newtown, Colorado 80906 • (719) 555-1234

Sylvia Valley

4605 Anywhere Drive • Newtown, CO 80915 • Home (719) 555-1234 • Cell (719) 123-4567

PROFILE
- Versatile lyric soprano singer with more than twenty years of experience.
- Proven ability to sing in both solo and chorus performances.
- Background in classical, opera, sacred, and popular music.

EXPERIENCE

SOLO
- Solo vocal recitals with a wide variety of music, including Broadway, opera arias, and classical
- Rehearsal soprano soloist with the CS Chorale for Mendelssohn's *Elijah,* Verdi's *Requiem,* and Beethoven's *Missa Solemnis,* 2001 – 2006
- Handel's *Israel in Egypt,* soprano I in duet for two sopranos, Colorado Springs Chorale, Donald Jenkins, Director, 2004
- Brahms' *Requiem,* soprano solo, Colorado Springs Chorale and Colorado Springs Philharmonic, Lawrence Leighton Smith, Director, 2003
- Beethoven's *Choral Fantasy,* second soprano solo, Colorado Springs Chorale and Philharmonic, Lawrence Leighton Smith, Director, 2003
- Robert Ward's *The Crucible,* Sara Goode, Opera Theater of the Rockies, 2002
- Douglas Moore's *Ballad of Baby Doe,* Samantha, Opera Theater of the Rockies, 2000
- Orff's *Carmina Burana*, soprano solos, Colorado Spring Children's Chorale and Youth Symphony, Dr. Anton Armstrong, Director, 2000
- Poulenc's *Gloria*, soprano solos, Soli Deo Gloria choir, Bob Crowder, Director, 1999
- Brahms' *Requiem*, soprano solo, Soli Deo Gloria choir, Edmund Ladouceur, Director, 1998
- Bach's *Magnificat,* "Quia Respexit," soprano solo, Soli Deo Gloria choir, Edmund Ladouceur, Director, 1997
- Vivaldi's *Gloria,* "Domine Deus," soprano solo, Soli Deo Gloria choir, Edmund Ladouceur, Director, 1996
- Sang the part of the youth from Mendolsshon's *Elijah* with the Soli Deo Gloria choir, Anna Hamre, Director, 1987
- Handel's *Messiah,* "He Shall Feed His Flock," Chapel Choir, Spangdahlem AFB, Germany, 1985

OPERA CHORUS
- *Puccini Spectacular,* soprano, Opera Theater of the Rockies, 2006
- *Le Nozze di Figaro,* soprano, Opera Theater of the Rockies, 2004
- *Daughter of the Regiment,* soprano, Opera Theater of the Rockies, 2003
- *Trial by Jury* and *The Crucible*, soprano, Opera Theater of the Rockies, 2002
- *Pagliacci*, soprano, Opera Theater of the Rockies, 2001
- *La Boheme*, soprano, Colorado Opera Festival, 1998
- *Carmen*, soprano, Colorado Opera Festival, 1997
- *Lucia de Lammermoor*, second soprano, Colorado Opera Festival, 1996

CHORAL
- Soprano with the Colorado Springs Chorale, Donald Jenkins, Director, 2001 – present
- Soprano with Soli Deo Gloria Choir, Colorado Springs, 1987 – 2001
- Soprano with the Abbey Singers, Colorado Springs, Judy Wescott, Director 1996 – 2000

VOICE TRAINING
- Pat Staubo, Colorado Springs, Colorado, 1997 – present
- Connie Heidenreich, Colorado Springs, Colorado, 1989 – 1997

135

LARRY D. SISK

3480 Hoofprint Road
Peyton, Colorado 80831

Telephone:
(719) 683-7522

PROFILE
- Seasoned construction superintendent with a comprehensive knowledge of the business and more than 30 years of experience in:
  - Commercial and residential building
  - New construction and renovations
  - Bid preparation and contract negotiations
  - Surveying
  - Job scheduling
  - Blueprint specifications
- Effective leader who is able to motivate employees and subcontractors to complete jobs on time.
- Skilled at evaluating margins to ensure profitability at project completion
- Proven ability to complete projects on time and under budget.

SUMMARY
- Supervised large commercial construction projects from bid through final walk-through.
- Responsible for project takeoffs, estimating, and development of project schedules and milestones.
- Sourced vendors, purchased supplies and equipment, and ensured timely delivery of materials.
- Evaluated blueprints and schematics; ensured compliance with regulations and specifications.
- Consulted with clients regarding design modifications and change orders; ensured customer satisfaction throughout the project life cycle.
- Interviewed, hired, scheduled, and supervised employees and subcontractors.
- Evaluated bids from subcontractors, ensured the quality of their work, and resolved problems.
- Implemented safety and quality control programs and regulations.
- As a business owner, was accountable for long-range planning, profit and loss, controlling costs, invoicing, recordkeeping, collecting accounts receivable, and monitoring financial performance.

SIGNIFICANT PROJECTS
- Biggs Kofford, CPA, Office Addition, $1.2 million (2005)
- Lake Point Medical Center, Design/Build Medical Office Building, $4.5 million (2003 – 2004)
- Falcon School District, Classroom Remodels, Gymnasium Additions, $1.9 million (2001 – 2003)
- Summit County Jail, New Detention Facility, Breckenridge, $7.5 million (2002)
- Santa Fe County Jail, New Detention Facility, Santa Fe, New Mexico, $8 million (1992)
- Evans Army Hospital, New Facility, Fort Carson, $95 million (1991)
- ADAL Computer Center, New Computer Facility, USAF Academy, $2.5 million (1990)
- Nixon Power and Sewage Disposal Plant, City Utility Project, $20 million (1988)
- American Numismatic Building, New Corporate Headquarters Building, $1.5 million (1986)
- Doherty High School, New Facility, $14 million (1985 – 1986)
- First Bank, New Building, $12 million (1982)

EXPERIENCE
Superintendent, Classic General Contractors, Colorado Springs, Colorado (2002 – present)
Estimator, BMC West, Colorado Springs, Colorado (2002)
Owner/Manager, Bulldog Construction, Peyton, Colorado (2001 – 2002)
Journeyman Carpenter, AA Construction, Colorado Springs, Colorado (2000 – 2001)
Journeyman Carpenter, Robert E. McKee Construction Company, Denver, Colorado (1999 – 2000)
Journeyman Carpenter, Desman Corporation (Chapman), Colorado Springs, Colorado (1999 – 2000)
Cement Finisher, Transco Pacific Company, Fort Carson, Colorado (1999)
Superintendent, Hibbitts Construction Company, Colorado Springs, Colorado (1999)
Carpenter Foreman, Sommers Building Company, Colorado Springs, Colorado (1999)
Journeyman Carpenter, Alvarado Construction Company, Denver, Colorado (1998 – 1999)
Ironworker, Bates Construction Company, Colorado Springs, Colorado (1998)
Superintendent, H.W. Houston Construction Company, Pueblo, Colorado (1997 – 1998)
Carpenter Foreman, McNally Construction Company, Colorado Springs, Colorado (1997)

EDUCATION
JOURNEYMAN CARPENTER, Southern Colorado State College, Pueblo, Colorado (1988 – 1991)
Completed a four-year carpenter apprenticeship program under the Carpenters and Joiners of America Local 515, Pueblo, Colorado

MILD STEEL ARC WELDER, Pikes Peak Community College, Colorado Springs, Colorado (1991)

Paragraph Style or Bullets

Good advertisements are designed in such a way that the reader's eye is immediately drawn to important pieces of information using type and graphic elements, including bold, italics, headline fonts, and so forth. Then the design must guide the reader's eye down the page from one piece of information to the next with the judicious use of white space or graphic lines.

In this science of typography, very long lines of text (longer than six or seven inches, depending on the font) and large blocks of text (more than seven typeset lines) are considered to be tiring to the reader's eye. If you look closely at textbooks, magazines, and newspapers, you will notice that the information is usually typeset in columns to reduce line lengths, and journalists intentionally write in short paragraphs because they are more reader-friendly.

How does this science translate into a résumé? As a general rule, you should keep your lines of text no longer than seven inches—five to six inches is even better—and your paragraphs shorter than seven lines of text each. Many people find it difficult to cram the description of a job and its accomplishments into a single paragraph while following this rule. Therefore, you will often see bulleted sentences used instead of paragraphs on résumés.

If you prefer the paragraph style, there are some tricks of the trade that can help make your résumé more readable.

1. List the job summary in paragraph form and then use bullets to highlight your achievements.

Provost and Dean of Faculties, Hofstra University . . . . 1990 – present
Interim Provost and Dean of Faculties, Hofstra University . . . . 1989 – 1990
In a position second only to the President of the University, the Provost is responsible for the entire academic area of the University, including all of the Colleges and Schools, Libraries, Honors Program, Center for Teaching Excellence, Computer Center, Scott Skodnek Business Development Center, and the Joan and Arnold Saltzman Community Services Center. Accountable for developing and managing an annual budget of $80+ million.

- *Successfully negotiated two five-year contracts with the University faculty* (1991–1996, 1996–2001) as the chief negotiator. Completed negotiations three months before the expiration of the existing contracts. The first five-year contract resulted in a nine-hour teaching load for faculty at a manageable economic cost to the University. The present contract has a unique incentive plan to promote early retirement, and the contract also provides compensation increases that are tied, in part, to the well-being of the University.

- *Currently leading the efforts to establish the Honors College,* which is a key aspect of our strategy for the future and an important factor in tailoring the profile of the entire class. The Honors College builds on the existing Honors Program and will be open to all qualified undergraduate students regardless of their major.

EDUCATION

CERTIFICATES
Imago Relationship Therapy, Institute for Imago Relationship Therapy (1991)
Clinical Fellowship in Hypnotherapy, Morton Prince Center for Hypnosis (1979)

Ph.D., BEHAVIORAL SCIENCE, Specialization in Psychotherapy (1983)
Florida Institute of Technology, School of Professional Psychology
- Dissertation: "Attitudes Toward Mental Illness by Student Nurses from Various Ethnic Groups"
- Honors: Graduate Assistantship (2 years)

MASTER OF SCIENCE, Psychiatric-Mental Health Nursing (1975)
Adelphi University, School of Nursing
- Thesis: "A Conceptual Model of Female Homosexuality from the Perspective of Analytical Psychology"
- Honors: NIMH Traineeship for Graduate Study, Sigma Theta Tau

BACHELOR OF SCIENCE IN NURSING, Major in Psychiatric Nursing (1973)
State University of New York at Stony Brook
- Honors: Graduated cum laude

ASSOCIATE OF APPLIED SCIENCE IN NURSING (1971)
Kingsborough Community College, City University of New York
- Honors: Salutatorian (third in a class of 1,000), Phi Theta Kappa, Dean's List, President's Award, Department of Nursing Award

---

ADMINISTRATIVE EXPERIENCE

DIRECTOR, NURSING ADMINISTRATION PROGRAM (1999 – present)
Seton Hall University, South Orange, New Jersey
- Developed a dual degree program with the Stillman School of Business offering an MSN/MBA as a collaborative degree program.
- Created a Master of Nursing Education program offered completely online through SetonWorld-Wide, the virtual university branch of Seton Hall.
- Completed a comprehensive revision of the Master of Science in Nursing Case Management program.
- Developed a grant proposal to obtain federal funding for the Nursing Administration graduate program.

DIRECTOR, HEALTH SERVICES ADMINISTRATION (1997 – 1999)
Nebraska Health Services, Omaha, Nebraska
- Directed the graduate program in Health Services Administration; responsible for operations management, budgeting, curriculum design, faculty supervision, and student recruitment initiatives.
- Developed and implemented a complete redesign of the curriculum based on market analysis.
- Involved in developing innovative new Internet-based distance learning programs.
- Created a program that allowed students to obtain dual graduate degrees.
- Developed incentives and interfaces between the undergraduate and graduate programs of the college to prevent loss of graduate students to competitive schools.
- Member of the Heartland Healthcare Executive Group; revitalized this regional chapter of the American College of Healthcare Executives, developed relationships with healthcare leaders in the community, and served as faculty advisor.

DIRECTOR, BEHAVIORAL HEALTH SERVICES (1993 – 1996)
Broward General Medical Center, Ft. Lauderdale, Florida
- Responsible for the administrative and clinical management of the behavioral health department of the fourth largest integrated health care delivery system in the nation.
- Directed the 98-bed inpatient service, crisis stabilization unit, psychiatric emergency services, specialty treatment unit, and mental health initiatives within primary health centers.
- Developed a consultation and liaison service to trauma and other hospital departments.
- Managed an expense budget of more than $7 million and a staff of 135 FTEs.
- Developed a re-engineering plan that modernized the care delivery model and restaffed the department, saving $400,000 a year in salary and benefit expenses.
- Absorbed all of the county mental health services valued at $4 million.
- Rewrote the department's policy and procedure manual; implemented a new quality assurance program.

2. Divide your experience into related information and use several shorter paragraphs under each job description.

EXPERIENCE

EXECUTIVE DIRECTOR OF ASSESSMENT (May 2002 – present)
Colorado Springs School District 11, Colorado Springs, Colorado
Direct all operations related to research, planning, assessment, evaluation, technology integration, and technology support for every school in the district (elementary, middle/senior high, and charter schools). Participate in the development of long-range strategic plans for the district and the department. Develop assessment methodology, reporting systems, and related utilization of technology.

Serve as a liaison between the Research Center of the University of Colorado at Colorado Springs and District 11's Board of Education. Develop and lead the Coordination Committee responsible for bringing IT and Instruction together on a district level. Oversee the Evaluation Unit that monitors district programs, task forces, and initiatives. Meet weekly with instructional services to align technology integration and assessment with the needs of literacy resource teachers and instructional specialists.

Accomplishments

Significantly revitalized the Assessment Unit by improving communication and implementing changes based on feedback from performance measurements. Personally conducted teacher telephone surveys throughout the year to evaluate service delivery. Piloted the concept of Building Assessment Teams to promote better utilization of assessment data. Improved service delivery by aligning the work of technical support, network administration, and the call center.

Fiscal Responsibility

Set budget priorities for two units; accountable for a total of $2.5 million in district funds. Actively campaigned for the 2002 bond issue.

3. Use left headings instead of centered headings to make the line lengths shorter (like in the sample above). This won't work, however, when the shorter line length forces your information into very long paragraphs. It is better to have longer line lengths and shorter paragraphs.

Bullets are a good way of presenting information on a résumé. Bullets are special characters (• ✦ ▪) used at the beginning of indented short sentences to call attention to individual items on a résumé. Short, bulleted sentences are easier to read than long paragraphs of text, and they highlight the information you want the reader to see quickly. Bullets also add some variety to a résumé and make it just a touch more creative.

In both MS Word and WordPerfect for Windows or Macintosh, clicking on "Insert" gives you access to a myriad of special characters that are not found on your keyboard.

On the following pages are sample résumés designed using paragraph formats, bulleted styles, and combinations thereof.

Sean M. Michaels

4533 Anywhere Drive • Newtown, Colorado 80918 • (719) 555-1234 • E-mail: seda@protypeltd.com

PROFILE
- Dependable system administrator with more than four years of experience.
- Proven troubleshooter who gets to the root of the problem quickly.
- Known for being able to see the big picture without getting lost in the details.
- Effective team leader with strong communication and interpersonal skills.
- Hold a current secret security clearance.

TECHNOLOGY

Networks: Microsoft Certified Systems Engineer (MCSE), Windows 2003, #2306869

Operating Systems: Windows 95/98/2000/NT/2003

Applications: MS Word, Excel, PowerPoint, Access, Outlook, Internet Explorer, MS Project, Front-Page, Terminal Services, Document Management Extensions (DME), Ghost Utility, Procurement Desktop (PD^2), Defense Messaging System (DMS), VisioTech, VisioPro, Automated Business Service System, and various government financial applications (IAPS, PBAS, InfoConnect, JOCAS II)

EXPERIENCE

SYSTEM ADMINISTRATOR, L-3 Communications, Schriever AFB, Colorado (1998 – present)
Provide system administration support for a large research and development network with 1,200 computers and 900 users. Install, maintain, and troubleshoot NT 4.0 and Windows 2000 workstations, laptops, and peripherals (printers, scanners, CD-RW drives, JAZ and ZIP backups, etc.). Lead a team of 20 technicians on various engineering change projects. Provide technical expertise to all personnel within the organization.

Hardware Experience:
- Troubleshoot hardware failures and resolve hardware conflicts (IDE and SCSI).
- Install peripherals and upgrade hardware on desktop workstations.
- Design and install workgroup networks: run cabling, configure ports and network protocols, add accounts to the domain, and verify connectivity.

Software Experience:
- Install Windows-based operating systems and applications on a 2,000-node Ethernet network.
- Configure workstations for WAN/LAN network connectivity.
- Install, configure, maintain, and optimize software applications and resolve conflicts.
- Engineered the Windows 2000 upgrade and interoperability with the NT 4.0 environment.
- Provide user support for MS Office and industry-specific applications.

CABLE INSTALLATION TECHNICIAN, Superior Design, Schriever AFB, Colorado (1998)
Assigned to Schriever by a temporary staffing firm. Surveyed, planned, and led installation teams on various cable engineering projects. Installed and terminated category 5 and fiber optic cable for up to 400 workstations per job. Interpreted cable trace schematics, subflooring and ceiling blueprints, power diagrams, and cable tray layouts. Accountable for equipment, installation tools, and cable materials.

SENIOR MEDICAL SERGEANT (E-6), U.S. Army, Fort Carson, Colorado (1988 – 1998)
Managed all medical care, training, and readiness for an operational detachment. Ordered and inventoried medical equipment and supplies valued at more than $40,000. Ensured that all team members were medically ready for deployment to foreign countries, including immunizations and medical records. Established mobile satellite communications as an air defense artillery missile crewman for three years before cross-training into the medical field.

EDUCATION

BACHELOR OF SCIENCE IN INFORMATION TECHNOLOGY
Colorado Technical University, Colorado Springs, Colorado (2001 – present)
University of Colorado, Colorado Springs, Colorado (2000)
Pikes Peak Community College, Colorado Springs, Colorado (1998 – 2000)
- Currently one year from completion of the degree
- Relevant course work completed: C++ Programming, Database Applications, Introduction to Networking, Client/Server Systems, Network Administration, Client/Server Operating System NT

MICHAEL T. SIMS, CPA

PROFILE

- Results-oriented financial management professional with solid experience in the telecommunications industry.
- Certified Public Accountant with more than 12 years of Fortune 100 corporate strategic planning, financial analysis, reporting, accounting, and auditing experience.
- Graduate of the prestigious Thunderbird Executive Program (International MBA).
- Extensive international business experienced throughout Asia, Europe, Mexico, and Canada.

STRENGTHS

- Strategic planning, management consulting, business support, process improvement, superior customer service, financial analysis, reporting, auditing, accounting, and budgets.
- Highly organized change agent with the ability to implement innovative ideas to achieve positive solutions.
- Decision maker with the commitment to create a climate for success and the ability to bring order to chaos.
- Team leader who is able to motivate others toward achievement of an organization's vision and goals.
- Effective trainer and coach, able to present concepts clearly to all audiences—from entry-level staff to CEOs.

Financial

- Financial planning and forecasting experience in all aspects of corporate finance, including cost centers, employee benefits, new business proposals, and revenue accounting.
- Skilled in the re-engineering of business accounting processes to streamline reporting procedures.
- Experienced in spreadsheet modeling of corporate financial statements, including income statements, cash flow statements, and balance sheets.
- Background in cross-functional operations of management, marketing, research and development, information technology, manufacturing, and human resources.

Technology

- Macro understanding of three converging industries: telecommunications, computers, and cable television.
- Proficient in the use of numerous computer applications and operating systems, including Windows, DOS, Lotus, Excel, MS Word, WordPerfect, PowerPoint, Office 95, communications (Netscape, Internet, Dow Jones News Retrieval, America Online, CompuServe, Easytriev, RAMIS), Lotus Notes, etc.

PROFESSIONAL EXPERIENCE

AG COMMUNICATION SYSTEMS *(A joint venture of AT&T and GTE)*, Phoenix, Arizona (1984 – present)
Financial Benefits Specialist (January 2006 – present)
Manager of employee benefits accounting and finance for this $310 million company involved in the development, manufacture, and marketing of software for the telecommunications industry. Full responsibility for the management of $400 million in corporate benefit plan assets. Prepare annual budgets, quarterly forecasts, and long-range plans for all benefits and executive compensation programs, including health, 401k, savings, and pension plans. Ensure accurate financial accounting of the defined benefit and contribution plans, as well as compliance with all federal tax and regulatory plan filings.

- Lead finance support for employee benefit design activities, including transition to flexible benefits, selection of healthcare providers, implementation of a cash balance pension plan, and 401K changes.
- Enhanced major forecasting processes for $45 million of annual employee benefits and compensation.
- Improved communications and trust between benefits department and primary customer, controller, treasurer, financial planning and analysis, external auditors, pension trustee, and medical consultants.

Manager of Business Analysis and Planning, Senior Financial Analyst (July 2001 – January 2006)
Supervised the financial management of the Network Services Division with $43 million in sales, $3 million in services inventory, and a staff of 500. Responsible for the forecasting, reporting, and analysis of sales, direct costs, period costs, and services inventory. Involved in the preparation of the annual budget and salary plan, rolling annual forecast, five-year business plan, and reconciliations of actual to target.

- Relocated business planning and analysis function from Illinois to Arizona and reduced staff by one-third to realize $80,000 in annual cost savings.
- Introduced and implemented streamlined reporting procedures, significantly improving presentation of financial information to senior management.

ADDRESS

6734 West Anywhere Avenue, Newtown, Arizona 85308-5505   (602) 555-1234

PROFESSIONAL EXPERIENCE

AG COMMUNICATION SYSTEMS (continued)
Continuation: Manager of Business Analysis and Planning, Senior Financial Analyst
- Converted $16 million of revenue recognition and $6 million of inventory accounting from manual to computerized processing.
- Simplified accounting and planning processes, improving reporting and saving $400,000 annually.
- Created a monthly sales through margin report which uncovered $2.7 million in cost overstatements.
- Set up and maintained monthly financial reporting and forecasting controls for $20 million in software sales.
- Prepared balance sheet and cash flow statement for the 2004 – 2006 business plan.

Special Projects: Responsible for diverse special projects, including the financial planning, analysis, and reporting treatment for software accounting and hardware warranty reserves, restatement of the 1994 budget, finance benchmarking, and the creation of finance key indicators. Lead support person in financial planning, analysis, and reporting for the research and development/product development organization. Served as financial representative on a special two-month project in the research and development of a business plan for the startup of a new wireless business.
- Researched and prepared business case analysis and financial statements, including pro-formas, net present values, and internal rate of returns calculations to determine revenue requirements for business startup.
- Introduced accounting policy changes regarding revenue recognition, software accounting methodologies, and hardware warranty reserves.
- Reduced financial support costs by $100,000 for 2004 through improvements to the financial planning, analysis, and reporting of the company's $49 million R&D cost center.
- Recommended that all R&D labor be consolidated from 30 different departments into one department to simplify planning, reporting, and analysis.
- Successfully reduced closing cycle by 25% as acting manager of general accounting and financial planning.
- Administered and facilitated the change from a micro- to a macro-based total company budget for 1995.
- Participated in the creation of the company's three strategic quality initiatives as finance representative on a cross-functional Quality Focus Team.
- Upgraded financial management to Microsoft Excel and Windows environments.

Marketing Financial Analyst, Supervisor of Accounting Operations/Services, Senior Financial Analyst, Financial Analyst, Staff Auditor/Senior Auditor (1994 – 2001)
Consolidated the sales and margin financial plans and monthly actual reporting. Directly forecasted $160 million of sales and presented monthly actual results, forecast, and variance data to VP of Marketing. Maintained and controlled the general ledger system and established the new general ledger for the joint venture between GTE and AT&T. Prepared quarterly SEC reporting to GTE. Served as member of the Finance Quality Committee.
- Implemented the first local area network in finance which improved departmental efficiency and accuracy.
- Reduced the number of records in the new joint venture general ledger by 75%.

ESMARK, INC., Chicago, Illinois (1993 – 1994)
Staff Auditor: Performed compliance audits to support Arthur Young's data on year-end financial statements.

EDUCATION

MASTER OF INTERNATIONAL MANAGEMENT—EXECUTIVE PROGRAM (2005)
American Graduate School of International Management, Thunderbird, Glendale, Arizona

BACHELOR OF SCIENCE IN ACCOUNTING (1993)
Northern Illinois University, Dekalb, Illinois

CONTINUING EDUCATION: Committed to life-long learning and self-development. Attended lectures by Tom Peters and former British Prime Minister Margaret Thatcher. Attended Dr. Deming's Quality Seminar, Dale Carnegie's Effective Public Speaking and Human Relations workshops, and seminars on employee benefits sponsored by the American Institute for International Research and the American Institute of Certified Public Accountants. Participated in GTE 3-5 day training programs on risk analysis, forecasting and strategy, financial analysis, and managing for results.

Executive Résumés

Webster defines an executive as "a person whose function is to administer or manage affairs of a corporation, division, department, group of companies, etc." This can be the president, director, chief executive officer, chief financial officer, chief information officer, any C-level executive, controller, executive director, vice president, general manager, treasurer, principal, owner, and the list goes on.

Generally, a person in such a position has strategically worked his or her way to the top echelons of management over a period of at least ten years. Executives tend to have many relevant past positions, credentials, achievements, published articles, speaking engagements, community service activities, or other important qualifications.

In order to reflect this experience, an executive résumé is almost always more than one page. In fact, an executive résumé can be as long as it needs to be in order to convince the reader that the candidate has what it takes to manage an organization effectively. The first page is the most important and convinces the reader to continue onto page two. If your résumé extends to a third page, it should contain only backup information that isn't critical if it doesn't get read.

Just because an executive résumé is long doesn't mean it should be wordy. The same good writing described in Step 8 (Chapter 9) is even more important in an executive résumé. Because the number of applicants for an executive position is generally not as large as for lower-level positions, every word of an executive's résumé will be read many times before a decision is made. Make sure every word you write serves a purpose!

There are some alternate styles that can help an executive manage a résumé that is getting too long. You can create a one-page summary that highlights your entire career and can stand alone. It is generally in a functional style with a simple listing of work experience.

Follow that one-page summary with a couple of pages that describe each job in detail, focusing on accomplishments using the CAR format (Challenge, Action, Result). Or, create a separate document listing critical leadership initiatives (success stories) or technology case studies. A brief narrative biography can be used instead of a résumé for networking purposes where a three-page résumé would be overkill.

On the next five pages are two examples of executive résumés. The first is a three-page résumé with standard formatting, and the second is an executive résumé with a more succinct, result-oriented style in a functional/chronological combination format.

DAVID A. SMITH, JD, LL.M., CPA

5797 South Anywhere Street • Newtown, Colorado 80111
Home: (720) 555-1234 • Cellular: (720) 123-4567 • E-mail: dsmith@protypeltd.com

---
EXECUTIVE SUMMARY

Chief Financial Officer and Strategic Business Executive with 15+ years of proven achievement driving solid revenue and bottom-line gains through expert financial, legal, and operational contributions to merger and acquisition transactions, new business development, turnaround operations, and high-growth ventures. Quantifiable results in the areas of

Negotiations • Board/Investor Relations • Effective Communications
Cost Containment • Integration Planning • Results Analysis • System Conversions/Upgrades
Public/Private Infusions • Equity/Debt Financings • Financial Reporting

Aggressive, results-focused, strategic leader offering a unique blend of operations, financial, and legal expertise producing significant financial gains and meeting operational objectives. Led dynamic growth and expansion efforts for investments of Goldman Sachs and other investment firms. Championed bankruptcy workouts and business turnarounds. Full P&L responsibility for multiple divisions in multi-million-dollar organizations. Intrinsic leadership skills fostering top performance and efficiency through team-focused strategies.

PROFESSIONAL EXPERIENCE AND ACHIEVEMENTS

VICE PRESIDENT, LEGAL AND BUSINESS SERVICES (2000 – present)
Coram Healthcare Corporation, Denver, Colorado

Spearheaded aggressive financial, legal, and operational turnaround for the nation's second largest supplier of infusion therapies. Streamlined and maximized budgetary accountability for $75 million in legal affairs, merger and acquisition activities, business development, SEC reporting, human resources, compliance, risk management, and administrative departments.

- Achieved and surpassed investor EBITDA and capital/debt restructuring goals.
- Initiated, negotiated, and closed $230+ million of capital restructurings at critical stages of the bankruptcy workout.
- Delivered a 23% EBITDA increase through combined M&A revenue enhancements and cost reductions.
- Enhanced cash flow 13% and contribution margins 9% by restructuring multiple departments for improved efficiencies.
- Infused business with $41.5 million cash by leading divestiture of non-accretive divisions.
- Negotiated a successful $18+ million resolution of $28+ million in tax liens.
- Produced 7% shift in core business and revenue quality through trend analysis and deployment of a benchmarking financial model to branch operations.

SVP BUSINESS AND LEGAL AFFAIRS / CHIEF FINANCIAL OFFICER (1998 – 2000)
ExchangeBridge.com, Atlanta, Georgia

Achieved financial, legal, and operational goals for this telecommunications e-business startup. Raised venture capital and implemented core business strategies focusing on cash flow, M&A activities, return on investments, business line mix, and same-store EBITDA levels. Led business development initiatives for an aggressive marketing strategy that created new distribution channels for product lines.

- Strengthened cash position by leading $75+ million in business development efforts and divestiture of multiple Web sites and by transferring intellectual property for publishing and pharmacy-based businesses.
- Accelerated return on investment from 3.6% to more than 28%, dramatically exceeding investor goals and building momentum for the eventual sale of the company to a strategic partner with full payout to investors.
- Brought the company from the brink of bankruptcy by structuring the workout of payroll tax liens, realigning staff functions, and negotiating favorable arrangements with vendors.

143

- Raised financings for senior and subordinated mezzanine debt restructurings required for merger of an insurance-based business utilizing discounted cash flow variable analysis.
- Championed five-fold increase in EBITDA, 20% improvement in receivable collections, and 33% enhancement of inventory turns, achieving business turnaround despite rapidly decreasing cash flows (high growth, low margins) and culminating in a profitable exit event for investors.
- Ensured SEC compliance and registration of an IPO offering. Minimized operational challenges associated with post-closing integrations by consolidating all due diligence efforts.

SENIOR VICE PRESIDENT, FINANCIAL AND LEGAL AFFAIRS / GENERAL COUNSEL (1992 – 1998)
Meridian Corporation, Memphis, Tennessee

Led team efforts for expansion and integration planning, including consolidation of financial, operational, and administrative functions for the nation's largest home healthcare company with 12,000+ employees and $500+ million in revenues. Negotiated and closed 75+ M&A transactions for management services divisions, producing debt/equity infusions. Consolidated $50+ million budgetary responsibility for financial services, marketing, legal, back office, and administrative departments.

- Spearheaded strategic three-year expansion for 350+ locations in 34 states and three countries by developing effective M&A growth strategies, leading due diligence, and reducing integration timelines to less than 150 days.
- Orchestrated $500+ million industry consolidation/merger through negotiations with industry leaders and alignment of investor and shareholder objectives.
- Reduced costs 15% by introducing stringent resource management and budgeting policies, reorganizing the sales force, and eliminating unproductive administrative support functions.
- Negotiated and closed $250 million syndicated debt restructuring and $85 million equity capitalizations.
- Decreased Medicare denials 13+% as chair of the Compliance and Risk Management Committees with rollout of improved financial reporting guidelines to all branch operations.
- Led successful integration of financial and telecommunications arrangements across more than 200 locations.

SENIOR ASSOCIATE / FIRST-LEVEL PARTNER (1990 – 1992)
McDonnell Boyd, LLC, Memphis, Tennessee

Directed and implemented complex capital/debt financings and restructurings, consolidations, divestitures, public and private stock placements, and M&A transactions. Provided counsel and led legal compliance initiatives, litigation strategies, executive compensation, and intellectual property and employment law issues. Furthered SEC reporting experience.

- Piloted $250+ million merger of hospital chains involving complex bond restructuring requirements.
- Charted a successful $50+ million expansion of Canadian and Latin American transportation business lines.
- Structured and navigated workout of a commercial carrier logistics-based company.

SENIOR ASSOCIATE (1988 – 1990)
Allen & Scruggs, LLC, Memphis, Tennessee

Directed commercial litigation, securitizations, SEC filings, and healthcare issues. Negotiated and consummated commercial, tax, and M&A arrangements, offerings, compliance, and intellectual property issues. Represented clients before federal and state courts and regulatory agencies.

- Maneuvered negotiations and closing for a $25+ million nationwide franchising program.
- Managed troubled debt restructurings and bankruptcy court filings for multiple clients.
- Drafted $100+ million multinational purchase/sales export agreements for expansion of business lines into Japan, Mexico, and Latin America.

EDUCATION

LL.M. IN TAXATION (1988)
Washington University School of Law, St. Louis, Missouri

JURIS DOCTOR (1985)
University of Memphis School of Law, Memphis, Tennessee

BACHELOR OF ARTS, PSYCHOLOGY AND ACCOUNTING (1982)
Christian Brothers University, Memphis, Tennessee

AFFILIATIONS AND PUBLICATIONS

Certified Public Accountant	1989, 250+ hours Continuing Education Units (CEU)
Tennessee Bar Association	1985 – 2001, Young Lawyers Division, Chairman of Child Waiting Room Project, Chairman of Oversight Committee, ADR Section
Author	"Keeping the Secret in Trade Secrets," (April 1997), *ACCA Magazine*
Speaker	Financial Statements for Nonfinancial Attorneys, Trade Secret Protection, M&A Planning, Integration Activities and Timelines: Application Service Provider Issues and Practical Solutions
Community Relations	Homeowners Association, First Vice President (2001 – 2002) Chaired homeowners committee of county government board (1998 – 1999) United Way Representative (1995 – 1997) Child Witness Waiting Room, County Government Liaison (1995 – 1996) Big Brothers Representative (1992 – 1995)

DARIN R. SMITH

PHILOSOPHY

"It's all about the food. A good manager will get out of the chef's way and let the food shine." Darin Smith

AREAS OF EXPERTISE

Food and beverage management
Hiring, supervision, and training
Purchasing and inventory management
Budgeting and effective cost control

EXECUTIVE QUALIFICATIONS

- Experienced General Manager with a passion for combining quality food and diverse menus with exceptional customer service.
- Confident leader who has served in every facet of the business, from the front to the back of the house.
- Self-motivated and focused with a powerful drive to succeed—at ease when working collectively with executive management.
- Highly focused, results-oriented professional with expertise in managing complex, chef-driven operations.
- Effective problem solver who is able to resolve issues before they become major roadblocks.

SUMMARY OF EXPERIENCE

KEY ACCOMPLISHMENTS

- History of successfully managing multi-unit, upscale, and volume restaurants and buffet operations generating millions of dollars in annual revenue.
- Turned around unprofitable operations by developing and implementing new processes, upgrading food service, and improving customer service.
- Built operations from scratch, including staffing, training, and operating policies and procedures.

OPERATIONS MANAGEMENT

- Accountable for strategic planning, profit and loss, cost control, budgeting, cash handling, and general record keeping.
- Maintained expenses at or below budget through accurate planning, purchasing, waste reduction, and cost-effective operating procedures.
- Recruited, hired, supervised, and motivated assistant managers, chefs, and 200+ staff members.
- Mentored and trained managers and chefs. Instituted high standards for the service staff.
- Developed innovative training programs that emphasized safety, organization, and the importance of exceptional customer service.
- Initiated systems of accountability, and perpetuated a firm, fair, and consistent management style that improved productivity and lowered turnover.

PURCHASING

- Estimated food and beverage costs, sourced suppliers, and purchased inventory, kitchen equipment, china, glass, and silver.
- Set product standards and ingredient specifications; structured purchasing and receiving processes and procedures.
- Solicited competitive bids and negotiated cost-effective contracts with major wholesale suppliers and boutique vendors.

WINE, SPIRITS, AND NONALCOHOLIC BEVERAGES

- Set standards, controls, and procedures for efficient beverage operations that consistently reduced liquor costs and excess inventory.
- Implemented a liquor pouring system that improved pouring accuracy and controlled costs.
- Served beverages in glassware that was appealing to customers while at the same time allowing cost-effective portion control.

CULINARY EXPERIENCE

- Managed the kitchens of fine-dining restaurants, including menu and recipe development, food preparation, and presentation.
- Planned and coordinated banquets, private/corporate parties, and off-site catering.
- Focused on highest quality ingredients and preparation, impeccable food appearance, and exquisite service.

146

EDUCATION   **CULINARY INSTITUTE OF AMERICA (CIA),** Hyde Park, New York
Associate of Science (1983)

PROFESSIONAL   **GENERAL MANAGER / OPERATING PARTNER, Outback Steakhouse,** Denver, CO (2001 – 2007)
EXPERIENCE   Took over a declining operation and turned it around, implementing standards that were higher than corporate expectations. Improved service and food quality, replaced service staff, and created new training programs. Expedited the food, checking every plate to ensure consistent products from the first customer to the last. Marketed this casual/family-style steakhouse by participating in community charity events, including golf tournaments, bike races, school career days, and athletic award banquets. Selected as Proprietor of the Year in 2005. Sold interest in the business at the end of the contract period when the company went private.

EXECUTIVE CHEF, The Peaks at Telluride, Telluride, Colorado (2000 – 2001)
Opened the culinary operations for this 181-room luxury alpine resort serving Rocky Mountain cuisine—staffed and furnished a kitchen serving two restaurants, purchased equipment, developed the menus and kitchen flow, set timing standards for cooks and servers, and created relationships with new vendors.

EXECUTIVE CHEF, The Lodge at Koele, Lanai City, Hawaii (1997 – 2000)
Recruited away from The Ritz Carlton and back to Rockresorts to manage the kitchen of a 102-room, world-class resort (#3 on the Zagat Survey of Top 50 Resorts). Rapidly promoted from Chef de Cuisine to Executive Chef after the departure of John Farnsworth. Oversaw the production of three sous chefs, an executive steward, and 40 employees. Prepared three meals a day in the formal dining room, in addition to private dining and banquets. Created a Guest Chef Program to promote the hotel with nationally known chefs such as Dean Fearing and George Marrone. Developed a Student Exchange Program to expand culinary education and a Community Farm Project that contracted with local growers for garden-fresh, organic produce.

"At the time of our visit and until recently, the kitchen was run by John Farnsworth, one of the most gifted chefs of his generation. His talent for using an amazing range of fresh ingredients, all local or homegrown, lives on in chef Darin Smith, who is creating the same deeply flavored, beautifully presented dishes." Suzanne Hamlin, Hawaii: Catch the Next Food Wave, **Food & Wine,** March 1999

"Since guests in both places have nowhere else to eat, the food at The Lodge and Manele Bay had better be good. And it is. Chef Darin Smith is intense. 'In The Lodge's fine dining room, I call my style Up Country Cooking. Continental on the terrace.' Smith makes the most of culled Lanai venison, smokes his own salmon, pheasant, turkey, and marlin that's startling. He raises his own pigs, keeps chickens for eggs, and grows papayas. Vegetables and herbs come from the hotel's private gardens, goat cheese from a nearby island." Kit Snedaker, **New York Post,** July 28, 1999

"All this serves as food for thought for Chef de Cuisine Darin Smith, whose extraordinary menus have been inspired by frequent visits to the fields. . . . Chef Smith manages to perk up even the mundane." Cheryl Chee Tsutsami, The Great Escape, **Aloha,** March/April 1999

RESTAURANT CHEF, The Ritz Carlton Mauna Lani, Kawaihae, Hawaii (1996 – 1997)
Member of the opening team responsible for hiring, training, setting up, and organizing the culinary department and complete kitchen operations for the American Grill Restaurant (Zagat #16).

EXECUTIVE SOUS CHEF, Carambola Beach Resort and Golf Club, St. Croix, USVI (1994 – 1996)
SOUS CHEF, The Greenbrier Resort, White Sulpher Springs, West Virginia (1992 – 1994)
SOUS CHEF, Keystone Ski Resort and Lodge, Keystone, Colorado (1990 – 1992)
Managed the kitchen operations of these Rockresorts, Inc., properties during alternating winter and summer seasons. The Greenbrier was a Mobil Five-Star Resort (Zagat #18) with banquets and dining rooms that accommodated 1,500 guests. Worked under Hartmut Handke, a Certified Master Chef.

Curriculum Vitae

Remember when I said there is an exception to every rule in the résumé business? Well, here's another one. In most cases, résumés should be concise and limited to one or two pages at the most. You will carefully select your information to provide a synopsis. In some professions, however, a much longer résumé is expected and the longer the résumé, the better your chances of getting an interview.

Those industries generally include medicine, law, education, science, and media (television, film, etc.). If you are applying for a job in a foreign country, long résumés with more detail and a considerable amount of personal information are the norm.

Such a professional résumé is called a *curriculum vitae* (CV) from the Latin meaning "course of one's life" (literally like running a race—and you just *thought* your life was a rat race!).

A successful CV will include not only education and experience but also:

- publications (books, magazines, journals, and other media)

- certifications and licenses

- grants and research

- professional affiliations

- awards and honors

- presentations, and/or courses taught

Anything relevant to your industry is appropriate to use on a CV, and the résumé can be as long as it needs to be to present the "course of your life."

A CV—or any résumé with multiple pages for that matter—must contain a header with your name and page number on each successive page. Should the pages become separated, the reader should be able to easily put your subsequent pages in their proper order and with *your* résumé!

Let's take a look at a sample CV.

CAROL S. KLEINMAN , Ph.D., R.N.

PROFILE	• Experienced university professor and academic administrator. • Able to bring real-world nursing and healthcare administration experience to the classroom. • Effective team player with strong communication and interpersonal skills. • Known for dynamic presentation style and the ability to reach any student.
TEACHING EXPERIENCE	**ASSOCIATE PROFESSOR** (1999 – present) **College of Nursing, Seton Hall University**, South Orange, New Jersey • Developed and delivered the first completely online College of Nursing course in multimedia format—"Theoretical Basis of Advanced Practice Nursing." • Teach graduate courses in nursing and health services administration. **ADJUNCT CLINICAL PROFESSOR** (1999 – present) **Department of Nursing, Essex County College**, Newark, New Jersey • Guide undergraduate students through clinical rotations in psychiatry. **PROFESSOR OF GRADUATE NURSING** (1997 – 1999) **Clarkson College**, Omaha, Nebraska • Taught selected courses in health services administration, all courses in the nursing administration major, and core courses in graduate nursing curricula. • Consistently received among the highest student reviews of all the faculty in the college. **ADJUNCT PROFESSOR** (1993 – 1997) **School of Nursing, Barry University**, Miami, Florida • Taught core courses in the graduate nursing curriculum. **ASSISTANT PROFESSOR AND COURSE COORDINATOR** (1978 – 1986) **School of Nursing, City College of New York** • Coordinated teaching team in upper junior level integrated nursing course. • Taught all psychiatric content throughout the undergraduate nursing curriculum, including clinical teaching in psychiatric inpatient settings. • Member of the Course and Standing Committee; Chair of the Evaluation Committee; Member of the Community Mental Health Liaison Committee.
COURSES TAUGHT	**GRADUATE NURSING COURSES:** • Nursing Theories and Concept Development • Theories and Concepts of Advanced Nursing Practice • Nursing Research • Social Context of Healthcare • Theories and Concepts of Nursing Administration • Psychosocial Assessment and Intervention in Primary Care • Thesis Development **GRADUATE HEALTH SERVICES ADMINISTRATION COURSES:** • Operations Management • Organizational Theory and Behavior • Human Resources Management • Reimbursement and Managed Care • Forces in Healthcare • Thesis Development
GRANTS AND RESEARCH	• Health and Human Services, Division of Nursing, Online MSN/MBA, December 2001. • Health and Human Services, Division of Nursing, Online MSN, Health Systems Administration, December 2001. • Developed research proposal for "Leadership styles and staff nurse retention" approved for implementation at Clara Maass Medical Center.
ADDRESS	18 Anywhere Court, Anytown, NJ 07747, Phone: (732) 555-1234, E-mail: drcsk@protypeltd.com

EXPERIENCE **(continued)**	**EXECUTIVE DIRECTOR** (1992 – 1993) **American Day Treatment Centers of Miami**, Florida • Directed all administrative and clinical operations of a freestanding, for-profit center that provided adult, adolescent, and geriatric partial hospitalization programs. • Developed this new program from the ground up, including definition and marketing of products, programs, and services. • Responsible for managing the construction project, purchasing capital equipment, and staffing. • Administered a \$2 million budget, achieving profitability within twelve months. **DIRECTOR, OUTPATIENT SERVICES** (1986 – 1992) **Green Oaks Psychiatric Hospital**, Dallas, Texas • Created and directed the outpatient department of a 106-bed psychiatric hospital, including adult, adolescent, and chemical dependency partial hospitalization programs. • Developed and implemented programs and services, making them profitable in less than a year. • Grew the program to 25 staff members in a dedicated 10,000 sq. ft. office space with a \$2 million budget and 50 patients per day. • Responsible for strategic planning, marketing, referral development, and regulatory compliance. • Elected to the national Board of Directors of the Association for Ambulatory Behavioral Healthcare.

SELECTED **PRESENTATIONS**	• Business and Health Administration Association Conference, Chicago, Illinois, February 28, 2002. • "Education for future nurse leaders." Keynote presentation for the Council of School Presidents, New Jersey Nursing Students, Inc., November 2002. • "Education for nurse leaders of the future." New Jersey State Nurses Association, Atlantic City, New Jersey, April 2001. • "Roles, power, and opportunities for men in nursing." American Assembly of Men in Nursing, Seattle, Washington, December 2000. • "Graduate education for the 21st century nurse." Poster presentation for the Fourth State of the Art of Nursing Conference, University of Nebraska Medical Center, April 4, 1999. • "Psychological aspects of menopause." Grand Rounds, Department of Psychiatry, Broward General Medical Center, January 16, 1997. • "Enhancing and expanding established partial hospitalization programs." American Association for Ambulatory Behavioral Healthcare Seminar; March 17–18, 1994; August 16–17, 1994; February 18–19, 1993; August 24–25, 1993; March 4–5, 1992, August 10–11, 1992. • "Setting up partial hospital programs for accreditation and other key aspects of program success." Texas Association of Partial Hospitalization Annual Meeting, April 26, 1991. • Kleinman, C., and Halperin, D. "Cults: Fact or fiction?" Southwestern Conference on Cult Issues, Dallas, Texas, April 10, 1990.

SELECTED **PUBLICATIONS**	• Kleinman, C. (Manuscript under review). "Understanding men's advantages in nursing." *Nursing Leadership Forum.* • Kleinman, C. (In press). "Nurse executives." *Journal of Health Administration Education.* • Kleinman, C. (1982). State Board Review Examination: Grant-funded development of 240 test items for New York State nursing examination, City College of New York.

AFFILIATIONS	• Council on Graduate Education for Administration in Nursing, National Treasurer • Institute for Nursing of New Jersey, Member, Board of Trustees • Organization of Nurse Executives of New Jersey, Membership and Fund Raising Committees • Bureau of Health Professions, Division of Nursing, Health and Human Services, Peer Reviewer • New Jersey Student Nurses, Inc., Faculty Advisor • East Orange School District, Member, Health Advisory Committee • Healthcare Foundation of New Jersey, Clinical Fellowship Grant, Project Director • American Organization of Nurse Executives • American Nurses Association • American Psychiatric Nurses Association • Association of University Professors of Health Administration

Designing the Perfect Résumé

Even though content is important, many times well-qualified people aren't considered for positions because a poorly designed résumé didn't grab the reader's attention long enough to make sure the words were read. Just the opposite can be true as well. Even if your qualifications aren't the greatest, a well-designed résumé improves your chances of getting an interview because it stands out in a crowd of poorly designed ones.

The choice of overall style, font, graphics, and even paper color says something about your personality. In this chapter, you have already seen some résumé designs to help you find ways to express your unique personality on paper. Now, I will show you a few more examples.

If you want additional design ideas, then you should read the third edition of *Designing the Perfect Résumé* (Barron's, 2006), with more than 260 sample layouts. It also covers in great detail the various elements of design.

Lisa Schenck

PROFILE	• Self-motivated sales professional with more than 15 years of proven experience.

PROFILE
- Self-motivated sales professional with more than 15 years of proven experience.
- Top performer with a strong background in building new territories and using creative marketing approaches.
- Respected for the ability to get to the decision maker and close the sale.
- Demonstrated ability to create client loyalty beyond the sales relationship.
- Entrepreneurial thinker who works well independently or as part of a team.

EXPERIENCE

SALES REPRESENTATIVE, Waxie Sanitary Supply, Denver, Colorado (2005 – present)
- Sell paper products, chemicals, equipment, and cleaning supplies to large corporate clients, including The Pepsi Center, Coors Field, Invesco, Coors Brewery, casinos, hospital, and various other market segments.
- Formulated a two-year strategic sales plan for territory growth and built the territory from zero to $1.2 million.
- Created and conducted onsite training programs for end users focusing on the safe use of chemicals and equipment.
- Made sales presentations to upper-level management based on comprehensive needs analyses.

SALES REPRESENTATIVE, Unisource, Denver, Colorado (1997 – 2005)
- Sold paper products, chemicals, and cleaning supplies to large corporate and government clients, including hospitals, hotels, casinos, City of Denver, and Coors.
- Formulated a strategic plan for the territory and grew the account base by 350% through effective cold calling and account development.
- Created and conducted sales presentations to upper-level management, assessed their needs, and developed unique customer applications.
- Successfully regained former customers through effective marketing and follow-up.
- Designed and executed training programs for key clients.
- Achieved the President's Club through exceptional sales performance; ranked the number one salesperson in the Denver metropolitan territory.

SALES REPRESENTATIVE, Moore Business Forms, Denver, Colorado (1993 – 1997)
- Sold customized business forms to companies in the Denver territory.
- Increased sales to existing customers and developed the territory by 178%.
- Designed special forms to fit proprietary computer systems.
- Created a forms management program for the Poudre Valley Hospital.

SALES REPRESENTATIVE, Pitney Bowes, Denver, Colorado (1990 – 1993)
- Developed markets for Pitney Bowes copiers throughout 20 zip codes in the Denver metropolitan area.
- Consistently exceeded production quotas by as much as 250%, producing nearly half a million dollars a year in sales.
- Honored as one of the top five Pitney Bowes salespeople in the state of Colorado.
- Completed a comprehensive Pitney Bowes professional sales training program.

EDUCATION

BACHELOR OF ARTS IN BUSINESS MARKETING
Colorado State University, Fort Collins, Colorado

8641 Anywhere Lane • Newtown, Colorado 80124
Phone: (303) 555-1234 • Cellular: (303) 123-4567 • E-mail: lisor@protypeltd.com

SUZANNE DAVIS

210 Anywhere Drive ✦ Newtown, Colorado 80906
Home: (719) 555-1234 ✦ Cell: (719) 123-4567 ✦ E-mail: sdavis@protypeltd.com

PROFILE

✦ Experienced multimedia sales director with demonstrated success in:
- Brand definition
- New product development
- Marketing plan creation
- Market penetration
- Online advertising
- Strategic market research
- Product positioning
- Franchise building
- Sales management

✦ Innovative thinker who is willing to step outside the box and take a risk.

✦ Proven sales leader with a strong background in building new territories and using creative marketing approaches to increase revenue.

EXPERIENCE

METRO NEWSPAPERS, FREEDOM COMMUNICATIONS, Colorado Springs, Colorado
Director, Major Accounts and Motion Pictures/Entertainment (May 2002 – present)

✦ Recruited by the publisher of *The Orange County Register* to join the new Metro Newspaper Division, Freedom Media Enterprises (FME). FME is an integrated information and media company designed to service marketing and advertising needs in new and exciting ways offering one central account contact for three markets—*The Orange County Register* (Santa Ana), *The Gazette* (Colorado Springs), and *The Tribune* (Phoenix).

✦ Developed the business plan, sales plan, policies and procedures, execution, and implementation of the new organization.

✦ Developed and managed a revenue budget of more than $30 million.

✦ Grew incremental revenues to $3.1 million in the first five months of operation.

FREEDOM COMMUNICATIONS, Newspaper Division, Colorado Springs, Colorado
Vice President, Corporate Sales (June 2000 – April 2002)

✦ Recruited by *The Gazette's* parent company to develop a new business venture to generate advertising for 28 newspapers (1.1 million total circulation), 6 Internet portals, 12 Hispanic publications, and 10 military newspapers nationwide.

✦ Wrote the business plan, policies and procedures, sales plan, and job descriptions.

✦ Hired, trained, and managed four account managers and an office manager.

✦ Created strategic and tactical marketing plans for the branding of Freedom Communications and generated more than $1.7 million in new revenue in the first year.

✦ Sourced contacts, developed sales presentations, made sales calls, and captured significant market share.

THE GAZETTE, Colorado Springs, Colorado
Director, Display Advertising (January 1996 – May 2000)

✦ Built a national advertising division from the ground up and managed major accounts, generating $24 million in annual advertising revenue.

✦ Hired, and managed a team of sales managers responsible for 40 account executives.

✦ Developed the *Home in Colorado* magazine that won the 1999 Addy Award for best in-house publication with more than four colors.

✦ Partnered with The Broadmoor (a Mobil five-star, five-diamond resort) to deliver *The Gazette* to guests every day; created a four-color, in-room *Broadmoor Magazine* for guests that generated significant income for the paper.

✦ Instrumental in securing advertising for the interactive division of the newspaper (Colorado springs.com).

✦ Created partnerships with cruise lines and travel agencies to give the newspaper travel section a more national feel and to offer new opportunities to readers.

154

EXPERIENCE   **LOS ANGELES TIMES**, Los Angeles, California
(continued)   **Advertising Sales Manager, Entertainment Category** (May 1994 – December 1995)
- Recruited from *The Orange County Register* because of the phenomenal success of its news entertainment section.
- Managed a team of six sales associates responsible for selling advertising space in the entertainment *Calendar* section that generated $150 million in annual revenue.
- Developed strategic plans for future growth and franchise protection.
- Created and promoted unique online advertising programs that were ahead of their time.
- Implemented performance management and team-building strategies that improved morale, reduced turnover, and increased individual sales revenue.

THE ORANGE COUNTY REGISTER, Santa Anna, California
Sales Manager, Major Accounts Division (June 1992 – May 1994)
- Recruited, hired, and supervised a staff of 14 account executives.
- Succeeded in growing revenue to more than $50 million a year from department, grocery, electronics, and small/medium specialty stores (Target, Macy's, Homestead House, etc.).

Retail Territorial Manager (June 1990 – May 1992)
- Managed six regional sales managers responsible for generating local advertisements from retailers throughout Orange County.

Sales Manager, Entertainment Division (January 1988 – May 1994)
- Developed and launched the Show Section, an entertainment tab that competed directly with the *Los Angeles Times Calendar* section.
- Grew the insert from 80 to 124 pages through aggressive advertising sales.
- Created significant advertising revenue with innovative partnerships, promotions, and special events.

EDUCATION   **SAN FRANCISCO STATE UNIVERSITY**, San Francisco, California (1984 – 1988)
- Completed three years of full-time undergraduate studies.

PROFESSIONAL DEVELOPMENT
- **Landmark Forum Education** (2002)
- **Community Leadership Forum**: Better Business Bureau (2001, 2002)
- **Associated Press Institute**: Publishing Your Own Newspaper (1999)
- **Center for Creative Leadership**: Leadership Development Program (1 week, 1998)
- **University of Southern California**: Management Institute (1995)
- **Aubrey Daniels**: Performance Management Training (1993)

AFFILIATIONS
- NAA Advertising Committee Board
- Better Business Bureau Board of Directors
- CASA Fund Raising Committee
- Denver Ad Federation

9980 Anywhere Trail
Newtown, Colorado 80809

Phone: (719) 555-1234
E-mail: kblack@protypeltd.com

PROFILE

- Experienced network administrator with broad knowledge of technical and training concepts, principles, and methods.
- Detail-oriented troubleshooter who gets to the root of the problem quickly.
- Known for the ability to create process efficiencies and getting the job done on time.
- Effective team player with proven communication and interpersonal skills.
- Hold an Interim Top Secret security clearance with access to Sensitive Compartmented Information (SCI).

TECHNICAL

Certification: Microsoft Certified Systems Engineer (MCSE)

Networks: Windows NT, Windows 2000, Windows for Workgroups, Exchange 5.5, Proxy Server 2.10, Microsoft System Management Server (SMS), Norton Ghost

Software: MS Word, Excel, PowerPoint, Outlook, Internet Explorer, Remedy, FrontPage, MS Mail, Netscape Navigator

EXPERIENCE

NETWORK ADMINISTRATOR (2001 - present)
Remtech Services, Inc., Cheyenne Mountain AB, Colorado
Manage the daily operations of two classified networks with a total of 1,000 users, ensuring that resources are used efficiently. Maintain file servers, e-mail, backups, permissions, and security. Continuously monitor the network and troubleshoot any problems to minimize downtime. Create user accounts, write procedures, and handle network vulnerability issues. Install, configure, and optimize software applications and resolve conflicts using standard installation techniques and Ghost images. Develop packages to distribute upgrades and service patches using SMS.

- Discovered a physical problem on one of the e-mail servers, moved all users to the backup server, discovered another problem on the backup server, replaced them both, installed and configured the operating system and software, and migrated users to the new server.
- Recommended the purchase of a third-party administration tool (Hyena), which saved significant time.
- Currently helping to create an accreditation package for the network.

NETWORK ADMINISTRATOR (2000 - 2001)
Honeywell Technology Solutions, Inc., Schriever AFB, Colorado
One of six administrators responsible for 3,000 users on an unclassified network. Installed, set up, and supported software products; installed service packs and hot fixes. Monitored network servers and responded to and resolved problems. Managed network/exchange accounts and share permissions. Provided input to generate and update project documents.

- Assist on special projects, such as network security, Windows 2000 testbed, and SMS packages.

LAN SYSTEMS ANALYST (1998 - 2000)
Honeywell Technology Solutions, Inc., Schriever AFB, Colorado
Provided level-three help desk support for a 3,000-user, Windows NT/95 LAN via telephone, SMS, and on-site visits. Trained new users. Maintained a computer maintenance log documenting each user request, detailed problem description, and resolution. Analyzed information to determine potential for enterprise-wide problems/solutions. Assisted the network administrator with creating user accounts and share permissions.

EXPERIENCE

LAN Systems Analyst (continued)
- Served as the focal point for troubleshooting help desk DMS/Exchange and rewriting help desk procedures.
- Webmaster for the help desk intranet Web page.
- Part of a team responsible for migrating all users from MS Mail to Exchange/Outlook.

STAFF ASSISTANT (1990 – 1998)
AlliedSignal Aerospace, Phoenix and Tempe, Arizona
Rapidly promoted through four departments, culminating in Product Safety/Integrity and Materials Management. Provided first-line support for users experiencing PC hardware and software problems. Increased employee productivity by fixing 90% of problems immediately instead of waiting 24 hours for IS technicians. Surveyed department personnel to determine how applications would be used, then developed and taught customized Microsoft Excel, Word, and PowerPoint.
- Researched and recommended software solutions so employees could either telecommute or work additional hours at home, which improved employee morale. Installed 20 copies of pcANY-WHERE and provided user training and help desk support.
- Designed and linked multiple Excel worksheets to provide monthly operating reports.
- Member of the team that implemented the total quality reward and recognition process in the Engines Department.
- Served as a member of the Policies and Procedures team that produced a desktop manual of the most important procedures for the credit administrators based on a survey of the department.
- Honored with seven recognition awards for commitment to teamwork, initiative, process improvements, and customer satisfaction.

EDUCATION

BACHELOR OF SCIENCE, INFORMATION SYSTEMS (1996)
University of Phoenix, Phoenix, Arizona

PROFESSIONAL DEVELOPMENT
U.S. Air Force: Windows 2000 Accelerated (November 2001), GCCS Advanced System Administrator (UNIX) (July 2001), GCCS Security Administrator (UNIX) (July 2001)

Solutech: Deploying Windows 2000 (January 2000)

ExecuTrain: Intermediate FrontPage 98 (July 1999)

New Horizons: Windows NT 4.0 Administration (October 1998)

AlliedSignal: Microsoft Master Trainer, TQL I and II Train the Trainer, Total Quality Facilitation, Situational Leadership, Managing Multiple Priorities, TimeMax Life Management, Managerial Techniques

Melissa Hardy

STRENGTHS
- Experienced loan processor and investigator with exceptional customer service skills.
- Responsible and dedicated worker who learns quickly.
- Effective team player with strong interpersonal/communication skills; highly proficient in Spanish.
- Proficient in WordPerfect, Windows 95, MS-DOS, MS Office, E-mail, and proprietary database and contact management software.

EXPERIENCE

DEALER SERVICE REPRESENTATIVE   2004 – present
AmeriCredit Financial, Colorado Springs, Colorado
- Serve as a loan officer, working directly with car dealerships to sell loans to their customers.
- Call on 4 to 5 dealers per day in the Colorado Springs and Pueblo territory, generating sales of as much as $4 million per month.
- Supervise the branch during the absence of the manager.
- Promoted from customer service representative responsible for loan processing and verification of employment, credit history, and other loan data.

LOAN PROCESSOR/ADMINISTRATIVE ASSISTANT   2004
World Class Homes and Mortgage, Colorado Springs, Colorado
- Entered data for loan applications and Loan Handler computer files.
- Made weekly customer courtesy calls to update customers on the status of their loan.
- Answered phones and customer inquiries; set appointments with prospective customers.
- In charge of coordinating subordinations and preparing associated paperwork.
- Ordered titles, payoffs, mortgage ratings, appraisals, and evidence of insurance.
- Designed and updated database of all clients; organized paperwork in stacking order.
- Helped start the business from the ground up; ordered office furniture and supplies.

LOAN PROCESSOR AND INVESTIGATOR   2003 – 2004
Champion Financial Services, Colorado Springs, Colorado
- Processed vehicle loans, verified calculations on buyer orders, gathered stipulations from customers, and prepared paperwork.
- Verified employment and residency, checked credit ratings, requested proofs of income, and investigated incoming applications for completeness and accuracy.
- Communicated with dealerships regarding stipulations and rollbacks.
- Determined Blue Book and NADA values of vehicles.
- Made ten-day calls to remind customers of first payments and processed requests for deferred payments.
- Answered questions from customers, resolved complaints, and communicated with Spanish-speaking customers.
- Designed an improved filing system for home office loans.

SALES REPRESENTATIVE   2003
MCI Telecommunications Corporation, Colorado Springs, Colorado
- Sold long distance services and Continental Airlines frequent flyer programs.
- Set goals in a highly competitive environment.
- Received Player of the Month award for highest sales.
- Won a trip to Orlando, Florida and other incentives for sales achievements.

CUSTOMER SERVICE REPRESENTATIVE   2001 – 2002
Maxserve, Inc. (for Sears), Tucson, Arizona
- Provided customer service and telephone sales of appliance parts.
- Entered data into the computer and researched part numbers.
- Used communication skills to determine correct parts from customer descriptions.

ADDRESS   5390 Anywhere Drive, Newtown, Colorado 80918, (719) 534-0570

Carol R. Florio

P.O. Box 1234 • Monument, CO 80132 • (719) 555-1234 • florio@protypeltd.com

PROFILE
- Experienced landscape artist with a strong background in:
  - Xeriscape
  - Desert gardens
  - Water conservation
  - Low-water-use plants
  - Efficient irrigation systems
  - Wildlife habitats
- Proven ability to build trust and to sell new concepts to customers.
- Self-motivated professional with a strong work ethic and a passion for the environment.
- Effective team player with excellent communication and interpersonal skills.
- Knowledge of Windows, MS Word, Excel, Publisher, Outlook, and Internet Explorer.

EXPERIENCE

LANDSCAPING
- Certified Desert Landscaper, Phoenix Desert Landscape School, Desert Botanical Gardens.
- Experienced in the identification of low-water-use plants, appropriate maintenance of plants and irrigation systems, proper fertilization and weed control, and identifying and controlling plant diseases.
- Designed and installed a water-efficient landscape for a Habitat for Humanity property located in Guadalupe, Arizona. Used xeriscape principles to design the landscape and installed an efficient irrigation system. Planted low-water-use trees, shrubs, and desert wildflowers.
- Renovated an old landscape to a new design compatible with the limited water supply of the Sonoran Desert.
- Recycled and relocated existing plants that were appropriate to the design and image of the new landscape.
- Removed high-water-use plants and installed new plants that functioned to provide shade, screening, privacy, seasonal interest, color contrast, and a wildlife habitat.
- Retrofitted the existing bubbler irrigation system to a drip system and upgraded it with an automatic timer to reduce water use.

SALES AND MANAGEMENT
- Successfully sold resale and new residential real estate. Licensed Real Estate Broker in Colorado.
- Consistently achieved annual Top Producer and won the Million-Dollar Producer awards.
- Built a client base through prospecting, referrals, cold calling, and direct mail campaigns.
- Demonstrated the features and benefits of properties and managed all of the details required to bring a transaction to successful close, including the negotiation of purchase offers and contracts.
- Accountable for long-range planning, profit and loss, budgeting, controlling costs, accounts payable, accounts receivable, operations, and customer service.

EDUCATION

CERTIFIED DESERT LANDSCAPER (1998 – 1999)
Phoenix Desert Landscaper School, Desert Botanical Gardens, Phoenix, Arizona
Successfully completed three semesters to earn the CDL designation.

UNDERGRADUATE STUDIES (1980 – 1985)
Arizona State University, Tempe, Arizona
Completed three years toward a Bachelor of Fine Arts degree.

JONES SCHOOL OF REAL ESTATE, Colorado Springs, Colorado (2001)

WORK HISTORY
Real Estate Broker Associate, Prudential Professional Realtors, Monument, Colorado (2001 – present)
Desert Landscaper, Phoenix, Arizona (1999 – 2001)
Real Estate Agent/Broker, West USA Realty, Phoenix, Arizona (1992 – 2001)
Real Estate Agent/Broker, ERA Realty, Scottsdale, Arizona (1987 – 1992)
Real Estate Agent/Broker, Coldwell-Banker Real Estate, Phoenix, Arizona (1985 – 1987)

Howard E. Hyde

1223 Anywhere Drive, Suite A • Newtown, CO 80906
Home: (719) 555-1234 • Cellular: (719) 123-4567
E-mail: hehyde@protypeltd.com

PROFILE

- Results-oriented senior executive with expertise in:
  - Organizational development
  - Strategic planning
  - Change management
  - Marketing/sales
  - Problem solving
  - Customer service
  - Line management
  - Staffing
  - Training and development
- Conceptual thinker who can see the whole picture, create a vision for the enterprise, and generate commitment from employees.
- Respected for the ability to lead business units through dramatic turnarounds and periods of high growth.

EXPERIENCE

PRESIDENT (2000 – present)
The Center for Customer Focus, Colorado Springs, Colorado
Developed a successful business that provides consulting and training services to organizations desiring to become more customer focused. Create and present workshops and seminars that help client organizations dramatically improve their competitive advantage by creating more value for their customers. Analyze client needs, develop innovative solutions, and serve as a change agent. Recruited, hired, and supervised a staff of four employees in addition to independent contractors. Accountable for operations management, business planning, profit and loss, accounting, marketing, and customer service functions.

- Developed measurement technologies that provided a systems approach to the measurement of a company's values and beliefs, its perceptions of service and quality, and the employees' perception of the organization's customer orientation.
- Successfully marketed services to clients such as Del Webb, NorthStar Print Group, Madison Fireplace and Lighting, Long Island Pipe, among others.
- Exceeded revenue and profit goals by setting high goals and mobilizing a strong work ethic.

GENERAL MANAGER, MARKETING STRATEGY AND CORPORATE MARKETING (1998 – 2000)
Control Data Corporation, Minneapolis, Minnesota
Selected to develop a complete plan for transforming the culture of the company from a product-driven organization to a customer-driven one. Conducted extensive secondary research at Harvard, Stanford, and the Kellogg graduate schools of business, and visited numerous customer-driven companies to broaden the knowledge base.

- Designed a measurement instrument to define discrete customer-driven factors and implemented a survey to measure the current culture of the company.
- Consulted with internal business units to strengthen executive marketing skills, develop marketing as a core competency, and improve financial performance.
- Created executive/employee development programs and modified human resource processes (compensation, performance appraisals, internal communications) to reinforce the desired culture.
- Developed and implemented a uniform strategic planning process that served as a model for other business units.

GENERAL MANAGER, MARKETING AND ACADEMIC EDUCATION (1995 – 1997)
Control Data Corporation, Minneapolis, Minnesota
Managed the marketing department of a business unit that promoted computer-based education in the academic marketplace. Analyzed the market, defined market segments, and developed a marketing strategy to meet the needs of each segment. Created formal criteria for advertising agency selection, interviewed agencies, and selected finalists to compete for the account.

- Instituted account planning processes and increased the sales force by 30%.
- Achieved 100% of goal and increased revenue by 152%.
- Developed a new marketing communication strategy with the ad agency that significantly increased product awareness in the market.

EXPERIENCE (continued)	**GENERAL MANAGER, GOVERNMENT SERVICES DIVISION** (1993 – 1995) **Control Data Corporation**, Minneapolis, Minnesota Provided direction for a division that marketed educational computer services and hardware to the government sector.

GENERAL MANAGER, GOVERNMENT SERVICES DIVISION (1993 – 1995)
Control Data Corporation, Minneapolis, Minnesota
Provided direction for a division that marketed educational computer services and hardware to the government sector.
- Developed and implemented the division's first marketing strategy and restructured prices.
- Reduced the number of market segments covered to focus on those segments with a higher growth rate and where the company could provide more value.
- Created a program to retrain unemployed steelworkers in Pittsburgh, which was so successful that President Reagan visited the operation to show how government and the private sector can partner to improve performance.
- Succeeded in lobbying to change federal legislation for the industry from cost-based to performance-based pricing.
- Produced the first profits in the division's history, increasing revenue by 166% in the first year and 183% in the following year.

GENERAL MANAGER, LEARNING CENTER DIVISION (1990 – 1993)
Control Data Corporation, Minneapolis, Minnesota
Assumed full profit and loss responsibility for 52 education centers that delivered computer-based training programs to various market segments.
- Attained 130% of revenue objectives and improved the bottom line from a loss position to a 12% pretax profit.
- Promoted from General Manager of Field Sales Operations for the Business Center Division, which marketed computer hardware, software, and training programs to small business markets.
- Built the division from the ground up, including leasing and renovating the facility and hiring staff.

GENERAL MANAGER, WESTERN REGION (1987 – 1990)
Control Data Corporation, Irvine, California
Managed four educational services divisions that included five Control Data Institutes, twelve computer-based learning centers, a consulting business, and a seminar business. Directed 175 full-time employees, as well as more than 100 supplemental employees and consultants.
- Took the region from the worst to the first region in the country by dramatically improving sales, profitability, and quality in all four divisions.
- Selected as the top regional manager; the region won 18 of the 23 top performance awards at the company's annual 100% Club event.

EDUCATION

MASTER OF BUSINESS ADMINISTRATION
Pepperdine University, Malibu, California
Graduated with a 4.0 GPA on a 4.0 scale

UNDERGRADUATE STUDIES IN ELECTRICAL ENGINEERING
University of Illinois, Chicago and Champaign-Urbana, Illinois

AFFILIATIONS

- Board of Directors, The Braas Company, Inc. (7 years)
- American Society of Training and Development, Current Member
- National Speakers Association, Current Member
- Colorado Speakers Association, Current Member
- American Marketing Association, Former Executive Member
- Sales and Marketing Executives International, Former Director
- Institute for the Study of Business Markets, Former Member
- The Pricing Institute, Former Advisory Board Member

PHILLIP W. SMITH

Home: (719) 555-1234 ▪ Cellular: (719) 123-4567 ▪ E-mail: psmith@protypeltd.com
1234 Fossil Drive ▪ Anywhere, Idaho 80918

QUALIFICATIONS

- Results-oriented manager with a strong background in operations, marketing, sales, logistics, purchasing, and inventory control.
- Proven achiever with a strong work ethic and drive to succeed.
- Flexible team player who enjoys the challenge of change and is committed to lifelong learning.

EXPERIENCE

GENERAL MANAGER

JANIKING, Boise, Idaho (2003 – present)

Purchased a franchise commercial cleaning business and grew revenue by 300% while holding down another full-time job. Accountable for strategic planning, profit and loss, expense control, marketing, and customer service. Recruited, hired, trained, and supervised 12 part-time employees and one full-time assistant manager.

- Generated contracts with 22 office and light industrial businesses through cold calling, Yellow Page advertising, word of mouth from satisfied customers, and JaniKing national accounts.
- Awarded Franchise of the Year for the Colorado region; selected for the President's Club (top 10% of sales nationwide); achieved Crown Club status (top 25% of sales nationwide).

PRODUCT & MARKETING MANAGER

COOK COMMUNICATIONS, Boise, Idaho (2001 – 2003)

Managed the purchasing and reselling of inspirational products to retailers, mass merchants and nontraditional CBA channels. Developed annual and semi-annual marketing plans based on extensive market research. Designed and produced displays, sales tools, and promotions to ensure constantly fresh merchandising of products. Wrote and managed a $370,000 marketing budget and provided input for the sales budget. Managed a J.D. Edwards inventory control program that handled cost accounting, inventory reporting, sales forecasts, customer service, and tracking of sales and returns. Served as a liaison between Cook Communications and the third-party logistics partner. Provided direct customer service for independent distributors and handled their special order needs. Managed order fulfillment, shipping, and receiving.

- Determined product assortment, purchased more than $3 million of inventory, and set prices to ensure profitability.
- Managed an aggressive sales team that increased revenue from $4.5 million in 2001 to $6.2 million in 2002.
- Lowered cost of goods sold to 50% by negotiating deals with suppliers and ensuring lower printing costs for books printed on demand.
- Reduced inventory obsolescence to 1.5% of revenue by aggressively negotiating returns with vendors and reducing SKU counts from 1,150 to 470.
- Achieved an average of 75% sell-through for all products.

INVENTORY PLANNER

COOK COMMUNICATIONS, Eden Prairie, Minnesota (1992 – 2001)

- Managed inventory control, purchasing, and database integrity.
- Hired, trained, and supervised a warehouse manager and 12 employees.
- Supervised moves of the entire operation from Eden Prairie to Denver in 1992 and then again to Colorado Springs in 1995.

162

WAREHOUSE MANAGER	**COOK COMMUNICATIONS**, Eden Prairie, Minnesota (1988 – 1992) • Managed the warehousing, receiving, and distribution of more than 1,150 items of inventory. • Worked closely with customers to ensure timely delivery of orders within a 48-hour shipping window. • Consistently shipped more products with fewer resources.
SHIPPER & ORDER PULLER	**COOK COMMUNICATIONS**, Eden Prairie, Minnesota (1986 – 1888) • Originally hired as an Order Puller but was quickly promoted to Shipper based on strong work ethic and attention to detail. • Performed order fulfillment, shipping, and receiving.

EDUCATION

UNIVERSITY OF DENVER, Colorado (1991)
Completed 1 semester of Purchasing Management courses

DR. MARTIN LUTHER COLLEGE, New Ulm, Minnesota (1982 – 1985)
Completed 2½ year of study toward a bachelor's degree in elementary education

PROFESSIONAL DEVELOPMENT
Inventory Control, APICS, 6 weeks (1996)

JULIE HARRIS, MS.Ed.

1234 Twin Gulch Court • Harrison, CO 80922
Phone: (719) 555-1234 • E-mail: julieh@protypeltd.com

PROFILE

- NASP Certified School Psychologist who sets high standards and motivates students to achieve success.
- Well-organized professional with extensive experience in special education populations.
- Effective team player with proven listening, interpersonal, and communication skills.
- Knowledge of Windows, MS Word, PowerPoint, Excel, and computerized IEP programs.

EDUCATION

Ed.S. IN SCHOOL PSYCHOLOGY (August 2003)
University of Northern Colorado, Greeley, Colorado
Relevant course work: Psychological Testing and Measurement, Abnormal Psychology, Theories of Personality, Seminar in School Psychology, Community Psychology and Social Systems, Legal and Ethical Issues, Psychological Consultation–Theory and Practice, Evaluation of Psychological Services, Child and Adolescent Psychology, Behavioral Approaches to Professional Psychology, Theories of Counseling, Intellectual and Cognitive Assessment, Family Systems, Infant and Toddler Neuropsychology, Evaluation and Correction of Individual Reading Problems

MS.Ed. IN SPECIAL EDUCATION (1999)
Old Dominion University, Norfolk, Virginia
Emphasis on learning disabilities and emotional disabilities
Licensed Special Education Teacher K–12 (Colorado)

BACHELOR OF SCIENCE IN PSYCHOLOGY (1995)
University of Maryland, Heidelberg, Germany

CONTINUING EDUCATION

- Depression: Comprehensive Assessment and Treatment of Children, Adolescents, and Adults, Medical Educational Services, 8 hours (2003)
- ADHD: Beyond the Label–Assessment, Treatment, and Educational Interventions, Medical Educational Services, 8 hours (2003)
- Crisis Response and Intervention, National Emergency Response Team, 16 hours (2002)
- Threat and Suicide Assessment, CSSP, 8 hours (2002)
- Special Education Law, Law Advisory Council, 8 hours (1999)

INTERNSHIP

SCHOOL PSYCHOLOGY INTERNSHIP (2002 – 2003)
Harrison School District 2, Colorado Springs, Colorado
- Completed an intensive 1,200 hour internship in an elementary school, middle school, and alternative night high school program.
- Provided psycho-educational assessment, individual and play therapy, and direct/indirect consultation.

PRACTICUMS

- Cognitive Assessment, Gorman Middle School, Harrison District 2, Colorado Springs, Colorado (Fall 2000)
- Personality Assessment, Colleagues and Families, Colorado Springs, Colorado (Spring 2001)
- Individual Counseling, Buena Vista Elementary School, Colorado Springs District 11 (Fall 2001)
- Systems Intervention, The New Horizons Alternative School, Harrison District 2, Colorado Springs, Colorado (Spring 2002)

164

EXPERIENCE   **SPECIAL EDUCATION COORDINATOR** (1999 – present)
The New Horizons Alternative School , Colorado Springs, Colorado
- Coordinate special education services for 7–12th grade students with learning and emotional disabilities.
- Develop intervention, program, and transition plans.
- Write Individualized Education Plans (IEPs) and psycho-educational reports.
- Facilitate multi-disciplinary team meetings and taught annual classes in psycho-educational assessment at the District 2 New Staff Institute.
- Supervise, train, and evaluate special education student teachers as a cooperating teacher for the University of Colorado at Colorado Springs.
- Serve as acting administrator in the absence of the principal.
- Certified ACT administrator and Accommodations Coordinator (1999 – present).
- Member of the interviewing and hiring team for new teachers and paraprofessionals (1999 – present).
- Member of the District Literacy Team responsible for developing a new literacy program, including curriculum and tests (2001 – 2002).
- Member of the District Transition Team that provided career and continuing education services to special education students between 18 and 21 years of age (1999 – 2000).

HONORARIUM INSTRUCTOR (2001 – present)
University of Colorado , Colorado Springs, Colorado
- Teach Psycho-Educational Assessment to graduate students and professional educators in the Masters of Special Education Program.
- Developed and implemented a unique hands-on curriculum, examinations, and multimedia presentation materials.

SIED TEACHER (1998 – 1999)
Southeast Cooperative Educational Program , Norfolk, Virginia
- Taught emotionally disabled students in 7–8th grade programs for the most at-risk students (expelled, violent, economically disadvantaged, and prison populations).

MENTAL HEALTH WORKER, TEACHER'S ASSISTANT (1998)
Southeast Virginia Training Center , Chesapeake, Virginia
- Worked with nonverbal adults in classroom and residential settings.
- Taught sign language to improve the communication abilities of adult autistic residents.

DISCIPLINE COORDINATOR, TEACHER'S ASSISTANT (1997 – 1998)
Chesapeake Bay Academy , Chesapeake, Virginia
- Served as an intervention specialist for this private school for learning disabled and ADHD children. Investigated incidents, determined disciplinary actions, and developed classroom interventions to prevent future problems.
- Assisted in teaching second and third grade classes for the first half of the year before being promoted to discipline coordinator for the entire K–12 population.

SENIOR AIRMAN (1990 – 1997)
United States Air Force (honorably discharged)
- Desert Storm Veteran who served four years as a paralegal and three years as a vehicle mechanic.

AFFILIATIONS   • National Association of School Psychologists

Brandi Black

1234 North Corona Street
Colorado Springs, CO 80907

E-mail: thx1138@springs.net

Home: (719) 555-1234
Cellular: (719) 123-4567

SUMMARY

- Experienced buyer with a diverse knowledge of clothing, jewelry, accessories, and shoes.
- Proven ability to evaluate trends and to know what customers want to buy.
- Effective team player with strong communication and interpersonal skills.
- Knowledge of Windows, MS Word, Excel, Outlook, Adobe Photoshop, and Quicken.

EXPERIENCE

TERRA VERDE, Colorado Springs, Colorado (1997 – present)
Terra Verde is a lifestyle boutique selling upscale furniture, gifts, women's clothing, shoes, jewelry, and accessories in the historic district of downtown Colorado Springs.

Lead Buyer (2000 – present)
- Make assortment selection and buying decisions regarding jewelry, accessories, and shoes. For two years, also served as the clothing buyer.
- Attend shows to find new lines and products, including among others:
  - New York: The Boutique Show, Accessoriestheshow*, Accessories Circuit, Femme, and Moda Manhattan
  - Los Angeles: California Market Center, New Mart Fashion Week, and LA Shoe Show
  - Las Vegas: The WSA Shoe Show
- Ensure excitement in each area by keeping up with trends and bringing in new and different lines/products.
- Reorder merchandise to maintain a constant flow of goods for sale, anticipating needs during strong sales periods.
- Receive and track merchandise, take physical inventory counts, and design displays.
- Process special orders and keep customers informed of status.
- Evaluate cost of goods sold and set prices to ensure profitability.
- Oversee the accurate pricing of inventory by staff.
- Provide sales support on the floor by assisting customers with their buying decisions.
- Open and close the store, handle cash and credit card transactions, and make recommendations for changes in processes and procedures.
- Facilitated a 400% growth in sales through assortment selection and accurate pricing.
- Helped the store to win *The Independent* newspaper's "Best of Issue" and silver award for "Best Jewelry Store."

Sales Staff, Back-Room Support (1997 – 2000)
- Greeted customers and introduced them to the store's merchandise.
- Used suggestive selling techniques to increase sales volume.
- Wrote sales tickets and accepted payments.
- Provided back-room support by receiving shipments, gift wrapping, and shipping orders.

EDUCATION

UNDERGRADUATE STUDIES (1998 – 2001)
University of Colorado, Colorado Springs, Colorado
Completed all but the senior year toward a Bachelor of Arts in Fine Arts

ENTREPRENEURIAL TRAINING COURSE (May – August 2001)
Small Business Administration, Colorado Springs, Colorado
Mi Casa, Business Resource Center for Women, Colorado Springs, Colorado
Course work included: Secrets to Becoming a Successful Small Business Owner; Legal Structure, Taxes, and Organizational Matters; Key Marketing Decisions and Research; Pricing, Financial Forecasting, and Credit; Marketing Mix; Marketing Plan and Analysis/Internet; Budgets and Projections; Record Keeping; Sales and Customer Service; Marketing Materials and Tools; and Business Plan Completion

$\mathcal{E}$ric Thomas

4113 Anywhere Drive

Phone: (719) 555-1234

Newtown, CO 80918

PROFILE
- ✦ *Dedicated manager with a strong background in service and consumer product industries.*
- ✦ *Proven experience in business administration, event management, economics, and supervision.*
- ✦ *Energetic team player with the ability to communicate clearly and work well with others.*
- ✦ *Self-motivated professional with a demonstrated work ethic and dedication to lifelong learning.*
- ✦ *Experienced international traveler (four continents) with an appreciation for other cultures.*
- ✦ *Proficient in Windows, MS Word, Excel, Outlook, Access, Works, Netscape, and Telnet.*

EXPERIENCE

BUSINESS ADMINISTRATOR, Roche s.r.o., *Prague, Czech Republic (2004 – 2007)*
- ✦ *Selected as a consultant for a contract to demonstrate Western business concepts for the Czech division of the third largest pharmaceutical company in the world.*
- ✦ *Conducted an internal audit of executive, mid-management, and staff-level personnel processes and made recommendations to executive management to improve the company's organic growth.*
- ✦ *Predicted a 7.2% growth in a shrinking market if recommendations were implemented.*
- ✦ *Evaluated stock supplies and recommended actions to save $27,000 in overstock.*
- ✦ *Designed the division's Web site to harmonize with corporate identity pieces.*

EXHIBITION COORDINATOR, Joly, *Prague, Czech Republic (2003 – 2004)*
- ✦ *Recruited by the AIESEC for a six-month internship with this exhibition company specializing in hunting and fishing events.*
- ✦ *Designed the layout and wrote the content for the company's Web site.*
- ✦ *Planned and managed an event for 10,000 participants, including 40 international companies.*

RESEARCH ASSISTANT, Murdoch University, *Perth, Australia (2002 – 2003)*
- ✦ *Conducted research on the Phillips Curve, working side by side with the noted Dr. Robert Leeson.*
- ✦ *Analyzed data, created formulas, and drew conclusions relating to the Asian crisis and its effect on Australian higher education for the Center for Labour Market Research.*

OWNER, GENERAL MANAGER, College Pro Painting, *Denver, Colorado (2001 – 2002)*
- ✦ *Developed this franchise operation from the ground up, generating $80,000 in one summer.*
- ✦ *Recruited, hired, and supervised three crews with a total of 13 employees.*
- ✦ *Accountable for long-range planning, budgeting, controlling costs, collecting accounts receivable, and monitoring financial performance.*
- ✦ *Scheduled, planned, and coordinated large projects, maximizing resources and ensuring customer satisfaction.*
- ✦ *Developed new accounts through flyers, direct mail, referrals, and cold calling.*
- ✦ *Achieved the highest customer satisfaction rate in the four-state mountain region as measured by surveys.*

PREVIOUS EXPERIENCE *(1998 – 2001)*
Foreman and Painter, *College Pro Painting, Colorado Springs, Colorado*
Volunteer Youth Soccer Referee, *Chargers Soccer Club, Colorado Springs, Colorado*

EDUCATION

BACHELOR OF ARTS, University of Colorado, *Boulder, Colorado (1999)*
- ✦ *Major in Economics (Major GPA 3.6)*
- ✦ *Study abroad at Murdoch University, Perth, Australia (Spring/Fall Semesters 1998)*

Gloria R. Conner

PROFILE
- Experienced, hard working flight attendant with a great customer service attitude.
- Able to foster cooperative relationships and generate enthusiasm.
- Skilled in taking the initiative—self-confident and conscientious.
- Traveled extensively in the United States, Hawaii, Mexico, and Europe.

RELEVANT EXPERIENCE

FLIGHT ATTENDANT
Frontier Airlines, Denver, Colorado (1998 – 2007)
Western Pacific Airlines, Colorado Springs, Colorado (1997 – 1998)
- Provided top-of-the-line service to airline customers during flights.
- Assured the safety and comfort of passengers on domestic and international flights.
- Greeted passengers, verified tickets, recorded destinations, and directed passengers to their assigned seats.
- Explained the use of safety equipment, served meals and beverages, and performed other personal services.
- Evaluated passengers for those who might pose a possible security risk, and ensured the safety of the flight deck and pilots.
- Interviewed candidates for flight attendant positions and made hiring recommendations.
- Certified for CPR, first aid, automated external defibrillator, water ditching, and self-defense.

STAFF ASSISTANT, DRUG COMMISSION OFFICER
United States Anti-Doping Agency, Colorado Springs, Colorado (2000 – 2002)
United States Olympic Committee, Colorado Springs, Colorado (1997 – 2000)
- Assisted drug commission officers in the collection of samples to test for performance-enhancing substances in athletes who compete in Olympic, Paralympic, and Pan American games and/or train in the United States.
- Traveled throughout the U.S. to conduct doping controls both in competition and out of competition without notice.
- Monitored urine collection to ensure the integrity of samples, reduced the chances of sample contamination, and maintained the security of each sample up to shipment.
- Completed forms with personal data, drug use history, sport, and other information.

FOOD AND COCKTAIL SERVER
Maggie Mae's Restaurant, Colorado Springs, Colorado (1995 – 1997)
McKay's Restaurant, Colorado Springs, Colorado (1994 – 1995)
- Provided high-quality customer service in family-style restaurants.

PHYSICAL AND HEALTH TRAINER
Straub Clinic and Hospital, Inc., Wahiawa, Hawaii (1993 – 1995)
Darmstadt Military Community, Darmstadt, Germany (1990 – 1993)
- Taught aerobics and helped people to reach their health and fitness goals.

EDUCATION

FLIGHT ATTENDANT TRAINING, Frontier Airlines, Denver, Colorado (1998)
- Completed three and a half weeks of flight attendant training

FLIGHT ATTENDANT TRAINING, Western Pacific Airlines, Colorado Springs, Colorado (1997)
- Completed three and a half weeks of intensive training

---

303 Huaka Street • Kihei, Hawaii 96753 • Email: alohagirl737@msn.com • Cellular: (720) 951-0570

168

Chapter 14

Electronic Résumés

The Internet has changed the way the world does business, and job searching is no exception. You can now find job openings anywhere in the world in a matter of seconds. According to The Conference Board, there were 4,104,800 unduplicated online job advertisements on 1,200 major Internet job boards at the beginning of 2008. The International Association of Employment Web Sites (*www.employmentwebsites.org*) lists more than 40,000 premier job sites on the Internet that meet their strict membership requirements.

There have been massive changes in the recruiting industry over the past decade. Recruiting and job seeking transitioned from paper-based to electronic, and huge online job boards spurred a massive increase in online résumé submissions. Résumés themselves changed just as dramatically. Instead of paper résumés, digital résumés are the main contact medium for 70 percent of the nation's employers. You now need electronic résumés in several formats to manage your online job searching. The only thing that hasn't changed is the purpose of a résumé. It is still a marketing instrument to promote your personal *brand*.

According to *U.S. News & World Report*, more than 1,000 unsolicited résumés arrive every day at most Fortune 500 companies, and before the days of résumé databases and applicant tracking systems, 80 percent were thrown out after a quick review. It was simply impossible to keep track of that much paper. Instead of opening and reading thousands of résumés, companies now accept them via e-mail or collect them on their Web sites, creating massive databases of résumés.

In order to make certain you have the right tools for this new world, this chapter will cover several kinds of electronic résumés. The first type is a generic computer file that you create specifically to cut and paste your résumé into those little e-forms on the Internet—an ASCII text version. Sometimes these ASCII text files are what job sites expect you to "browse" for

> The Internet has created a nationwide job network that requires a new set of job-hunting skills.

and upload. The second includes your MS Word document and Adobe Acrobat PDF file, which you use to attach to e-mails or upload when a Web site allows you to "browse" for a résumé. The third is an e-folio or an HTML résumé that is posted on the Internet at your own Web site, on your blog, or at a networking site like MySpace, Facebook, or LinkedIn.

I don't recommend digital video résumés for the average job seeker, so this chapter won't even address them. I feel that video résumés cause more harm than good in most cases, since very few candidates are skilled in front of a camera. The exception might be a television broadcaster, news anchor, actor/actress, or model. If you fall into this class, then you already know how to maximize the media, so you just need to find the technical help to create the right kind of digital file and upload it to the Internet.

Controlling Your Online Identity

You never know when someone will "Google" you before an interview. (Do you Google someone before a first date? I thought so!) All a hiring manager needs to do nowadays is to enter your name in any major search engine and see what pops up . . . or what doesn't! Hopefully, what he or she finds is good. If you want to control what a hiring manager sees, then a well-designed and promoted e-folio and/or blog could be your answer. These Web tools allow you to have more control over your online image.

Research shows that at least 63% of recruiters and hiring managers conduct Google searches on applicants before interviewing them. They are looking for articles you have written, blogs, leadership roles you have taken, evidence of volunteer activities, awards, recognitions, newspaper/journal articles that mention your name, confirmation of employment history and education, criminal record, and the list continues.

In light of this trend, you must learn how to manage your online identity. That means controlling every word you write on the Internet and in e-mails, and choosing Web tools that will enhance the position of information *you choose* to appear when your name is Googled.

Blogging and Online Networking

Do you write a regular blog of your own, or do you comment on other people's blogs? Do you participate in online forums, chat rooms, or message boards? Are you registered at social networking sites (LinkedIn, Facebook, MySpace, Ryze, Ecademy, Jobster, Friendster, and others), at lense sites (Squidoo), or profile aggregating sites (Zoominfo, Ziggs)? If so, do you consciously think about your career with every word you write on the Web? If not, then you should.

If you were to conduct a Google search on your name today, what would you find? Would your career expertise pop up first? Or will you find embarrassing photographs from college or something inappropriate that your children posted about you at their MySpace page?

Blogs are powerful promotional tools. Search engines like them because they are updated frequently, so they are considered more relevant and rank higher in search engines. Blogs are often linked to other blogs, and the more cross-links a site receives, the higher it ranks in search engines. All of this is great if you are writing about your industry, but if you happen to mention a wild drunken party while you were in college or post photographs of half-naked bodies or mention drug use, then your career could be in jeopardy. The rule is, if there is something you don't want a potential employer to read someday (even ten years down the road), then don't blog about it, don't write it on a message board, and never put it in your LinkedIn, MySpace, or Facebook profile. You should also watch what your children are saying about you online.

Even if you have made such mistakes in the past, it is never too late to begin cleaning up your online image. Start by creating a professional blog that you update at least once a week. Two or three times a week is even better. Kirsten Dixson, technology guru for Kennedy Information Systems' Career Management Alliance, believes that blogs are an excellent platform to promote your personal online brand, to build visibility and credibility. A blog can give hiring managers a free trial of your expertise, and it establishes you as a subject-matter expert in your industry. This good publicity can begin to bury some of your past indiscretions on the second and third pages of a Google search.

One caveat, however. If you are not a good writer, forget blogging, unless you have an endless source of free editing and proofreading services from a friend or colleague. Even if you are a good writer, unless you are a Web site designer by trade, hire a professional to help you create your blog layout and initial content. A bad blog can do more damage than not having one.

The ASCII Text Résumé

When you type words onto a computer screen in a word processing program, you are creating what is called a *file* or *document*. When you save that file, it is saved with special formatting codes like fonts, margins, tab settings, and so on, even if you didn't add these codes. Each word processing software (like Microsoft Word) saves its files in its own native format, making the file readable by anyone else with the same software version or with some other software that can convert that file to its own native format.

Only by choosing to save the document as a generic ASCII text file can your document be read by anyone, regardless of the word processing software he or she is using. This is the type of file you should create in order to send your résumé via e-mail.

An ASCII text file is simply words—no pictures, no fonts, no graphics—just plain words. If you print this text, it looks very boring, but all the words that describe your life history are there, just as they are in the handsome paper résumé you created to mail to a potential employer or take to an interview. This computer file can be sent to a potential employer in one of two ways.

First, you can send the file directly to a company's recruiter via an e-mail address. Second, you can use this file to post your résumé onto the Internet at a company's Web site or to a job bank in answer to an online job posting (such as at *Careerbuilder.com*). In any case, the file ends up in the same type of computerized database in which the e-mailed résumés have been stored.

There are many advantages to e-mailed résumés. First, they save you money over conventional mailing of a paper copy of your résumé with a cover letter. Second, they are faster, getting to a potential employer in only seconds instead of days. And, lastly, your résumé will be accessible every time the hiring manager searches the résumé database using keywords. Your résumé will never again languish in a dusty filing cabinet.

A recent survey conducted by the Society of Human Resource Managers found that one-third of human resource professionals would prefer to receive résumés by e-mail—and your job is to make them happy!

Steps for Creating an ASCII Text File of Your Résumé

To make sense of this topic, you must first understand the difference between a native word processing format and an ASCII text file. ASCII (pronounced "askee") is an abbreviation for American Standard Code for Information Interchange. It is a universal code that nearly all computers understand. ASCII text files are very generic—they have no special fonts, margins, tabs, bold, italic, or other formatting codes added. When you create a file in a word processor (like Microsoft Word), on the other hand, the program automatically formats and saves its files in a "native" format. This native format includes codes that not all computers or software programs can read.

Don't use any special bells and whistles when you type your ASCII text résumé in a word processing program. That means don't use boldface, underline, italics, fonts, font size, margin settings, etc. Tabs will disappear when you convert your file to text, so use your spacebar to move words over instead of tabs. Rather than trying to force lines into bulleted phrases, I recommend using paragraphs and generous white space on an ASCII résumé.

Also be careful of the "smart quotes" that many word processing programs automatically place when you press the " key on your keyboard. These special characters will not translate when you save your file as ASCII text. That includes mathematical symbols, em-dashes, en-dashes, and any character that does not appear on your keyboard.

Your choices for bullets are also limited to the characters on your keyboard. Some of the better symbol choices to highlight lines of text are ~, *, +. You can use special characters from your keyboard to create dividers, like a series of ~~~~~ or ----------- or ===== or ********.

Do not set full justification on an ASCII résumé. Instead left justify all lines so the right margin is ragged.

You can't control how someone else's e-mail software will format your message at the other end. If you force lines in your e-mail message to end at 60 characters, they won't display properly on someone else's smaller screen (like a Blackberry). When you type your résumé text, let your sentences "wrap" to a new line so the pasted text will adjust itself to the width of the e-mail message screen or electronic form on the Internet. Use the "enter" key to add extra white space between paragraphs and sections but not at the end of lines within a paragraph. That way, you can be sure the lines will break correctly and your ASCII résumé will look neat on the screen.

Don't worry about the page breaks that your word processor shows you. They won't matter once the text is pasted into your e-mail or into an electronic form on the Internet, since the text adjusts itself to fit the available space.

An ASCII résumé can be longer than one page, but remember that you have one screenful of space (about 15 lines) to grab your reader's attention and motivate him or her to click down to the next screen. You should start with a summary of your qualifications and achievements at the top of your résumé and then list your chronology of experience.

If you have already created a neat, formatted paper résumé and have saved it on your computer, it is easy to strip it of all the codes by saving it as an ASCII text file. In most word processing software, you can select "Save As" from the "File" menu and choose "ASCII Text" (or "MS DOS Text"). Remember to save the file under a new name with a "txt" extension. You don't want to save over your formatted paper résumé and lose all that hard work! See the screen shot on the next page for the process in Microsoft Word.

Screen shot of Microsoft Word used with permission of Microsoft Corporation.

In Corel WordPerfect, the best file type to select is "ASCII (DOS) Generic Word Processor," which maintains the wrap at the end of lines. If you choose "ASCII DOS Text" in WordPerfect, the file will be saved with hard returns at the end of every line of text and it won't wrap correctly when pasted into an e-mail or e-form on the Internet. Just as in Microsoft Word, after you have saved the file as a "txt" file, you must then open it again and clean up the text.

Now that you have a generic file on your computer screen, you need to be careful how you save that file, or your word processor will still add hidden codes that will make your file jumbled on the Internet. You must always remember to "Save As" from the "File" menu or your word processor's default format will take over. Repeat the instructions above for saving the file as an "ASCII (DOS) Generic Word Processor" in Corel WordPerfect or "MS DOS Text" in Microsoft Word.

On the following pages are sample résumés created in word processing programs but saved as ASCII text files and then cleaned up. You will notice that they are nothing special to look at and are more than one page long, but hiring managers are accustomed to seeing these generic files and aren't expecting beauty. Their e-mail software will probably change the font (which you can't control), so your résumé won't look quite as bad as it does on your screen.

RENA D. SMITH
1234 Wild Trap Drive
Colorado Springs, Colorado 80925
Home: (719) 555-1234
Cell: (719) 555-5678
E-mail: rena.smith@protypeltd.com

PROFILE
~~~~~~
Proven team leader with a strong background in telecommunications customer service.
High-energy professional who enjoys the challenge of solving complex problems.
Experienced supervisor with a reputation for team building, coaching, and mentoring.
Strengths: detail oriented, flexible, analytical, self-motivated, and articulate. Experienced in
Windows, MS Word, Excel, Netscape, Internet Explorer, and Vision software.

EXPERIENCE
~~~~~~
QWEST (Formerly US WEST Communications), Denver, Colorado
Excelled in supervisory positions for this telecommunications leader over a 25+ year career.
Awarded numerous certificates, stock options, and bonuses for excellence in service.
Achieved President's Club twice, an honor reserved for the top 10 percent of employees
nationwide.

LEAD PROCESS ANALYST
Federal Government Division, Colorado Springs, Colorado (2005 to present)
Provide tier-two technical support to sales personnel in all 50 states. Handle escalated and
chronic problems for federal government customers, including missed deadlines, facility
issues, and special projects. Required to respond within one hour of being contacted and to
provide constant feedback to all parties involved. Collaborate with internal departments and
nationwide customers to manage large projects. Serve as a member of the Emergency
Response Team for 14 states in the Qwest network. On call 24/7. Received recognition for
exceptional service. Fill in for supervisors and peers during absences. Assist in coaching
customer relations managers in the Federal Government Customer Care Group. Received a
Certificate of Appreciation for coordinating the NATO project in 2007.

PROCESS MANAGER
Construction/Engineering Staff, Denver, Colorado (2003 to 2005)
Evaluated whether the Perigon initiative (a legacy system upgrade) and its four component
projects will improve productivity, cost effectiveness, contractor accountability, accuracy
and quality of work, and the ability to interface with current systems. Created 30 user guides
to provide standard methods and procedures for each type of user. Assisted in deploying the
new systems in 14 states, including user demonstrations and training programs. Worked
closely with creative services to develop a training video to educate users on new systems;
responsible for scripting, editing, music and graphic selection, and content. Collaborated
with field, construction, and engineering staff to ensure a smooth transition of work and to
develop productivity measures for system users.

CONSTRUCTION MANAGEMENT CENTER SUPERVISOR
Colorado Springs, Colorado (2001 to 2003)

Supervised the Construction Management Center for the southern and western Colorado territories. Processed 400 to 500 construction jobs a month, including scheduling, monitoring, updating, tracking, and ordering of materials for the office and outside plant cable. Supervised 10 analytical associates, 2 clerical contractors, an administrative assistant, network technician, and job force manager. Worked closely with engineers, senior executives, and other internal/external customers to maintain work flow and certification standards. Responsible for reports, held orders, designed services, and database maintenance. Served as management's representative to the union; responded to discrimination, performance, and attendance issues.

CENTRAL OFFICE MANAGER
Colorado Springs, Colorado (1994 to 2001)
Managed the daily operations of a 1,500 square-mile territory with 24 offices and 3 area codes that included Colorado Springs, Glenwood Springs, and Idaho Springs. Supervised, coached, and trained 17 technicians, ensuring safety, productivity, and quality performance. Coordinated the scheduling and completion of all central office jobs. Responsible for meeting design service and delayed order commitments. Managed several projects to convert switches from analog to digital and to upgrade, add, or remove central office and power equipment. Succeeded in reducing staff overtime by changing work schedules to better meet customer demand and by cross-training technicians.

NAC/MPAC MANAGER
Colorado Springs, Colorado (1993 to 1994)
Managed the Number Assignment Center (NAC) and the Machine Performance Assignment Center (MPAC). Supervised a system support group of 15 employees responsible for assigning telephone numbers and tracking central office equipment. Collaborated with engineers to add or replace central office equipment.

EDUCATION
~~~~~~
REGIS UNIVERSITY, Colorado Springs, Colorado (1996 to 2000)
Courses in business management

CONTINUING EDUCATION
Computers: Microsoft Word, Excel, PowerPoint, Internet Explorer, Outlook
Leadership: Quality Team, Leadership Renewal, Team Problem Solving, Initial Management Course, Team Building, Project Management, Labor Relations
Training: Train the Trainer, Detailed Quality Engineering

AFFILIATIONS
~~~~~~
Executive Women International, Vice President and various committees. Coordinated the national conference hosted by the Denver chapter. Selected the location, lodging, meals, hospitality room, and conference agenda.

Silver Key, Board of Directors, 7 years.

Pikes Peak Community College, Marketing Committee.

MATTHEW C. GELLER
1234 Knoll Lane, Apt. 123
Colorado Springs, Colorado 80917
Home: (719) 555-1234
Cellular: (719) 555-5678
E-mail: mcgeller@protypeltd.com

BACKGROUND
==
Experienced Engineer with a strong background in:
* Electro-mechanical systems
* Research and development
* Hydraulics and pneumatics
* Robots and robotic controllers
* Lasers
* Optics
* Servo systems
* Precision measuring instruments
* Extremely close tolerances
Eight years of experience servicing medical equipment in the
field and factory, including x-ray, mammography, hematology,
and immunoassay systems. Experienced with FDA inspections and
regulations for the inspection of prototype medical equipment.
Extensive expertise in module integration at the system level.
Collaborated with R&D engineers to build and test prototyped
enhancements to existing systems.

STRENGTHS
==
Adaptable engineer who can readily transfer skills and bring a
fresh perspective to any industry. Effective communicator with
the ability to provide exceptional customer service at all
levels. Experienced trainer with extensive hands-on and classroom technical experience. Proficient in Windows, MS Word,
Excel, PowerPoint, Outlook, and Internet Explorer.

MEDICAL EXPERIENCE
==
ENGINEERING SERVICE TECHNICIAN (2002 to 2005)
Lorad, Inc., Danbury, Connecticut
Directed a team of eight electro-mechanical technicians in the
construction and testing of mammography and x-ray equipment.
Spent 50 percent of time providing field service to downed
equipment in a large territory with ten hospitals. Collaborated with R&D engineers on design improvements and prototype
enhancements for new product lines. Met with customers to
determine liability for warranty problems and negotiated
settlements. Trained new technicians, field engineers, and
customers on equipment and tool repair. Helped write assembly
and repair procedures for factory and field service personnel.

Installed and monitored systems at hospital beta test sites. Provided technical phone assistance to service engineers. Performed system upgrades in both field and factory settings.

SENIOR ENGINEERING SERVICE TECHNICIAN (1997 to 2002)
Miles, Inc., Tarrytown, New York
Led a team of 15 electro-mechanical, electrical, and test technicians in the research and development of hematology and immunoassay systems. Conducted quality control inspections of in-production and finished modules. Managed materials and production control for the entire product line. Worked closely with design engineers on product improvements and prototype development. Responsible for troubleshooting and repairing all electro-mechanical, cable, hydraulic, and pneumatic problems. Wrote all training manuals for new electro-mechanical assemblies. Trained domestic and international field engineers on electro-mechanical systems and served as an expert resource for field service engineers. Transferred systems from an R&D environment to the production plant in Puerto Rico—trained, installed, and retrofit legacy systems. Accountable for controlling inventory of parts and maintaining repair logs of systems. Installed systems at beta testing sites for FDA approval; collaborated with FDA inspectors on revisions to new systems before production release.

TECHNOLOGY EXPERIENCE
==
SENIOR FIELD SERVICE ENGINEER (2000 to 2008)
SVG Lithography, Wilton, Connecticut / ASML, Tempe, Arizona
Stationed at an Intel chip-manufacturing site in Colorado Springs in order to troubleshoot and maintain SVG lithography equipment (valued at $10 million) from component to system levels. Installed new tools as they arrived at the site, and performed lithographic testing to ensure tools meet customer specifications. Performed system upgrades and modifications at the request of customer and/or factory. Provided technical phone assistance to other sites and managed all warranty issues. Diagnosed and repaired computerized electro-mechanical systems. Maintained and tracked precision-calibrated tools used for system repairs. Trained new employees on all tool phases from module replacement to troubleshooting down to the component level. Interviewed, made hiring recommendations, supervised, and evaluated 10 engineering technicians. Prepared daily and weekly site reports and part repair logs; met with senior customer engineers daily. Wrote training manuals for certain modules and documented repair procedures. Developed an automated journal system that tracked weekly repair time using Excel.

Key Accomplishments: Helped identify a duct work error that was costing Intel $100,000 per shift because of contamination blowing up from the sub-fab. Saved Intel $250,000 by changing

motor coils in the system rather than replacing the entire
module. Cleaned vacuum ports, which prevented replacement of
the system, saving Intel an additional $250,000. Received a
Silicon Valley Group award in recognition of outstanding
contributions to the MSX and REA build process.

COMPUTER TECHNICIAN / ENGINEERING TECHNICIAN (1988 to 1992)
TAD Technical Services, Poughkeepsie, New York
Assigned to IBM to manage a team of five electro-mechanical
technicians in cabling and power supply installation on
million-dollar mainframe computer systems. Served as a repair
technician for all electro-mechanical, cabling, and power
supply issues. Collaborated with design engineers on product
improvements. Performed quality control inspections on cabling
with a 98 percent defect-free rate for the entire group.
Rewrote assembly procedures, enabling a reduction in build
time from eight hours to four hours or less. Responsible for
materials management and production control in designated
area. Trained new employees on cabling and power supply system
installation and quality control.

EDUCATION
===
UNDERGRADUATE STUDIES (1995 to 1998)
Duchess Community College, Poughkeepsie, New York

PROFESSIONAL DEVELOPMENT
General Industry Safety and Health (10 hours, 2001)
* OSHA/SVG Safety
* Lockout/Tag Out
* Walking and Working Surfaces
* Physical Hazards
* Job Hazard Analysis
* Chemical Hazards
* Hazardous Energies
* Egress and Fire Protection
* Electrical Safety
* Personal Protection/PPE

Micrascan Training (2006):
* Computerized Electro-Mechanical Systems
* Environmental Control Systems
* Preventive Maintenance
* Reticle Handling
* Wafer Handling
* Lithography
* Beam Delivery System
* Robotic Handling

How to Compose and Send an e-Mailed Résumé

You may be thinking, "I can do that. I'll just skip this section." Don't! Even though the process itself is pretty basic, there are a few tricks of the trade that you shouldn't miss, so please read this section completely.

You can type your entire résumé into an e-mail message from scratch, but why would you do that when you have already typed it, spell checked it, and used your word processor's grammar function? When you are composing a cover letter and/or résumé for e-mail, it is always much better to start with your word processor since you can use its powerful grammar and spell check features to make certain your document is perfect before e-mailing it to a potential employer.

After you have created this perfect résumé in your word processor and saved it in ASCII format, open the ASCII file again in your word processor. Click on "Edit" and choose "Select All." Then click on "Edit" and choose "Copy."

Open your e-mail software. After you have typed in the address where you will be sending your message and added your subject line, click on the message box so your cursor is active in the large white space. Then select "Edit" and choose "Paste." Your text will appear in the message box.

Now you are ready to attach your Microsoft Word file and click on "Send." Most e-mail programs will automatically log on for you and send your message, or you can schedule it to send later. Here are some screen shots from MS Word and America Online to walk you through the process.

Screen shot of Microsoft Word used with permission of Microsoft Corporation.

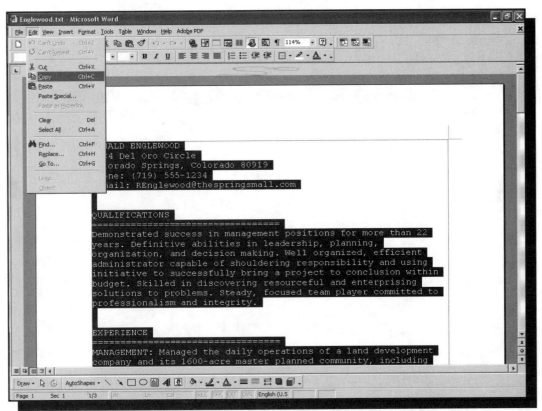

Screen shot of Microsoft Office used with permission of Microsoft Corporation.

Copyright 2004, America Online. Used by permission.

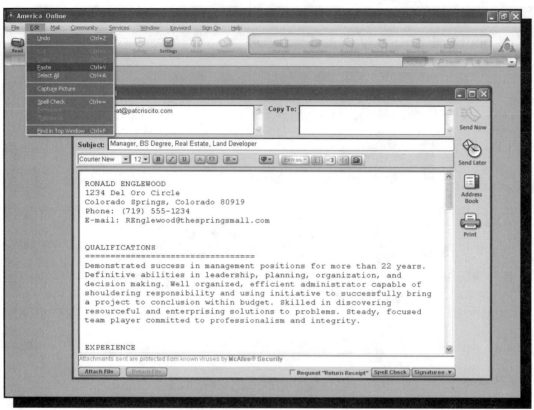

The subject line is a valuable tool for introducing who you are and what you do. Don't neglect this line. You can use it for your objective statement, to reference the job opening for which you are applying, or to show that you are updating a résumé you have sent previously. Never leave a subject line blank, since that is the hallmark of spam (junk mail). I know that I never open e-mail messages sent to me without a subject line, and I've heard the same comment from many recruiters.

What about a cover letter? Remember that e-mail is intended to be quick, so don't precede your pasted résumé with a long-winded cover letter. A simple paragraph or two that highlights your best qualifications and tells your reader where you heard about the position is all you need. I recommend that you limit your cover letter to no more than two paragraphs, although there are exceptions to every rule in the career business. Here's a sample cover letter that you can paste above your résumé in an e-mail:

> *I found your posting for a Customer Service Manager (Job #12343) on the Internet at Indeed.com and would appreciate your serious consideration of my qualifications. I have more than thirteen years of operations management experience that included budget analysis and tracking ($13 million), expense control, staffing, training, and customer service. I have succeeded in significantly controlling costs and maximizing productivity in all my jobs. I could also bring to this position my team spirit, ability to manage multiple priorities with time-sensitive deadlines, and strong communication skills.*

Pasted below is the text version of my résumé and attached is the MS Word document as your advertisement requested. I look forward to hearing from you soon.

Sincerely, Jane Doe

Now, experiment. Send the résumé to yourself or a friend, print it, and see what it looks like. Also look at it on your computer screen. If the text and spacing didn't translate correctly, this is the time to fix it. Save it again and then try the e-mail one more time. Once it is perfect, you are ready to use the file in e-mail and on the Internet.

MS Word and PDF Résumés

You may be asking why you can't just attach a Microsoft Word file to the e-mail message and forget about this cut and paste thing. First of all, when you attach a file to an e-mail message, the recipient of your e-mail will see only what you have typed in the subject line and your brief cover letter in the message box saying that your résumé is attached. When he clicks on the icon to "Download Now," your résumé will be saved on his hard drive. Later, he will have to remember that he has a file to view, recall where he saved it on the hard drive, and then open a word processor like Microsoft Word in order to view your résumé. Wouldn't you much rather have him begin reading the text of your résumé the minute he opens his e-mail? If he wants to see the formatted version, he can always download your MS Word document and look at it later.

There is also the chance that the recipient won't have the right software to open your file, either. For many years, I have known a small, niche recruiter without a large office staff. He never invested in the Microsoft Office software, so every time he received an attached MS Word file, he would send it to me to print and then he would collect the paper printouts once a week or so. He didn't have Adobe Acrobat on his system until just last week, even though it's free at *www.adobe.com*!

Speaking of Adobe Acrobat (PDF) files, there was a time when applicant tracking software could not interpret PDF files, so résumés sent in that format were never added to the databases. That is changing now. The majority of these software packages have now become capable of importing PDF files, but there is still no 100% guarantee.

There was a time when recruiters were afraid of viruses in attached files, but nearly all companies have implemented antivirus software or realize that they can choose not to download an attached file if they are concerned. That is why you should always paste the ASCII text version of your résumé below your brief cover letter in the body of the e-mail message, even when you are attaching a PDF or MS Word file.

You should send only one attachment with any one e-mail, and that file should be your MS Word or PDF résumé. Some people still have difficulty with "zipped" (compressed) files. When you attach more than one file to any e-mail, it is automatically compressed into a single file for transmission over the Internet. At your recipient's end, you have to be confident that the person's e-mail software will automatically "unzip" the files. Although it is becoming more likely that the decompression will be automatic, I can't guarantee it in every case. For that reason, I recommend that you send only one file attached to your e-mail. It is better to be safe than sorry.

Sending ASCII text e-mail across the Internet is relatively painless, but attaching binary files can get complicated. First, both you and your recipient must have the same (or newer) version of the software used to create your "pretty" résumé. For instance, if you created a résumé in Microsoft Word 2007 and your recipient has Word 95, she won't be able to open the file at all.

What if you used a unique font to design your Word résumé, but your recipient's computer doesn't support that font? Then your résumé will adjust to a new default font, and your résumé will look different from how you created it. The newer versions of MS Word and WordPerfect now allow you to embed TrueType fonts (but not Adobe Type One fonts) in documents, which helps prevent this problem. However, you must set up each document in MS Word by clicking on "Tools," "Options," "Save," and "Embed TrueType Fonts." In WordPerfect, you check the "Embed Fonts" box on the "Save As" option.

There are many things you can't control when sending e-mail. You can't control whether the recipient's printer definition will reformat your MS Word file. And you can't control how your recipient's e-mail software decodes your MS Word file. In order to send files across the network of computers that make up the Internet, binary files must be encoded in a special way before they are sent and then decoded when they are received at the other end. Each file is broken into tiny packets of information and sent across various parts of the Web. At the recipient's end, those packets must be put back together again . . . and in the right order!

Most e-mail software will automatically encode an attached file, so it is invisible to you. However, sending between different platforms (PCs, Macintosh, UNIX) can sometimes cause problems with decoding.

There are so many things that you can't control when sending binary files across the Internet that you want to take the safest route possible. And that route is to cut and paste your ASCII text file into the e-mail message screen. Then it is okay to attach an MS Word document to the e-mail. Your reader can choose to download it or not, but you haven't lost anything because your résumé is being read right on the screen.

Let's take a look at how you attach a file in Microsoft Outlook below. It is as simple as clicking on the paper clip and telling Outlook where to find the file you want to attach. That file can be stored on your hard drive, a CD-ROM, flash drive, or some other digital storage medium. Once you select the file, it is automatically attached to your e-mail message and ready to be sent.

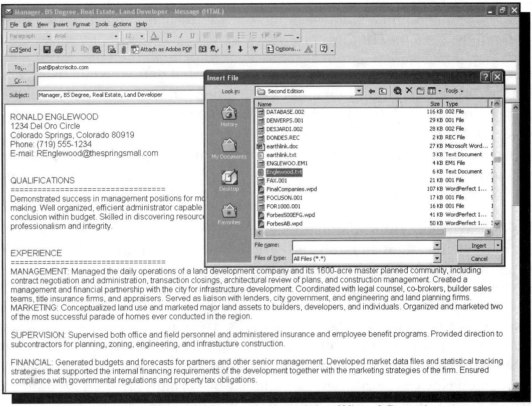

Screen shot of Microsoft Outlook used with permission of Microsoft Corporation.

HTML Résumés and e-Folios

Imagine a musician playing her latest composition from the Internet, a teacher incorporating a video of his teaching style, a poet reading clips from her poetry, or an entertainer demonstrating his latest dance steps. The creative juices are flowing! Web-based HTML résumés and e-folios are the perfect places to showcase skills that are better seen (or heard) in all their glory.

If you are a C-level executive, self-employed consultant, computer programmer, Web site developer, graphic designer, artist, sculptor, actor, model, animator, cartoonist, poet, writer, or anyone who would benefit by the photographs, graphics, animation, sound, color, or movement inherent in a Web-based portfolio, then you should definitely read this chapter. If you don't fall into one of these categories, read the rest of this chapter anyway, because you will be surprised how an e-folio can enhance your job search and help you manage your career even while you are currently employed.

If you want to control what a hiring manager sees when you are "Googled," then a well-designed and promoted e-folio is your answer. It allows you to control your online image. This part of the chapter will show you how to create and manage your e-folio or Web résumé.

A Web Résumé or an e-Folio?

A Web résumé is simply your paper résumé converted to a Web site using HTML codes. It is rather basic without a lot of extra information. Instead of having a single page on your Web site, however, a Web résumé is usually divided into sections that are accessed through hyperlinks from an introductory page—Career Objective, Summary, Skills, Experience, Education, Affiliations, etc. You can add information that you couldn't include in your paper résumé, but the more information you add, the more like an e-folio your Web résumé will become.

If you have more information about your career than you can practically include in a résumé, then an e-folio is a great option for making this additional information available to a potential employer. An e-folio provides visible evidence of your knowledge, skills, abilities, and core competencies.

You've heard the old saying, "A picture is worth a thousand words." That is the primary advantage of an e-folio. They are more tangible with links to PDF files, scanned images, and video/audio downloads. You can talk about what you've accomplished in words (either on paper or verbally) from now until doomsday, but nothing makes an impression like tangible, visual backup, especially today when so many recruiters and hiring managers are skeptical of claims made on résumés.

Another advantage of an e-folio is the first impression it makes. Dr. John Sullivan, Head Professor of Human Resource Management in the College of Business at San Francisco State University, says that "because portfolios take some effort, they demonstrate a degree of commitment on the part of the candidate that is not required in a résumé . . . so it improves the quality of new hires."

Most of us think of artists, models, actors, and photographers when we think of a portfolio, but that's not the case today. Everyone should maintain a portfolio. More and more employers are asking to see concrete evidence of the experience, skills, education, and accomplishments shown on your résumé, especially during the interview. I've even had employers ask recent MBA graduates for copies of their school term papers or other special projects and writing samples.

For years, in my own practice, I've been advising my clients to keep an "I Love Me" file with performance evaluations, job descriptions, letters of recommendation, thank you notes from customers, vendors, or supervisors, sales statistics, growth charts, writing samples, awards, honors, scanned product images, photographs, or even three-dimensional items that expand on or support the outline that is inherent in their résumés. If you have collected this information during your entire career, then you have the foundation for an e-folio that will help you sell your special abilities and manage your entire career. If you haven't, then create an e-folio with whatever you do have or can get your hands on now. It's never too late to start collecting for your "I Love Me" file.

A Web résumé or e-folio is just another type of e-résumé, but it cannot take the place of your paper résumé, ASCII text résumé, and MS Word or PDF file. In today's busy world, most recruiters and hiring managers have so little time to read résumés that they are turning to applicant tracking systems to lighten their load. Unless they are highly motivated, they won't take the time to search for and then spend fifteen minutes clicking their way through a multimedia presentation of someone's qualifications, either online at your Web-based e-folio or on a CD-ROM you might mail to them.

The real purpose of an e-folio is to provide extra information for when a potential employer is trying to narrow down his or her applicant pool. You can even direct the hiring manager to your Web site during an interview. You are more likely to be Googled at the weeding-out stage, which is either just before an interview offer or after the interview. That is when an e-folio becomes truly valuable. It might just tip the scales when a hiring manager is trying to choose between you and someone else.

You can always direct your reader to your e-folio by listing the URL on your résumé, letterhead, personal business card, and e-mail signature. Or place your URL in the appropriate field on job boards so recruiters can click on the link to get more information about you—information that you control. Just don't expect to get a job offer by simply creating a Web résumé or e-folio and waiting for a recruiter to find you. You must still be proactive in your job search by signing up for job agents on the major job boards, applying for each job that interests you, and networking like crazy.

Besides keeping your résumé in front of recruiters by being on the Internet all of the time, a well-planned e-folio is great for formal employment interviews, networking, informational interviews, performance assessments and evaluations on your current job, admission to colleges and universities, easily accessed information for your references, and an archive that lets you download your résumés from anywhere in the world (think Hurricane Katrina), among other functions. It is a professional self-marketing tool that can help you manage your entire career.

An e-folio is especially useful for entrepreneurs and consultants, since it can serve as a marketing tool for whatever products or services they sell. If you think about it, though, we should all be treating our careers as "entrepreneurial" ventures. When you take control of your career as a business owner controls his or her company, you make conscious choices about how to market your product—in the case of your career, that's *you*. Your résumé becomes your print advertising and your e-folio is your online brochure that convinces a "buyer" to call you instead of the "competition."

An e-folio is also a great career management tool that you don't have to save just for your job search. Imagine preparing for your annual performance evaluation with your current employer by reviewing the accomplishments you have collected in your "I Love Me" file and putting together either a paper-based or Web-based portfolio. When it is time to sit down with your supervisor and talk about what you have achieved this year, you can take control of the discussion by making a "sales presentation" of your accomplishments and tangible examples of work samples. What an impression you will make! You've got a raise!

Don't wait for your annual evaluation to think about using this tool. Many companies have implemented performance assessment programs that are ongoing with periodic meetings throughout the year to assess goals, milestones, and incremental achievements toward objectives.

If your company isn't that progressive and barely uses annual performance evaluations, let alone performance goal setting, then make yourself stand out in the crowd of other employees by being proactive. Develop your e-folio or paper portfolio and set the meeting with your supervisor yourself. Take charge of your career path and show your entrepreneurial spirit. Remember that entrepreneurship is all about "ownership," and you can own your career whether or not you own the business for which you work. This kind of independent thinking is often rewarded with promotions and/or pay increases that reflect your value to the company. It also makes your job more secure, since you have proven value to your employer. With downsizing the norm in today's workforce, the more valuable you are, the less likely you will be laid off. Companies are in the business of making money. If you make your employer more money than you cost to keep around, it just makes business sense that you will be retained.

The key to an effective portfolio is to research the company you will be interviewing with first. Determine what their needs might be and then select key items for your portfolio that you think would be of special interest to that employer. The portfolio you take to the next interview might be totally different, although it doesn't necessarily have to be different if you are applying for the same types of jobs in the same or similar industries. However, you must be able to tell a coherent story with the information. Make sure there is a connecting thread so you can easily transition from one item to the next. Keep it short—no more than 15 minutes—half of that time is even better. Practice before the interview!

When developing an e-folio, avoid photographs, proprietary/confidential employer information, personal information, family photographs, or negative comments about previous employers. If your Web site developer recommends a design that includes automatic background music or a lot of Flash programming, think twice before agreeing. They tend to be irritating to site visitors.

Portfolio Ideas by Job Type

Everybody's portfolio will be different, especially across industries and job titles. Even when two people share the same position in the same company, they shouldn't expect the contents of their portfolios to be the same. We each have our own unique backgrounds, qualifications, and accomplishments. However, there are some basic items that will appear in all portfolios:

1. **A résumé**—Your résumé (or bio in some cases) generally serves as the foundation of your e-folio. If it is well written, your résumé determines the basic outline for your Web site and helps you decide what sections to include. Don't simply rehash your résumé verbatim in your e-folio, however, or there is no point to your Web site. Summarize and expand on your résumé with job descriptions, employer reviews, work samples, problem-solving examples, organizational charts, leadership examples, customer survey results, proposals, business plans, and so on.

2. **Proof of achievements**—These can be charts or graphs if your accomplishments are quantifiable (like in sales and positions with P&L responsibility, i.e., bottom line results), copies of publicity, articles you have written, photographs, videos, company newsletters, white papers, special projects, newspaper or magazine articles, thank you letters from supervisors/ customers/vendors, performance evaluations with key accomplishments highlighted, honors, awards, and so on. If any of the information you want to use is copyrighted by someone else, you will need to get written permission to use it on your Web site first.

3. **Credentials**—This is where you back up your education, special training, licenses, certifications, and other credentials with scanned images of your diplomas, certificates, transcripts (for some positions), and other proof documents. Lists of major course work and select projects might be included if you are a recent graduate with little experience.

4. **Recommendations**—Scan your letters of reference from past employers, current supervisors, key customers or vendors, and other people who know your work well. Highlight key phrases or simply type a list of quotes

with the person's name, job title, and company. These third-party recommendations validate what you say about yourself in your own documentation.

It is easy to overdo both a hard-copy portfolio and an e-folio. It is sometimes hard to narrow down the items you want to include, so people have a tendency to make their portfolios much too long. Dr. Sullivan feels that a world-class portfolio has the following five characteristics:

1. It must be scannable in fifteen minutes or less.

2. It sells you with your work and your ideas.

3. It is customized for each job and each company.

4. It includes and highlights your accomplishments.

5. It excites the viewer.

Once your e-folio has the four basics, you can add other things to make it unique. Rather than repeat the items above for every industry, the lists below are in addition to your résumé, credentials, recommendations, and proof of accomplishments (although some items fall into this category just to give you more ideas). Use your imagination. These lists are just jumping off points for your own creativity, which is really what you are trying to display in your portfolio anyway.

Administrative Assistant	■ Lists of technical competencies
	■ Examples of various document preparation skills—correspondence, spreadsheets, PowerPoint presentations, forms, organizational charts, etc.
	■ Photos, agendas, budgets of events planned
	■ Letters of appreciation
	■ Certificates from classes, workshops, seminars, conferences
Antique & Art Dealer	■ Areas of expertise
	■ Select finds and sources
	■ Valuation/appraisal experience
	■ Restoration experience with photos
	■ International travel
	■ Import/export
	■ Apprenticeships and other hands-on experience
	■ Education and credentials
	■ Letters or comments from clients

Apartment Manager	▪ Photos of properties ▪ Size and types of units (luxury, family, senior citizen) ▪ Amenities ▪ Construction or renovation ▪ Occupancy rates ▪ Special promotions, events, and open houses ▪ Activities for residents ▪ Graphics representing impact on the bottom line
Architect	▪ Drawings, photographs, blueprints ▪ Styles ▪ Honors and awards ▪ Media coverage ▪ Professional affiliations ▪ Presentations ▪ Letters from satisfied customers and builders ▪ Acknowledgments from peers ▪ Parade of Homes participation
Artist	▪ Includes painters, sculptors, illustrators, designers, cartoonists, or anyone producing a visual art ▪ Mediums ▪ Education and special training ▪ Photographs of artwork ▪ Published works ▪ Reviews in magazines, newspapers, and other publications ▪ Lists and photographs of exhibitions ▪ Representations ▪ Museum collections ▪ Descriptions of style and artist philosophy ▪ Hyperlinks to online displays of artwork
Athlete	▪ Sports ▪ Media coverage ▪ Records and times ▪ Competitions ▪ Honors, awards ▪ Coaches, trainers
Attorney	▪ Areas of specialty ▪ Credentials—diplomas, licenses, etc. ▪ Track record of success ▪ Client testimonials ▪ Lists of significant cases

- Bar and court admissions
- Presentations
- Professional affiliations
- Volunteer work

Chef
- Menus
- Photographs of plated dinners and banquet presentations
- Thank you notes from customers
- Certificates of completion from special training programs
- Participation in stages and international programs
- Reviews in magazines, newspapers, and other publications
- Honors, awards, contests, chef's tables

Computer Professional
- Photographs of software packages or manuals
- Examples of a unique or difficult code and its result
- Screen shots of GUI interfaces
- Charts and graphs that show increases in productivity or profitability as a result of the finished product
- Technical skills divided into types
- Special projects
- Technical documents produced

Construction
- Areas of specialty
- Photos of completed projects
- Honors, awards, Parade of Homes, etc.
- Proof of licenses and bonding
- Letters from satisfied customers
- Community participation
- Professional affiliations

Customer Service Representative
- Letters from satisfied customers
- Awards for exceeding quotas
- Customer service scores
- Personality tests (like Myers-Briggs) that show an aptitude for working with people

Diplomat
- Negotiations, conflict resolutions, treaties
- Languages, cultures
- Special events
- Media coverage
- White papers, publications
- Pictures with famous people
- Noteworthy speeches and other presentations

Economist	<ul><li>Credentials are very important in this industry—education, degrees, training</li><li>Areas of expertise—energy, inflation, imports, employment, monetary policy, consumer theory, markets, profits, costs, public policy</li><li>Examples of research and analysis</li><li>Expertise with statistical analysis software</li><li>Sample spreadsheets, graphs, charts</li><li>Publications</li><li>Presentations</li><li>Publicity</li></ul>
Editor	<ul><li>Education and special training</li><li>Writing samples</li><li>List of own published works</li><li>Types of editing—fiction, creative nonfiction, trade, nonfiction</li><li>Editing samples—both hard copy and digital</li><li>Titles of books edited</li></ul>
Engineer	<ul><li>Drawings</li><li>Schematics</li><li>White papers</li><li>Research</li><li>Education and credentials</li><li>Media attention</li><li>Honors and awards</li></ul>
Event Planner	<ul><li>List of functions</li><li>Venues</li><li>Entertainment</li><li>Menus</li><li>Photos of decorations</li><li>Thank you letters and other kudos</li><li>Print promotions, invitations, newspaper coverage</li><li>Video clips</li></ul>
Executive	<ul><li>Executive summary</li><li>Management philosophy</li><li>Charts and graphs reflecting impact on the bottom line and performance improvement data</li><li>List of business competencies showing levels of expertise</li><li>Description of a major problem, your solution, and the result</li><li>Leadership examples</li></ul>

- Organizational charts showing subordinate personnel and areas of responsibility
- Affiliations and professional memberships with any leadership positions

Firefighter
- Certifications
- Areas of expertise
- Education and training
- Professional development
- Community involvement
- Special projects
- Professional affiliations
- Promotion record

Flight Attendant
- Photographs—head shot and full-body shot
- Special training
- Letters of appreciation from customers
- Recognition from supervisors
- Routes—domestic or international
- Languages and cross-cultural experience

Florist
- Lots of photographs that show quality of work
- Examples of different styles and types of arrangements
- Artistic designs using other media besides flowers
- Comments from satisfied customers

Groomer
- Photographs, photographs, photographs!
- Show dogs and champions
- Styles
- Humane treatment philosophy

Hospitality
- Lists or photos of hotels or restaurants managed
- Growth charts showing proof of impact on the bottom line
- Occupancy rates
- Letters of appreciation from satisfied guests
- Property improvements/construction/renovation
- Operating improvements
- News coverage
- Grand openings

Human Resources
- Employee benefits packages
- Interview worksheets
- Motivational and training programs

- Union negotiations
- Documentation of faster hiring or better retention
- Proof of lower costs for the hiring process
- Industry association participation
- Implementation of new technologies to manage the hiring process

Inventor or R&D
- Areas of expertise
- Patents
- Photographs of inventions
- Professional associations
- Presentations and academic assignments
- Publications and white papers
- Media coverage

Jeweler
- Photos! Photos! Photos!
- Design specialties—rings, necklaces, bracelets
- Materials expertise—gold, silver, platinum, precious stones, stone cutting, jewelry repair
- Testimonials from customers

Manufacturing
- Proof of product development
- Charts and graphs showing process improvements
- Implementation of new technologies and processes
- Safety improvement
- Quality control
- Volume increases
- Schematics, blueprints, designs, technical drawings

Marketing
- Marketing plans
- Advertising programs (video, print, voice)
- New media productions (Web sites, CD-ROMs)
- Focus group design and results
- Proposals
- Photographs
- Results, results, results!

Mechanic
- Areas of specialty
- Photos of body work or design
- Certifications
- Testimonials from satisfied customers
- Location of shop with map

Minister
- Religious philosophies
- Family photos
- Personal information about children and spouse

	▪ Sermon outlines
	▪ List of topics
	▪ Letters and comments from church members and leaders
	▪ Presentations and special teaching assignments
	▪ Media coverage
	▪ Video clips or radio broadcasts
Model	▪ Photos, photos, photos!
	▪ Copies of magazines or newspaper coverage
	▪ Fashion show advertisements and runway shots
	▪ Specialty areas
	▪ Languages, singing, acting, musical instruments, sports, etc.
	▪ Video tapes of commercial spots, movie appearances, etc.
Museum Curator	▪ Special events with invitations, photos, media coverage
	▪ Lists and photos of special exhibits
	▪ Fund-raising results
	▪ Speakers acquired
	▪ Permanent exhibits and acquisitions
	▪ Capital improvements
	▪ Advertising and promotions, including brochures, museum literature, television, radio, and print campaigns
Musician	▪ Recordings of performances and/or compositions made into sound files for the e-folio and CD-ROM
	▪ Reviews in magazines, newspapers, and other publications
	▪ Conservatory and special training programs
	▪ Performances
	▪ Honors, awards, contests
Nonprofit Sector	▪ Fund-raising
	▪ Event planning
	▪ Capital campaigns
	▪ Volunteer management
	▪ Areas of specialty
	▪ Low turnover of employees and volunteers
	▪ Publicity, media coverage
Photographer	▪ Photos! Photos! Photos!
	▪ Genre specialties
	▪ Recognitions, honors, awards
	▪ Exhibits (both solo and group)
	▪ Purchases—museum, gallery, business, individual
	▪ Media reports and reviews

Physician, Nurse, or Other Healthcare Practitioner	<ul><li>Licenses and other credentials</li><li>Degrees</li><li>Research projects</li><li>Grants, awards, and honors</li><li>Patient testimonials</li><li>Philosophies</li><li>Academic appointments and teaching assignments</li><li>Publications</li><li>Presentations</li><li>Professional affiliations</li><li>Community service</li></ul>
Police Officer	<ul><li>Special projects and committees</li><li>Community involvement</li><li>Areas of expertise</li><li>Education and special training</li><li>Awards and honors</li></ul>
Professor	<ul><li>Education and credentials are very important</li><li>Courses developed and taught</li><li>Research and development</li><li>Professional presentations</li><li>Publications—books, journals, and other periodicals</li><li>Special committees and projects</li><li>Student evaluations</li><li>Administrative responsibilities</li><li>Awards, honors, and other recognition</li><li>Community involvement</li></ul>
Project Manager	<ul><li>Lists of projects</li><li>Outcomes</li><li>Processes—needs analysis, resource allocation, project scheduling, product development, budgets, implementation</li><li>Letters from satisfied customers (internal and external)</li></ul>
Radio Broadcaster	<ul><li>Audio clips of shows, promos, jingles, etc.</li><li>Expertise with digital editing equipment and other technology</li><li>Examples of original scripts, journalism, and other writing</li><li>Community outreach</li><li>Promotions</li></ul>

Real Estate Agent	- Sales achievements—graphs, awards, honors - Areas of specialty - Success stories with photographs - Client comments
Recent Graduate	- Diplomas - Scholarships, grants, awards, honors - Samples of class papers, projects, reports, videos - Transcripts or lists of relevant courses - Course descriptions to add keywords and depth - Teacher evaluations - Community service projects - Clubs, honor societies, fraternities, and leadership positions
Sales	- Types of products sold, customers, and territories - Documented achievements—increased revenue or profits - Charts and graphs - Significant account acquisition - Number of leads generated and converted - Closing ratio - Letters from customers - Sale team-building exercises - Training and motivation programs developed and presented - Results, results, results!
Scientist	- Areas of specialty - Special projects - Inventions - Patents - Professional affiliations - Honors, awards, or other special recognition - News reports - White papers - Research - Grants - Presentations
Social Services	- Areas of specialty - Credentials, licenses, diplomas - Testimonials from clients helped - Professional affiliations - Volunteer work

Speaker	■ Video of key presentations
	■ Areas of expertise
	■ Topics, prices, and schedules
	■ Honors, awards, accolades
	■ Future speaking engagements
	■ Past audiences
	■ Invitations to share your expertise
	■ Thank you letters
	■ Membership in speaker organizations
	■ Photographs of you in action
	■ Brochures from events
Teacher	■ Teaching philosophy statement
	■ Lesson plans, syllabi, curricula
	■ Photographs of bulletin boards and learning aids
	■ Staff development projects
	■ Examples of special challenges and how you overcame them
	■ Degrees, transcripts, continuing education—credentials are really important in this industry
	■ Examples of community partnerships, legislative or volunteer work, and special committees
	■ Student portfolios or other proof of your legacy
	■ Affiliations and professional memberships
Television Newscaster	■ Lists of major stories covered
	■ Writing examples
	■ Video clips
	■ Areas of specialty—hard news, breaking news, feature stories
	■ Professional head shots
	■ Promotional materials created by the station
Translator	■ Writing examples
	■ Lists of special projects
	■ Areas of specialty
	■ Languages and levels of proficiency
	■ Teaching or tutoring programs developed and presented
	■ Letters of appreciation
Web Designer	■ Examples of Web sites to show off your designs
	■ Link to pages to emphasize what makes them unique—Java scripts, flash graphics, e-commerce features
	■ Letters from satisfied clients
	■ List of technical competencies
	■ List of projects and clients with hyperlinks to their sites

Writer

- Poems
- Excerpts from published works
- Media coverage
- Reviews
- Copies of articles in newspapers and magazines or hyperlinks to the online version of the article

e-Folio Sample

Kirsten Dixson of Brandego™ develops unique, executive-level portfolio services. Kirsten agrees that "an e-folio is much more effective when it does more than just reiterate a person's paper résumé." She is also adamant that the design of the Web site doesn't detract from its message. Kirsten says, "Brandego™ provides a comprehensive career-management solution that combines the best of personal branding, career portfolios, Web design, and direct marketing."

With Brandego's™ permission, on the following pages you will find an excellent example of a sophisticated e-folio throughout its various levels. For more samples, check their Web site at *www.brandego.com*.

When you develop a Web site for the first time, deciding what message you are going to convey and then laying out the flow of the site to facilitate delivery of that message is the key to an effective finished product. Patricia Moriarty (the sample e-folio that follows) is a specialist in education and technology curriculum integration, so her Web site focuses on her knowledge, skills, and abilities in this arena. Her site is laid out using the outline beginning on the next page.

1. INTRODUCTION

- A summary paragraph of history and qualifications.
- A list of areas of expertise.
- A keyword list of personal attributes or strengths.
- The introduction is the place for your personal branding statement, the unique value you bring to the job.

Patricia Moriarty
PORTFOLIO — Teaching for the 21st Century

| Intro | Vision | Career Highlights | Development | Endorsements | Résumé | Contact Info | ✉ |

Intro

Patricia Moriarty is an Education and Technology Curriculum Integration Specialist with 14 years of experience as a middle school educator. With her adaptive nature, she has made strong contributions in the areas of special education, math, language arts, social studies, and technology. Patricia is recognized for innovating and building programs from scratch and pioneering the use of technology in education. She was selected from 2700 applicants nationwide to be one of the 53 state representatives participating in NASA's prestigious Classroom of the Future Program. Her unique value is her ability to identify needs and team with diverse stakeholders-teachers, students, parents, administrators, school board, community, and committee members to influence positive change. The keys to Patricia's effectiveness are her true passion for education; her drive to ascertain the rationale for practices and pedagogy; and her desire to act as a guide for students to facilitate self discovery. Whether it is through staff development, training, teaching, learning, or evaluating, Patricia firmly believes that education is the essential ingredient to personal empowerment, growth, and ultimately, success.

Areas of Expertise

Grant Writing
Teaching
Technology Support & Integration

Teacher Training
Special Education
Creative Thinking & Problem-Solving

Attributes

visionary, creative, lifelong learner, insightful, committed, open-minded, generous, ethical

Patricia Moriarty · PO Box 963 · Exeter, NH 03833 · (603) 418-0023
✉

Copyright 2007 by Brandego™ LLC and Patricia Moriarty. Used by permission.

2. VISION

- A statement of personal philosophies about that work, which reveals values, vision, goal, purpose, etc.
- Notice that every page of the Web site contains:
  - Full links to every other page of the site.
  - Full contact information at the bottom of the page to make it easier for a potential employer to call.
  - A little envelope that jumps directly to a contact form that the viewer can use to send an e-mail immediately.
- The point is to make the site easy to navigate.

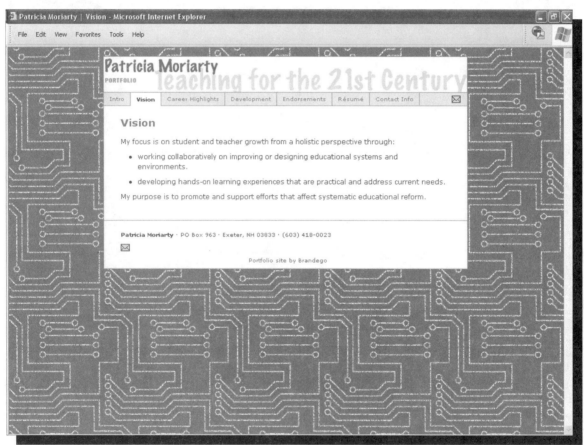

Copyright 2007 by Brandego™ LLC and Patricia Moriarty. Used by permission.

3. *CAREER HIGHLIGHTS*

- This section is not just a reiteration of the résumé.
- I especially like the fact that you don't have to use the "Back" button to return from the scanned images to the main page.
- Details of the NASA Classroom of the Future Program:
  - Challenge, Action, Results (CAR) statements
  - Scanned image of the citation
  - Scanned image of a newspaper article
- Details of the Technology Literacy Program:
  - CAR statements
  - Scanned image of a Compaq training certificate
  - Scanned image of a newspaper article
- Details of a New Hampshire Special Education Grant:
  - CAR statements
  - Quote from the parent of a former student
- Details of a State Work-to-School Grant:
  - CAR statements
  - Scanned image of a newspaper article
- Details of her study abroad:
  - CAR statements

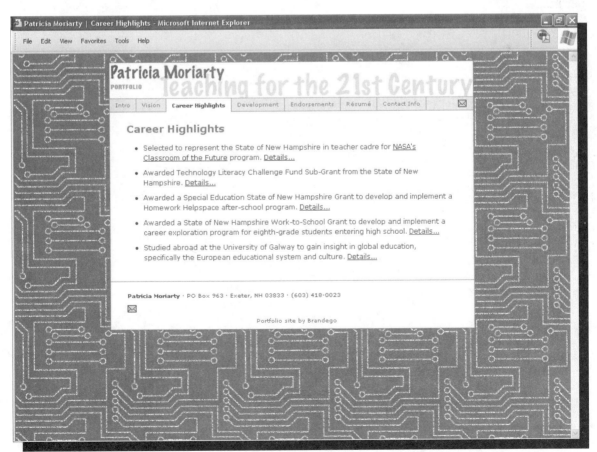

4. *DEVELOPMENT*

- Formal Education:
  - Scanned images of Master's degree
  - Scanned images of Bachelor's degrees
- Ongoing Professional Development:
  - Scanned images of various certificates

Patricia Moriarty
PORTFOLIO — Teaching for the 21st Century

| Intro | Vision | Career Highlights | **Development** | Endorsements | Résumé | Contact Info |

Development

Education

Master of Education, Instructional Technology-with honors (2002)
Lesley University, Cambridge, MA

Earned 14 Graduate Credits, NASA Educational Training (Summers 1998-1999)
Wheeling Jesuit University, Wheeling, WV

Bachelor of Arts, Elementary Education, Psychology concentration (1990)
Bachelor of Science, Special Education
Notre Dame College, Manchester, NH

Ongoing Professional Development

- State of New Hampshire Teacher Certification (1990-2005)
- NH Highly Qualified Teacher Certification for Social Studies and Language Arts
- Compaq Computer Technology Integration Leader Certificate
- Microsoft Certification Courses for Windows 98
- Critical Skills Teacher Certification
- NASA 2001 Teacher Cadre
- Member, National Education Association
- Member, Association for Curriculum and Supervision
- Member, New England League of Middle Schools. Developed and delivered a teacher workshop, Design and Implementation of a Successful Technology Program

B.A. Degree
Masters
Masters
Educator Certificate
Certificate

5. ENDORSEMENTS
- Quotes from former students.
- Quote from a parent of a former student.
- Quotes from colleagues.
- Quotes from an administrator.

6. *RÉSUMÉ*

- The complete paper résumé is re-entered here using HTML formatting.
- The reader can choose to download either a PDF, ASCII text, or MS Word version of the résumé.
- The ASCII text file can be downloaded by the viewer for input into computerized applicant tracking systems.
- The MS Word file is for recruiters who like to customize résumés before submitting them to their clients.

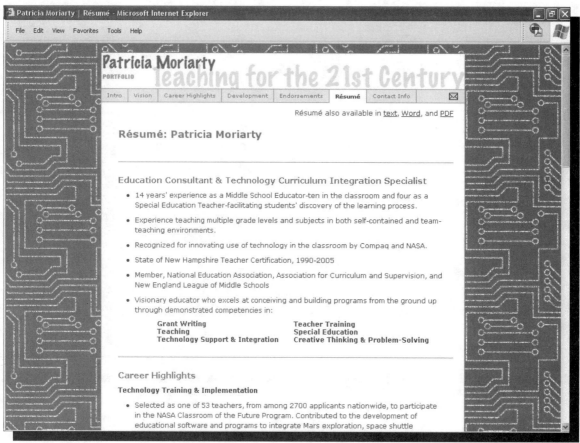

7. CONTACT INFO

- In addition to the full mailing address and telephone numbers at the bottom of the page, this page provides a form that the viewer can complete and e-mail directly.
- If you have only a cellular number, always identify it as a cell phone so the viewer knows they can try to reach you during business hours.

Copyright 2007 by Brandego™ LLC and Patricia Moriarty. Used by permission.

Chapter 15

The first rule of cover letters: Never use a generic cover letter with only "To Whom It May Concern." With tons of work on your desk, would you be interested in such a mass mailing? You would probably consider it junk mail, right? You would be much more likely to read a letter that was directed to you personally, and so would human resources professionals.

The second rule: Every résumé sent by mail or fax needs a personalized cover letter even if the advertisement didn't request a cover letter.

The third rule: Résumés sent by e-mail don't need a long cover letter. Use only a quick paragraph with three to five sentences telling your reader where you heard about the position and why your qualifications are a perfect fit for the position's requirements. E-mail is intended to be short, sweet, and to the point. Then, cut and paste your ASCII text résumé into the e-mail message screen instead of just attaching your MS Word file (see Barron's *e-Résumés* for detailed instructions on how to create and use an electronic résumé). Here is a sample cover letter for an e-mail message:

I found your posting for a Customer Service Manager (Job #12343) on the Internet at Monster.com and would appreciate your serious consideration of my qualifications. I have more than thirteen years of operations management experience that included budget analysis and tracking ($13 million), expense control, staffing, training, and customer service. I have succeeded in significantly controlling costs and maximizing productivity in all my jobs. My team spirit, ability to manage multiple priorities with time-sensitive deadlines, and strong communication skills would be true assets to your customer service program.

Pasted below is the text version of my résumé and attached is the MS Word document as your advertisement requested. I look forward to hearing from you soon.

Sincerely, John Doe

> *Never use a generic cover letter with only "To Whom It May Concern."*

This chapter will address several cover letter types. A letter to a recruiter requires different information than a letter in answer to an advertisement. A targeted cover letter that tells a story and captures your reader's attention is ideal when possible, but such letters aren't always practical (see the sample on page 224). Not everyone has the writing skills to produce an effective story, and the time involved in researching and writing the story would be impractical for mass mailings. A hard-hitting salesperson can write a dynamic cover letter, but not everyone is comfortable with that style and a good cover letter doesn't have to be "pushy."

Before we get into specific styles, let's cover some general rules that apply to most cover letters. The letters on pages 214–222 are general cover letters following these rules.

1. Customize each cover letter with an inside address (do not use "to whom it may concern").

2. Personalize the greeting (Dear Ms. Smith). Try to get the name of a person whenever possible. A blind advertisement makes that impossible, but in other cases a quick telephone call can often result in a name and sometimes a valuable telephone conversation. When you can't get a name, use Dear Recruiter, Dear Hiring Manager, Dear Search Committee, or Dear Sir/Madam.

3. Mention where you heard about the position so your reader knows where to direct your résumé and letter. The first paragraph of your cover letter is a great place to state (or restate) your objective. Since you know the specific job being offered, you can tailor your objective to suit the position.

4. Be a name-dropper. In the first paragraph, mention someone you know in the company. Hiring managers take unsolicited résumés more seriously when they assume you were referred by one of their employees or customers.

5. The second paragraph (or two) is the perfect place to mention specific experience that is targeted to the job opening. This is your "I'm super great because" information. Here is where you summarize why you are absolutely perfect for the position. Really sell yourself. Show your passion—employers hire for passion. Focus on accomplishments and proven performance that is specifically related to the company's requirements, or elaborate on qualifications that are not in your résumé but apply to this particular job. You should show a direct match between what the employer wants and what you have to offer. If you make mention of the company and its needs, it becomes immediately obvious that your cover letter is not generic. Entice the reader to find out more about you in your

résumé. Don't make this section too long or you will quickly lose the reader's interest.

6. The closing should be a concise call to action. Let the reader know what you want—an application, an interview, an opportunity to call. If you are planning to call the person on a certain day, you could close by saying, "I will contact you next Tuesday to set up a mutually convenient time to meet." Don't call on Mondays or Fridays if you can help it. If you aren't comfortable making these cold calls, then close your letter with something like, "I look forward to hearing from you soon." And remember to say, "Thank you for your consideration" or something to that effect (but don't be obsequious, please!).

Story Letters

If you are planning a direct mail campaign to 50 or 100 or 400 companies, this type of letter is not for you. It just isn't practical. However, you will have to admit that the letters on pages 223–229 are great attention getters. For those dream jobs that require something special, this is the way to go. In a story cover letter, you must be able to tell a good story and write it well. If writing is not your forté, you can hire someone to write the letter, but you must still do the research and have a general outline of the story.

Letters to Recruiters

There are two types of recruiters: retained and contingency. The difference is that retained recruiters are hired by a company and are then paid by that company whether they ever find the right employee for the position or not. Contingency firms are also paid by the company but only when they find a good match and the job seeker is hired. Most recruiting firms don't charge the job seeker, which means they are working for their client companies and not *you*.

Because their mission is not to find the perfect job for you but to find the perfect employee for their client, they have little interest in communicating with you unless you are a prime candidate for a position they are seeking to fill *now*. Don't call recruiters; they will call you if they are interested. This affects both the beginning and ending of your cover letter. If you don't have a person's name, use Dear Recruiter. You should resign yourself to waiting for the recruiter to call you, so "I look forward to hearing from you soon" is an appropriate closing for a recruiter cover letter.

In addition to the "I'm super great because" paragraph(s), you need to add another paragraph just before the closing that tells the recruiter your ideal position title, industry, salary, and geographic preferences. Check the cover letters on pages 230–231 for examples.

Dynamic Letters

Job openings that require a certain amount of dynamic spirit—such as sales—deserve a more dynamic letter. This can be accomplished in the opening paragraph. The rest of the letter is written like a standard cover letter but with a little more energy than usual. The last paragraph can be a bit more aggressive—you call the hiring manager instead of waiting for him/her to call you. See pages 221, 222, and 228 for examples of cover letters that exude confidence and power.

Thank You Letters

According to a recent survey, less than 20% of applicants write a thank you note after an interview. Of the recruiters surveyed, 94% said that a thank you letter would increase the applicant's chances of getting the job, or at least help him/her stay in the running, provided the applicant is otherwise qualified. Fifteen minutes of your time and a first-class postage stamp are very inexpensive investments in your career!

Thank you letters simply thank the interviewer for his or her time and reiterate some of the important things you learned about the company in the interview. Add some key qualifications that you forgot to mention in the interview, or emphasize some of the more important things you discussed. If the interviewer shared some information that gave you an insight into the company and its culture, mention how much you appreciated it.

A thank you letter should be short—three paragraphs at the most. Don't try for the hard sell. You had your chance in the interview. The thank you letter just reinforces what you have already said. See the examples on pages 233–235.

Letterheads

It is so easy to create a letterhead all your own and to make it match your résumé. Just copy into a new document the name and address you have already created for your résumé. It couldn't be simpler! It makes a very sharp impression when your cover letter and résumé match in every respect from paper color to font to letterhead.

Paper Colors

Color, like music, creates an atmosphere. Everyone knows that different colors evoke different feelings. Red can make a person feel warm, whereas blue does just the opposite.

Of course, you wouldn't want to use red in a résumé—although an artist could get away with just about any color. As a general rule, résumé papers should be neutral or light in color. After 27 years in the résumé business, I have discovered that brilliant white linen paper is still the most popular, followed closely by a slightly off-white and then by shades of light gray.

Just make sure that the color of the paper you choose is representative of your personality and industry and that it doesn't detract from your message. For instance, a dark paper color makes your résumé hard to read.

There is another reason to avoid dark-colored papers and papers with a background (pictures, marble shades, or speckles). Often companies will photocopy résumés for hiring managers, and dark colors or patterns will simply turn into dark masses that make your résumé difficult to read. If a company has multiple locations, the original résumé may even get faxed from one site to another and the same thing happens.

The type of paper (bond, linen, laid, cover stock, or coated) isn't as important, although it also projects a certain image. Uncoated paper (bond, linen, laid) makes a classic statement. It feels rich and makes people think of corporate stationery and important documents. Coated stock recalls memories of magazines, brochures, and annual reports. Heavy cover stock and laid paper can't be successfully folded and don't hold the ink from a laser printer or copier very well, so they must be handled gently. All of these factors play a part in your paper choice.

Regardless of the paper you choose, mail your résumé flat instead of folded. It costs a few extra cents in postage and a little more for the 9-by-12-inch envelope, but the impression it makes is well worth the extra cost. Thank you letters and other follow-up letters can be folded in standard No. 10 business envelopes.

JOANNE A. RIDGEWAY

4321 Dexter Avenue NE ◆ Massillon, OH 44646 ◆ (330) 555-1234 ◆ ridgeway@protypeltd.com

February 8, 2007

A letter in response to an advertisement with bulleted skills that address the advertised requirements.

Attention: Christine Simmers
Alder Agency
4321 Market Avenue North, Suite 101
Canton, OH 44702

Dear Ms. Simmers:

Your advertisement in *The Repository* on Sunday, February 6, 2007, for an administrative secretary/receptionist attracted my attention. Your ad stated you are looking for candidates with strong oral and written communication skills as well as experience in Word, Excel, and Access. As my enclosed resume indicates, my qualifications closely match your requirements as follows:

- ◆ **EXPERIENCE** of more than ten years in administrative/secretarial positions with advanced computer skills in all Microsoft Office programs including Word, Excel, and Access. As technical administrative assistant at PolyOne, I streamlined production of correspondence and product specifications in Word through use of custom templates, electronic forms, macros, autotext, and modification of toolbars. I am also proficient in spreadsheet applications using Excel. At PolyOne, I was also responsible for maintaining the customer specification database and providing reports to the department manager using Access.

- ◆ **EDUCATION** at The University of Akron/Wayne College reinforced my communication and business English skills. Membership in Toastmasters International, a public speaking group, strengthened my oral communication skills.

May I come in, at your convenience, so we can discuss my qualifications more fully? I can be reached at 330-555-1234 or by email at ridgeway@protypeltd.com. If I do not hear from you by next week, I will call to see if you have any questions and to check on the status of this opportunity.

Sincerely,

Joanne A. Ridgeway

Enclosure

Regina Openhence

125 S.E. Stanley Court • Palance, Utah 99999

208-555-1234 cell | *home 208-555-5678*

May 16, 2007

A letter in response to an advertisement.

Attention: Lindsey Harold
Codder County Bank
P.O. Box 9229
Palance, UT 99999

Dear Ms. Harold:

In response to your recent advertisement for an experienced Commercial Loan Officer, I have enclosed a copy of my résumé for your review. As you will note, I have spent more than twenty years in the banking industry in a variety of positions. My expertise is in working in the Commercial Loan Department and one-on-one with the customers, walking them through the loan process, educating them, and making sure they are receiving the fullest benefits possible.

I have achieved numerous accomplishments and have a record for developing a strong bottom line for the bank. My personal passion as a "people person" shines through in the successes I've achieved. I am computer literate, analytical, thorough, and well experienced in the complete loan process.

I would like the opportunity to meet with you personally where we may further discuss your bank's requirements and my qualifications. It appears from your advertisement that our needs may be a very close match. Please call me at your earliest convenience to schedule a time when we may meet and review how we may mutually benefit each other. Thank you for taking the time to review my résumé, and I look forward to meeting you personally.

Sincerely,

Regina Openhence

Enclosure

Jennifer Wallace

1234 Evergreen Dr. • Baltimore, Maryland 21032 • Phone: 410-555-1234 • jwallace@protypeltd.com

October 30, 2007

> A letter sent at the recommendation of a company employee.

Attn: Mary Ann Brown, Director of Sales
Marriott Corporation
3299 K Street NW, Suite 700
Washington, DC 20007

Dear Ms. Brown:

Connie Johnson, a sales director at Marriott ExecuStay in Washington, DC, suggested that I contact you regarding a marketing position with Marriott Corporation. I am familiar with Marriott's reputation as a leader in the hospitality industry as well as its variety of affiliate partners around the world. I have the knowledge, experience, and desire to uphold Marriott's world-renowned reputation for success, comfort, and quality.

As an independent consultant, I have utilized sales, marketing, and research skills to develop my business, negotiate contracts, and build positive relationships with various business leaders in my community. I am self-motivated and a great motivator of other people. I make people *want* to come to the gym, sweat, and eat right. Can you think of a better example of someone's ability to motivate others?

In addition to my entrepreneurial experience, I worked in foreign exchange and as a stock broker in a previous career. The companies I worked for placed me in managerial positions in marketing, development, and business operations. My supervisors entrusted me with significant autonomy and implemented many of my suggestions for improvements and new programs. One such "take it and run with it suggestion" I made involved setting up a foreign exchange office for the Olympics.

Ms. Brown, as you can see, I am a creative professional with great communication skills and I would be a positive asset to the Marriott Corporation. I'd like to pursue my formal introduction further with a personal interview. I'll contact you the week of February 7 unless I hear from you before then.

Thank you for your time and consideration and I look forward to speaking with you.

Sincerely,

Jennifer Wallace

Enclosure

MORGAN ALLEN

4708 Seminole Drive
Indian River, Florida 32999
914-555-1234
mallen@protypeltd.com

April 20, 2007

Mr. John Longfeld
Operations Manager
Call Center Corporation
1234 Telephone Road
Orlando, Florida 32801

> A letter for a confidential job hunt.

Dear John:

After a successful 10-year track record with Circle Technologies, I am discretely exploring new career possibilities that will capitalize on my call center operations, account management, and sales management capabilities. As part of that effort, I am contacting a few trusted colleagues to get your perspectives on the local market and seek your wisdom. Accordingly, I have enclosed for your reference a résumé that outlines my capabilities.

John, I believe that my key areas of expertise relevant to a new professional position include:

- *Managing call centers with up to 115 representatives and addressing a range of functions that have included inbound and outbound telesales, lead generation, order entry and fulfillment, customer service/customer care, and technical ("help desk") support.*

- *Assessing needs, defining project scopes, and developing contract specifications for providing services to corporate clients as an outside vendor.*

- *Managing the collection, tracking, and analyzing data related to the performance of and return on various direct marketing programs.*

- *Recruiting, hiring, training, and developing high-performing call centers and telesales teams that have delivered multi-million dollar revenues with high profit margins to my employers.*

My goal is to stay in the Greater Orlando / Central Florida region, and I am convinced that I can contribute to the success of a dynamic company. I would appreciate the opportunity to chat with you about my plans and get any insights you may be able to offer. I will call you early next week to arrange a mutually convenient time for us to have a conversation. Meanwhile, if you are aware of any opportunities that would be appropriate, please let me know whom to contact. Since no one at my current employer is aware of my plans, I trust your discretion.

Thank you for your time. I look forward to speaking with you soon.

Sincerely,

Morgan Allen

Enclosure

MICHAEL DOUGLASS CASSEDY

806.555.1234

9999 55th Street, Pheasant Run, Texas 79000 ✶ mdcassedy@protypeltd.com

January 6, 2008

My principal career goal is to obtain a high-impact leadership position that promotes the well being of U.S. citizens—a role that requires the ability to meet highly responsible challenges that contribute to ensuring national/international security.

Special Agent Recruiter
FBI Division of Federal Government
#1 Place Washington Avenue
Washington, DC 00999

RE: FBI Special Agent, Announcement # 003895703FBI

A letter for a government position with the FBI.

Dear Recruiter:

Officer and paratrooper training in the Special Reservists, a secret security clearance, a business degree, management experience, and a creditable background clearly translate to an FBI special agent position where structure, discipline, skill development, and applied knowledge are fundamental prerequisites. Proven trainability and promotability as a civilian and reservist also reflect noteworthy leadership skills.

Additionally, a reputation for maintaining the highest level of personal and professional reliability, dedication, bravery, and integrity also precedes me, character traits necessary to a position of this magnitude. The enclosed résumé and application package represent a sincere desire to become a member of the most elite investigative arm of the federal government, the FBI.

Augmenting my education, military training, experience, and character are skills that demonstrate leadership ability to:

- ✶ Build rapport and gain trust with others, ensuring strong business relationships.
- ✶ Set priorities and manage time in accordance with management goals.
- ✶ Perform well under pressure, where precision and choices are critical to positive outcomes.
- ✶ Make effective, timely decisions within the scope of authority.
- ✶ Anticipate needs / problems, assess progress, evaluate results, and apply knowledge for an efficient operation.
- ✶ Research / investigate the source of problems to create practical resolutions.
- ✶ Identify objective, organize resources, and direct efforts to achieve desired results.
- ✶ Analyze perspectives and assess risk factors to promote safety.
- ✶ Grasp and integrate organizational mission and values to help achieve company objectives.
- ✶ Share a vision, communicate goals, and delegate tasks to appropriate individuals to generate success.
- ✶ Enforce compliance with policy and procedure to maintain departmental credibility.
- ✶ Build a motivated work environment when tasks and procedures seem mundane.
- ✶ Work supportively as a productive team player to contribute to the mission.
- ✶ Remain flexible and adapt to change when transition becomes necessary.
- ✶ Focus on tasks through completion, including administrative paperwork.

I am confident that you will find me to be an excellent choice for FBI special agent and look forward to a mutually beneficial personal interview to further discuss your needs and my qualifications. In the meantime, thank you for your time and consideration.

Sincerely,

Michael D. Cassedy

Enclosure: Résumé

JANICE MOSS, RN, BSN

12345 Cherrytree Circle
Ashland, KY 41101

(606) 555-1234   moss@protypeltd.com
□□

December 6, 2007

> This letter writer is relocating and is cold calling on possible employers.

Ms. Mary Jane Archibald, RN, MSN
Director of Nursing
Baptist Hospital
310 Healthcare Row
Durham, NC 27701

Dear Ms. Archibald:

I learned of your facility through research in the Nursing '06 Career Directory and would be interested in exploring employment opportunities as a registered nurse in a cardiac stepdown or cardiac care unit at Baptist Hospital.

As you read my enclosed résumé, you will see that, for the last seven years, I have been employed at the Highland Medical Center in Ashland, Kentucky, one of the first facilities in the state to receive the prestigious Magnet Award for outstanding nursing care. I perform both staff nurse and occasional charge nurse duties on an intermediate care cardiac medical/surgical stepdown unit. In my position, I provide primary care nursing for 4–8 patients, particularly during the critical 24-hour postoperative period following open-heart surgery.

As a nursing team participant, I routinely respond to respiratory and cardiac codes in a calm, assertive, and well-organized manner. My dedication and enthusiasm for nursing enables me to create a supportive atmosphere that is beneficial to the well-being of patients who are experiencing the extreme discomforts associated with major surgery.

My references will confirm that I maintain excellent collaborative relationships with physicians and other staff professionals in carrying out care assignments for positive patient outcomes. Many of my patients have also written me letters of appreciation. I feel confident that my broad range of skills, acquired though my professional training and clinical practice, would be of value to Baptist Hospital.

Since I plan to be in North Carolina over the holiday season and into early January, may I ask for a few minutes of your time so that I could introduce myself and learn more about your facility and nursing staff needs? I will call you to schedule a mutually convenient interview time. However, if you wish to contact me before December 22nd, please feel free to call me at the above phone number.

Sincerely,

Janice Moss

Enclosure: Résumé

JENNIE A. HALL
12345 E. Cochise Dr. ■ Scottsdale, AZ 85259
Phone: 480-555-1234 ■ Email: hall@protypeltd.com

March 3, 2007

Chris Jones
Director of Personnel
City of Tempe
12345 E. University
Tempe, AZ 85282

Reference: Five reasons to interview me for Call Center Manager

Dear Mr. Jones:

As a proven Customer Service and Sales Call Center Manager, I offer the skills and abilities you need for the Call Center position.

Specifically, I bring you:

➤ Experience in large team operations management and project management as demonstrated by receiving AT&T's highest consumer service award and completing large, complex projects.

➤ Proficiency in exceeding sales and customer service objectives by 120 percent.

➤ Expertise in training large groups, team building, and coaching one-on-one gained by managing over 200 employees and team leaders with outstanding employee opinion survey results.

➤ Capability to utilize and lead process improvement techniques to improve performance by working with teams of 10 to 12 people.

➤ Bachelor of Science in Marketing.

Based upon these highlights and those detailed in my enclosed résumé, I am certain I would be a strong match for your requirements. I would enjoy meeting with you to discuss how my qualifications can meet the needs of the City of Tempe. I look forward to hearing from you soon.

Sincerely,

Jennie A. Hall

Enclosure

JOAQUIN BETANCOURT

501 Private Beach Drive   Home/Fax: 949.000.1001
Newport Beach, CA 92659   JBetancourt@protypeltd.com   Cell: 949.000.2002

August 5, 2007

> A letter requesting a senior management position in hospitality.

John E. Smith
Major Airlines
30 Rockefeller Plaza, Suite 1000
New York, NY 10112

                                RE: Senior Vice President of Onboard Services

Dear Mr. Smith:

Building corporate value, total quality guest environments, and workplaces that reflect a company's mission are my professional passion and expertise.

In January 2005, I was recruited by Multinational Hotels, Inc., to serve as Senior Vice President for Inter-American Operations and play a key role in the corporation's $4 billion startup. We envisioned and created an environment that thrives on the improvement process and breakthrough ideas that result from never accepting a formula just because "everyone else is doing it." Today, Multinational is the largest international hotel and leisure operations enterprise and is recognized by guests, trade publications, and the airline industry as the "World's Best Global Hotel Company."

I bring to the position of Senior Vice President of Onboard Services 20 years of proven strategic and tactical leadership in the hospitality industry. My strengths in operations management and complex negotiations are measured in multimillion-dollar revenue increases, earnings gains, reduced operating costs, and more competitive and sustainable market advantages. These core proficiencies are critical to meeting Major Airlines' financial, operating, market, superior customer service, and employee relations goals.

My team has successfully implemented innovative guest services programs that improve customer satisfaction and loyalty in collective bargaining environments. We consistently receive top approval ratings from management to front line staff. My participatory leadership style evolved from having worked through school as a doorman, busboy, server, line cook, and front desk agent. I can, and still do, walk in our employees' shoes. I do not ask any one to do anything I would not do.

As a frequent flyer, I have observed and experienced the best and the worst our industry has to offer. The same traveler who steps onto a plane also stays at our hotels. Our goals are the same—to provide an enjoyable, comfortable, safe, and hassle-free experience.

I appreciate your consideration and look forward to speaking with you regarding your search.

Sincerely,

Joaquin Betancourt

Enclosure: Résumé

John G. Warren

1ˢᵗ Avenue #4C – Long Island City, New York 11106 – Cell: 407-555-1234 – Home: 212-555-5678 – E-mail: jgwarren@protypeltd.com

September 12, 2007

Florida Hotel & Resort
3138 Terry Brook
Winter Park, Florida

> A letter used to gain a position in the hospitality industry without experience in that industry.

Re: General Resort Manager

Dear Employment Manager:

You need impeccable guest services, tenacious management, and a sincere desire to fulfill expectations to cement memorable experiences for customers in the hospitality industry. As an experienced General/Senior Manager with more than 10 years of experience ensuring excellent operations, propelling profits, and delivering superb service, I now offer you my assistance as your new General Resort Manager.

In order to annihilate your competition, retain your existing clientele, and win new ones, your hotel must service above the standards of your competitors and make an impression with competent and professional people. In addition, your facility must invite your existing and prospective guests with pleasing aesthetics and seductive comfort. Above all, every person in your team MUST exceed the expectations of every guest with which they interact. I offer to secure these essentials for your hotel and continue to uphold the professional image Florida Hotel & Resort exudes.

With an accomplished history under my current employer, I now seek an opportunity to contribute in the hotel industry with an upscale establishment like yours. Please review my attached résumé, and allow me to highlight the following. I have…

- ✓ Turned low-performing locations into profitable establishments that pleased directors, owners, and customers.
- ✓ Enhanced already successful establishments and produced in areas overlooked by other managers.
- ✓ Led large staffs by motivating them, infusing them with confidence, and leading them by example.
- ✓ Communicated with corporate and non-corporate personnel using language that is clear, sensible, intelligent, and persuasive.
- ✓ Developed a valuable reputation with a highly demanding clientele by delivering on promises and anticipating their comfort and service needs.
- ✓ Generated millions in annual gross by overhauling departments and decreasing expenditures.

The value I will bring to your hotel is not limited to the above. In me, you will gain a manager that can forecast financial, operational, and guest needs accurately, prioritize and manage intelligently, and own all responsibilities in your organization, which will lead to your continued success.

Thank you in advance for your time and consideration. I look forward to hearing from you.

Sincerely,

John G. Warren

222

MICHAEL MARTINEZ

123 London Street • Northern, IL 60099 • (847) 555-2222 • mmartinez@protypeltd.com

January 6, 2008

A broadcasting letter for an entry-level worker.

Human Resources
Felicity, Inc.
P.O. Box 49552
Chicago, Illinois 60110

Dear Hiring Professional:

As a child my playground was most often the family restaurant. I learned early on that success depends on a strong commitment to customer satisfaction, quality, and a constant focus on the bottom line. My recent experience includes retail management roles in book, video, and game product store environments. The range of my experience spans:

Retail Store Operations Management	Merchandising / Creative Product Display
P&L Responsibility / Budgeting / AP / AR	External Marketing / Publicity
Solutions-Focused Customer Service	Special Events Coordination
Shift Supervision / Opening and Closing	Editor / Author Monthly Catalog
Primary / Peripheral Sales	Solid Communication / Teambuilding Skills
Inventory Control / Purchasing / Loss Prevention	Strong PC and Database Skills

My contributions include:

- **Editor, author, creative designer for a 20-page monthly book catalog** including writing feature articles and book / product synopses.

- **Redesigned product displays** resulting in a **50% increase in sales** in targeted merchandise sales.

- **Awarded 35 recognitions for customer service and peripheral sales**; personally exceeded all other district stores in presales of select video product.

I have approached my work with a strong sense of urgency, working well under pressure and change. I am considered a team player who has a strong commitment to the people and the organization I work for.

The sum of my experience has provided me with the qualifications to contribute to your company's long-term success. I have enclosed my résumé in anticipation that you may be interested in adding an impact player to your team. I would welcome a personal interview. Thank you for your time and consideration.

Sincerely,

Michael Martinez

Enclosure

JOSE CASTELLANOS

June 26, 2007

> A great example of a "story" letter.

Ms. Cindy Smith
College Relations Manager
Hallmark Cards, Inc.
P.O. Box 123456
Kansas City, Missouri 64141

Dear Ms. Smith:

It was in my hometown of Bogotá, Colombia, that as a teenager I came into contact with Hallmark for the first time. Even though I was not aware of the vision, effort, and commitment of resources that had gone into the Mother's Day card I had purchased, I was a happy customer. I never thought to wonder about the logistics of how that card had gotten to that small store or why a company more than 3,000 miles away was able to appeal to me, a kid from another country, culture, and language.

Hallmark's aggressive market penetration in more than 100 countries and its striving to provide employees with a supportive and challenging environment to best develop and apply their individual skills demonstrate to me that Hallmark is a company well worth entrusting with my career. In addition, I am impressed and attracted by Hallmark's commitment to supporting the communities in which it operates.

In light of Hallmark's international interest, you may be interested in my background. I started a small business in Colombia, which tested my energy, creativity, and initiative. The business quickly grew to be competitive as a result of innovative marketing and operation strategies. I have since learned to speak English, obtained a Bachelor of Business Administration from a U.S. university, and worked in several countries in varied positions, successfully adapting to both the people and management styles of these countries. Furthermore, in order to be better prepared for today's complex business environment, I am pursuing a Master of International Management degree, which I will complete in December.

It is my hope that my solid academic and cultural backgrounds, business experience, and interest in the international arena will convey to you that I have the qualifications to make a valuable contribution to Hallmark's efforts to remain the worldwide leader of the social expression industry.

I would like to be part of the Hallmark team that once helped me express myself through that card I gave my mother, and to take part in expanding the company to reach even more people all over the world. I would appreciate the opportunity to interview with you during your upcoming visit to Phoenix and hope that you will give the enclosed résumé favorable consideration. Thank you for your attention.

Sincerely,

Jose Castellanos

Enclosure

Gloria R. Clawson

1234 Queen Anne Way • Colorado Springs, Colorado 80917 • (719) 555-1234

July 21, 2007

A dream job with little relevant experience.

United Airlines (AFA)
Attn: F/A Employment
Box 66100
Chicago, Illinois 60666

Dear Sir/Madam:

I have dreamed of being a flight attendant since I was sixteen, but something has always prevented me from fulfilling that dream. Now that I've had a little experience with Western Pacific Airlines, I'm confident that I qualify for such a position. I would very much like to work for United Airlines, which I feel is a well-established and reputable organization.

With my twenty years of public relations experience, I would be an asset to United. I am a highly qualified individual who is ready to move forward into a more professional career. As you will see from the enclosed letters of recommendation, I am a very efficient and conscientious worker. I have a particularly strong desire to travel and work with people. With my outgoing personality and infectious smile, I know I would make a great addition to your team.

My résumé can only highlight my qualifications. A personal interview will assure you of my potential value to your company. I look forward to hearing from you so we may take the discussions of this challenging position one step further.

Sincerely,

Gloria R. Clawson

Enclosure

LORNA HURLEY

1234 Saturn Drive #123 • Colorado Springs, Colorado 80906 • (719) 555-1234

October 19, 2007

> Making connections with the feelings of the reader and explaining why the job would be a good fit even though the writer is over-qualified.

Human Resources
USAA
1234 Telstar Drive
Colorado Springs, CO 80920

Ref Code: PC-COS-1234

Dear Recruiter:

I have long been a satisfied customer of USAA, as was my father before me, so when I noticed your advertisement for Customer Account Professionals in a recent edition of <u>The Gazette</u>, I was immediately attracted to the possibility of working for USAA again. I was a supervisor in the Communications Center in your San Antonio headquarters for two years before returning to Colorado Springs for family reasons.

Although I don't know your current hiring needs, I hope to explore the possibility of working for USAA as a customer service supervisor. I was a supervisor at Allstate insurance in the customer and agency service department, and all of my positions have involved a high level of customer service for both internal and external clients. At Allstate, I reviewed detailed policy information and relayed that information to both the insureds and their agents. I am accustomed to working in a fast-paced team environment with conflicting deadlines and have good computer skills. My college degrees and continuing professional development have prepared me for success within your customer service department.

Even though you might consider my qualifications too strong for this position, I want to assure you that I would enjoy the opportunity to learn USAA's Colorado Springs business from the ground up. I would welcome the opportunity for an interview to further discuss how my unique skills could benefit USAA. Thank you for your consideration, and I look forward to hearing from you soon.

Sincerely,

Lorna Hurley

Enclosure

GREGORY HUMPHREYS

5896 42nd Street ▪ Lubbock, Texas 79000
ghumphreys@protypeltd.com
806.555.1234 (C) ▪ **806.555.5678 (H)**

January 6, 2008

Mr. Gary Wintworth
Manager
ABC Company
5555 Main Street
Amarillo, Texas 78000

Dear Mr. Wintworth:

Your associate, Brady Williams, whom I met last Thursday at a Rotary Club meeting referred me to you in my quest to find out more about the telecom industry. It is with sincere interest that I request a 30-minute informational interview with you at your convenience. I am currently a manager with Intel but would like to make a transition to a related field and feel someone in a reputable company, such as yours, could enlighten me. As Brady speaks highly of you, I would very much respect any guidance you might offer.

I will call your office within the week to perhaps set up a date and time. Until then, thank you for your consideration.

Gratefully,

Gregory Humphreys

Enclosure: Business Card

Michael C. DeWitt

Permanent Address: 1234 Edgepark Road ◆ Vienna, Virginia 22182 ◆ Message: (703) 555-1234
Present Address: Jan Luykenstraat 1234 ◆ 1071 CR Amsterdam ◆ The Netherlands
Home: (+31) 20-555-1234 ◆ Work: (+31) 20-555-5678 ◆ E-mail: dewitt@protypeltd.com

February 17, 2007

A dynamic cover letter.

Mr. Mike Smith
Vice President, Sales
BT North America
1234 East 52nd Street
New York, NY 10022

Dear Mr. Smith:

Would you have an interest in an individual who has generated more than $50 million in global account revenues for a telecommunications leader, and who recently played a key role in the success of a new BT European joint venture? If so, I'd like to speak with you about how I can employ these skills and my knowledge of MCI/WorldCom to help BT North America achieve its revenue and business objectives in the new global marketplace.

As a successful sales and business development manager with MCI, I have a proven track record of delivering significant revenue and profit growth by building value propositions for advanced voice, data, and Internet applications. These skills have placed me within the top one percent of MCI's global sales force on three separate occasions.

In my current assignment as a member of the senior management team for Telfort in The Netherlands, I direct a group that, in just six months time, has been instrumental in contributing more than $10 million in revenue to this successful startup.

With my overseas assignment drawing to a close in April 2007, I have a strong interest in pursuing opportunities within BT North America. Should you have a current or emerging need for a proven contributor to your management team, I would appreciate your serious consideration of my qualifications outlined in the enclosed résumé.

My present travel plans call for me to be in the United States from 2/20 through 3/2. I would welcome the opportunity to meet with you in person and will contact you shortly to determine if this is convenient for you. I look forward to hearing from you soon.

Sincerely,

Michael C. DeWitt

Enclosure

228

KEISHA CHAMBER

1234 East Platte
Colorado Springs, CO 80903

Telephone:
(719) 555-1234

July 12, 2007

A networking letter requesting an internship or informational interview.

Stephen Smith
P.O. Box 1234
LaJunta, Colorado 81050

Dear Mr. Smith:

John Smith, Professor at UCCS, recommended that I contact you. I have just graduated from the University of Colorado at Colorado Springs with an undergraduate degree in geography and environmental sciences.

My studies, combined with my Olympic training have been particularly intense. I often devoted more than 30 hours a week to my sport and still found the time to pursue my degree and earn a 3.4 GPA. Unfortunately, this rigorous schedule didn't afford me the benefit of an internship, but it did provide me with the desire to achieve and the belief that consistent training improves performance. Now that I have graduated, I would like to spend the next year working for a company like yours and learning all there is to know about the GIS industry. I am available full time in whatever capacity you need.

The opportunity to work for your company would be a real asset to my career, and I would appreciate your serious consideration of my qualifications. If you don't see a fit with your organization at the present time, I would still like to have the opportunity to meet with you or someone in your company who could take a few minutes to provide me with some ideas for how I might break into and succeed in this industry. Thank you for your consideration, and I look forward to hearing from you soon.

Sincerely,

Keisha Chamber

Enclosure

TONY POLACEK

1234 Bridle Trail
Pueblo, Colorado 81005

Phone: (719) 555-1234
polacek@protypeltd.com

November 17, 2007

A letter to a recruiter. Note the third paragraph that is unique in letters to recruiters.

Mr. Stefan Smith
President
Management Search, Inc.
1234 S. Cook St., Suite 12
Barrington, IL 60010

Dear Mr. Smith:

Is one of your clients looking for a Human Resources or Labor Relations Manager with a proven track record of success in both manufacturing and high-tech services industries? Then you will want to review my qualifications.

As a successful human resource generalist with extensive labor relations experience, I have become well known for my ability to improve employee morale and increase trust between unions and management. I have negotiated and administered several collective bargaining agreements and was often called in to diffuse stalled bargaining processes. My dynamic leadership style motivates change within the corporate culture and builds support from within the ranks. These skills, plus many more, would be true assets to any company whether they are unionized or not.

My target job is at the middle-management level with an innovative company that could challenge my skills in human resource management, employee relations, and compensation and benefit administration. I have no geographic preferences and would be open to relocation. My salary requirements would of course depend on the city, but I would anticipate a base salary in the area of $60,000.

Should one of your clients have a current or emerging need for a member of their human resource management team, I would appreciate your serious consideration of my qualifications as outlined in the enclosed résumé. I am free to meet with you at your convenience and look forward to hearing from you soon.

Sincerely,

Tony Polacek

Enclosure

LEE DAVID MILLER

1234 Amstel Drive • Colorado Springs, Colorado 80907 • (719) 555-1234 • E-mail: ldmiller@protypeltd.com

August 13, 2007

A letter to a recruiter.

Mr. Scott Smith
Office Manager
Korn/Ferry International
1234 S. Wacker Drive, Ste. 12
Sears Tower
Chicago, IL 60606

Dear Mr. Smith:

After a 25-year career in a number of senior management positions with high-tech computer/communications companies in the Silicon Valley (and a short stint owning my own consulting company), I have seen many examples of great leadership and a few that were less than that. What seems to separate the truly successful senior executive from the mediocre is the degree of commitment he is able to instill in his people. I have been successful in building strong teams of productive professionals by creating comfortable, yet challenging environments that are stimulating and satisfying. Having participated in changes that have transformed the industry, I want to continue to be a part of this challenge in a senior leadership position that can take advantage of my in-depth knowledge of current technologies.

If one of your clients is looking for an experienced vice president or director who can motivate a team not only to meet but to exceed growth and financial goals, I am the person who can deliver those expectations and more. I am looking for a position that will continue to challenge me and give me the opportunity to lead a company into the 21st century. I have no geographic preferences and would expect compensation in the $130–175,000 range, exclusive of benefits.

The enclosed résumé will provide you with the details of my experience and accomplishments. I would welcome the opportunity for an interview to discuss how my skills and experience can meet your needs. Thank you for your consideration.

Sincerely,

Lee David Miller

Enclosure

231

DAVID F. KOVACH

August 16, 2007

Ms. Nancy Waite
COO, Executive Vice President
Ports of Call
3333 Quebec Street, Suite 9100
Denver, Colorado 80207-2331

Dear Ms. Waite:

Carol Ingwersen recommended that I forward a copy of my résumé for your review. I am very interested in returning to the travel industry in a sales capacity and would appreciate an opportunity to sit down with you to talk about the unique ideas I could bring to your sales process.

As you can see in my résumé, I have extensive sales and customer service experience, but what you can't see is that I have worked for travel clubs twice in my career. I succeeded in selling 450 memberships in only three months for The Diplomats in Des Moines, Iowa, and I worked as the membership director for the Texas Air Travel Club during my early career. With its own private jet and 2,500 members, the Texas Air Travel Club was very similar to Ports of Call. I developed some innovative ways of increasing memberships that would be valuable to your company.

Even though you don't have any current openings, I think you will find my ideas worthy of a trial even if you have to create a position for me. I will give you a call next week to see if there is a mutually convenience time we can get together to talk about the possibilities. Thank you for your consideration.

Sincerely,

David F. Kovach

Enclosure

SALLY RENE STEWART

5000 West 5th Street
Lubbock, Texas 79400
(806) 555-1234
srs@protypeltd.com

January 6, 2008

A thank you letter following an interview.

Ms. Jane Young
The Design Center
Merimax Interiors, Inc.
234 Waukegan Road
Lubbock, Texas 79402

Dear Ms. Young:

Thank you for the time you extended me during our interview last Tuesday. Our discussion was enlightening and enjoyable. I am sincerely interested in a designer position with Merimax Interiors, Inc., as I was impressed with your company's culture, growth options, and mission to provide creative yet functional interior designs to clients in the medical care industry.

As you may recall, my particular strength is a positive approach to my work and a commitment to excellence in any endeavor I attempt. The honors I attained during my college career at Texas Tech University reflect my quest for distinction. The prospect of putting my color and design knowledge to work in a business environment such as yours at Merimax Interiors, Inc., is thrilling.

If you have additional questions, please feel free to contact me at (806) 555-1234. I look forward to hearing again from you in the very near future.

Again, thank you for your interest in my qualifications for your designer vacancy.

Sincerely,

Sally Rene Stewart

David M. Hudson

4321 Oakmoore Avenue NE
Massillon, OH 44646
330-555-1234

February 10, 2007

A thank you letter following an interview.

Mr. Randall Killian
Manager, Prototype Operations
Topco Industries, Inc.
4231 Seabrook Ave. NW
North Canton, OH 44720

Dear Mr. Killian:

I would like to take this opportunity to thank you for the interview Thursday afternoon at your office and to confirm my strong interest in the CNC Machinist position.

After we spoke, it became increasingly clear to me that the position we discussed would be a good fit for my skills and interest. I recognize that this is a busy department with a demanding schedule and a need for accuracy and the ability to meet deadlines. I believe my background, experience, and skills will allow me to make a positive contribution in this department. I hope you will consider me for this position.

In closing, I would like to again thank you for sharing your valuable time with me. I am excited about the possibilities of this position and remain even more convinced of the potential for a good match. I would consider it a privilege to be an employee of a company with an excellent reputation such as Topco. I look forward to a favorable outcome.

Sincerely,

David M. Hudson

Amy Rigby
1234 Main Street, Annapolis, MD 21401
410-555-1234 • Rigby@protypeltd.com

July 15, 2007

A thank you letter following an interview for a nurse returning to the workforce.

Attn: Anne Johnson, Nursing Recruiter
Wayson Pavilion – Human Resources
Anne Arundel Medical Center
2001 Medical Parkway, Suite 350
Annapolis, MD 21401

Dear Ms. Johnson:

Thank you for taking time out of your busy schedule yesterday to discuss the pediatric temporary float pool clinical nursing position that is available. As we discussed, this is the perfect position where I can continue to develop my nursing skills but have the flexibility that I desire.

I am confident that I can make a positive contribution to the high quality of nursing care that is provided at AAMC. My experience working as a clinical nurse in the Pediatric Research Unit at Johns Hopkins University facilitated my ability to quickly and accurately assess patient needs and identify appropriate treatment plans. Being a team member on research protocols proved to me how important it is to clearly communicate patient needs and requirements, in writing and verbally, especially when numerous medical caregivers were involved. I learned the importance of patient advocacy and how to properly inform parents and caregivers how to monitor their children's medical needs and follow prescribed treatment plans upon hospital discharge.

These skills and more, combined with my Bachelor's Degree in Nursing from Johns Hopkins, more than qualify me for the position. I would consider it an honor and privilege to serve the staff, patients, and physicians that choose to affiliate themselves with Anne Arundel Medical Center.

Thank you for your time and consideration for this position. I look forward to speaking with you in more detail soon.

Sincerely,

Amy Rigby

1234 Ashwood Circle
Colorado Springs, CO 80906
Phone: (719) 555-1234
E-mail: lsteele@protypeltd.com

June 7, 2007

> A thank you letter that drops the name of the recipient's manager.

Ms. Jeanine Smith
Director of Sales and Marketing
The Cliff House
1234 Canon Avenue
Manitou Springs, Colorado 80829

Dear Ms. Smith:

Thank you for taking the time to interview me for the Sales Manager position at The Cliff House. As we discussed, I have built two successful businesses from the ground up and am very comfortable making cold calls, networking, and building a clientele from scratch. One of those businesses was a travel agency, where I worked closely with my counterparts in the hospitality industry and made high-level presentations to corporate prospects. This experience would translate well into the hotel industry here in the Colorado Springs area.

I had the unexpected pleasure of speaking with Craig Hartman on Friday, May 28, and got a positive feeling for the management culture at The Cliff House even before meeting you. I know that I would be a good fit in the Sales Manager position. Enclosed is a copy of my reference list, as you requested. If you have any further questions, feel free to give me a call. I look forward to hearing from you soon.

Sincerely,

Liz Steele

Enclosure

MATT C. LINCOLN
8899 1st Place – Lubbock, Texas 79416
(806) 555-1234
mattlincoln89@protypeltd.com

January 6, 2008

Mr. Jack Preston
Vice President
Cox & Preston Advertising
9986 Ave. G
Lubbock, Texas 79401

Dear Jack:

It is with mixed emotions that I present this letter of resignation. As you know, my parents have been ailing for the last three years. Considering their poor health, I have secured a position with Braxton and Braxton in New York City to be near them. I will relocate to that area in two months. However, it is my intention to remain in the office at for at least two to four weeks to ease the transition in filling my vacancy.

I want to express to you that my ten years with you and David have been rewarding and beneficial to my growth as a layout artist. You have both been great associates and mentors. I only hope my position with Braxton and Braxton will bring me as much job satisfaction.

Please let me know if there is anything else I must do to complete the resignation process.

Sincerely,

Matt C. Lincoln

Index

246